To: _____

From: _____

Date: _____

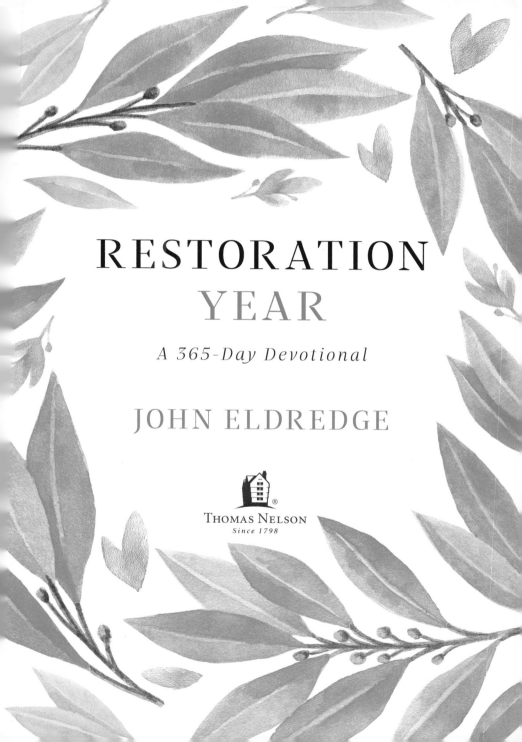

RESTORATION
YEAR

A 365-Day Devotional

JOHN ELDREDGE

THOMAS NELSON
Since 1798

Restoration Year

© 2018 John Eldredge

Published in Nashville, Tennessee, by Thomas Nelson. Thomas Nelson is a registered trademark of HarperCollins Christian Publishing, Inc.

Thomas Nelson titles may be purchased in bulk for educational, business, fund-raising, or sales promotional use. For information, please e-mail SpecialMarkets@ThomasNelson.com.

Unless otherwise noted, Scripture quotations are taken from the Holy Bible, New International Version®, NIV®. Copyright © 1973, 1978, 1984, 2011 by Biblica, Inc.® Used by permission of Zondervan. All rights reserved worldwide. www.Zondervan.com. The "NIV" and "New International Version" are trademarks registered in the United States Patent and Trademark Office by Biblica, Inc.®

Scripture quotations marked THE MESSAGE are from *The Message.* Copyright © 1993, 1994, 1995, 1996, 2000, 2001, 2002. Used by permission of NavPress Publishing Group.

Scripture quotations marked NASB are from New American Standard Bible®. Copyright © 1960, 1962, 1963, 1968, 1971, 1972, 1973, 1975, 1977, 1995 by The Lockman Foundation. Used by permission. (www.Lockman.org)

Scripture quotations marked NKJV are from the New King James Version®. © 1982 by Thomas Nelson. Used by permission. All rights reserved.

Scripture quotations marked NLT are from the *Holy Bible*, New Living Translation. © 1996, 2004, 2007, 2013, 2015 by Tyndale House Foundation. Used by permission of Tyndale House Publishers, Inc., Carol Stream, Illinois 60188. All rights reserved.

ISBN 978-1-4002-0948-4

Printed in China

19 20 21 22   DSC   10 9 8 7 6 5 4 3 2

JANUARY

A FRESH START

Is anything too hard for the LORD?
GENESIS 18:14

January 1. A brand-new year. It's the time of year we start thinking about making changes. This year, rather than writing a quick list of resolutions that we'll likely forget before February, maybe we should take a different approach. This is a good time for each of us to ask ourselves, *What do I want to be different this year?*

Sit with that for ten minutes. Let your heart surface and then . . . take it to Jesus in prayer. *Lord, come into this. Show me the way.* I will often ask God for his "theme" over my new year: *Jesus, what is the theme of this year?*

I do this every January, and it has proven a mighty rescue many times over. Usually, Jesus says one simple thing. One year I heard, "Love." All through the year, I found myself needing to return to the simple truth of love. Another year it was, "Restoration," and that was the year I took a short sabbatical and sought needed restoration.

Ask Jesus, *What is the theme of this year, Lord?* And when he speaks, write it down! Post it somewhere you will see it often. In very big letters.

WHAT EFFECT?

Long before [God] laid down earth's foundations,
he had us in mind, had settled on us as the focus of
his love, to be made whole and holy by his love.
EPHESIANS 1:4 THE MESSAGE

We exercise because we want to grow stronger; we take vitamins in the hope of being healthy; we attend language classes expecting to learn a new language. We travel for adventure; we work in the hope of prospering; we love partly in the hope of being loved. So why Christianity? What is the *effect* Christianity is intended to have upon a person who becomes a Christian, seeks to live as a Christian?

The way you answer that question is mighty important. Your beliefs about this will shape your convictions about nearly everything else. It will shape your understanding of the purpose of the gospel; it will shape your understanding of what you believe God is up to in a person's life. What is Christianity supposed to *do* to a person?

God wants to make people whole and holy, by his love. To make *you* whole and holy by his love. Whole, and holy—this is what you ache for.

Jesus—do I really believe this? What do I think you are actually up to in my life? Show me, Lord.

HEMMED IN

*You hem me in behind and before, and
you lay your hand upon me.*

PSALM 139:5

At the Fall, why did God curse Adam and Eve with an empti-ness that nothing would be able to fill? Wasn't life going to be hard enough out there in the world, banished from the Garden? It seems unkind. Cruel, even.

He did it to save them. For as we all know, the heart shifted at the Fall. Something sent its roots down deep into their souls—that mistrust of God's heart and resolution to find life on their own terms. So God thwarted them. In love, he blocked their attempts until, wounded and aching, they turned to him for their rescue.

Jesus has to thwart you too. Your controlling and your hid-ing; the ways you seek to fill the ache within you. Otherwise, you would never fully turn to him for your rescue. Oh, you might turn to him for a ticket to heaven when you die. But *inside*, your heart remains broken far from the One who can help you.

And so you will see the gentle, firm hand of God in your life hemming you in. Wherever it is you have sought life apart from him, he disrupts your plans, your "way of life" that is not life at all.

How has God been "hemming you in," disrupting the plans you have to make life work?

A HEART FOR HIS KINGDOM

God has made everything beautiful for its own time.
He has planted eternity in the human heart.
ECCLESIASTES 3:11 NLT

The thing you are made for is the renewal of all things. God has given you a heart for his kingdom—not the wispy vagaries of a cloudy heaven, but the sharp reality of the world made new. This is one of the most important things you can know about yourself. Did you know this about yourself? When was the last time you told yourself, as you looked in the mirror in the morning, *Good morning; you have a heart for the kingdom?* This explains so much; it will be such an enormous help to you. It explains your anger and all of your addictions. It explains your cry for justice, and it also explains the growing hopelessness, resignation, cynicism, and defeat.

If you will listen with kindness and compassion to your own soul, you will hear the echoes of a hope so precious you can barely put words to it, a wild hope you can hardly bear to embrace. God put it there. He also breathed the corresponding promise into the earth; it is the whisper that keeps coming to you in moments of golden goodness. But of course, the secret to your unhappiness and the answer to the agony of the earth are one and the same— you are longing for the kingdom of God. You are aching for God's promise of the restoration of all things.

Jesus—restore my hope this year. Renew my hope that you are going to renew all things, including my life.

ONE MORNING

*We who have run for our very lives to God have every
reason to grab the promised hope with both hands
and never let go. It's an unbreakable spiritual lifeline.*

HEBREWS 6:18–19 THE MESSAGE

The hope and promise of the restoration of all things has been planted in your heart—whether you are aware of it or not. It is the only hope strong enough, brilliant enough, glorious enough to overcome the heartache of this world.

One morning you will wake, and sunlight will be coming in through the curtains. You will hear the sound of birds singing in the garden; delicious scents of summer will waft in on the breeze. As you open your eyes you realize your body feels young and whole. No tormenting thoughts will rush in to assault you; you realize that your soul feels young and whole too. As you sit up to look around the bedroom filled with light, you hear the sounds of laughter and running water outside and you will know—it is going to be a wonderful day.

Only this hope can serve as the anchor for your soul. The renewal of all things, including *you*, is the only hope strong enough, brilliant enough, glorious enough to overcome the heartache of this world.

So chase it now with all of your being.

Take the time to pause here, and dream. When you imagine the first few moments when your life is restored, what are the first three things you will want to do? Who will you want to see?

GOLDEN GOODNESS

*"He is like the light of morning at sunrise on
a cloudless morning, like the brightness after
rain that brings grass from the earth."*

2 SAMUEL 23:4

What makes your heart awaken? For what awakens your heart is worth paying attention to.

Think about sunshine—what daily radiance is showered upon you through it, what immense golden goodness. Every single day, over so much of the planet. It saturates the world, warming the earth, raising the crops in the fields by silent resurrection, causing birds to break out in song with the dawning of each day. It bathes everything in light, which then enables us to behold and enjoy, to live and work and explore. What a gift sunlight is—coming and going. I love getting up in the darkness of early morning and praying through the dawn. As I find myself drawing nearer to God, the room begins to grow lighter while the spiritual air clears around me. With a final amen, the golden glowing light of sunrise fills the room like the presence of God.

Pause, and simply be still for a moment. Let the presence of God surround you, for he is always here with us. Let his love come to you again, as you simply quiet yourself in his presence. His love is like sunshine in our hearts.

A HEART FOR REDEMPTION

It is because of him that you are in Christ Jesus,
who has become for us wisdom from God—that
is, our righteousness, holiness and redemption.

1 CORINTHIANS 1:30

You have a heart for redemption. Your kingdom heart longs for restoration and reconciliation, for justice, for the recovery of all that has been lost. What is the redemption that your heart longs for on a global level? What passions arouse your heart? Is your heart for a people group? A community or nation? For the arts or sciences? You have very particular passions for justice and redemption, and they will be realized. Your heart needs to know this—they *will* be realized.

And what is the redemption your heart aches for on a personal level—for your family, your friends? What cries fill your prayers in the night? Oh, to see the day that alcohol no longer holds a family line in its grips; when abuse no longer tears a family apart. Nor poverty, or shame, or mental illness. You have very special and particular longings for redemption for those you love. And my dear friend—those longings were given to you by the God who shares them, and they too *will* be fulfilled.

The promise of redemption, of justice fulfilled, is yet another one of the great hopes of the coming kingdom.

Jesus, I give to you everyone I care about, and everything that matters to me. I release it all to your love, to rest my heart in you.

YOUR FIRST HOPE

"For I know the plans I have for you," says the
LORD. "They are plans for good and not for
disaster, to give you a future and a hope."
JEREMIAH 29:11 NLT

The renewal of all things is meant to be your first hope in the way that God is your First Love. If it isn't the answer to your wildest dreams, if you aren't ready at this very moment to sell everything and buy this field, then you have placed your hopes somewhere else. Nearly everyone has.

You cannot move forward in your search for the *palingenesia* until you face this as honestly as possible. *Palingenesia* is the Greek word for "renewal," which is derived from two root words: *paling,* meaning "again," and *genesia,* meaning "beginning."

If you're not honest about where you place your hope, this will just be a curiosity; interesting, but not the rescue your heart so desperately needs. You hear about the Renewal and think to yourself, *Well, isn't that nice; I'd never heard it put that way,* and go right on with your desperate search for the kingdom now.

Ask yourself: *Where is my kingdom heart these days? Am I embarrassed by it? What am I presently doing with it? What am I fantasizing about?* (Where you take your fantasies is a helpful way to know what you are doing with your kingdom heart.)

CASUAL HOPES

*The Spirit of God is arousing us within. . . . That
is why waiting does not diminish us. . . . But the
longer we wait . . . the more joyful our expectancy.*
ROMANS 8:23–25 THE MESSAGE

Have you taken the time to consider where your hope is placed? My friend, it is so important to know where your hope is placed these days. Knowing this helps it land in the right places.

When your hopes are in their proper places, attached to the right things, not only do you flourish better as a human being, but you're rescued from a thousand heartbreaks. For not all hopes are created equal; there are casual hopes, precious hopes, and ultimate hopes.

Casual hopes are the daily variety: "I sure hope it doesn't rain this weekend"; "I hope we can get tickets to the game"; "I really hope this flight is on time." Nothing wrong with this brand of hope; it is human nature to have it. I think it is the sign of a healthy soul when we often use the words "I hope." My wife does. "I hope this pie turns out," meaning she cares about the dinner she is hosting. "I hope we get to the Tetons next year," meaning she cares about dreams and family memories.

Hope shows your heart is still alive.

*O Jesus—what have I done with hope? Come and find my hope, Lord,
for I give it to you. I want my hope to be placed in you alone.*

PRECIOUS HOPES

*Hope deferred makes the heart sick, but
a longing fulfilled is a tree of life.*

PROVERBS 13:12

Hope is so precious. It is your lifeline. Casual hopes show you your heart is alive, but they are nothing when compared to your precious hopes: "I hope this pregnancy goes well"; "I hope God hears my prayers for Sally"; "I hope the CT scan turns out to reveal nothing at all." Precious hopes are far deeper to your heart, and they tend to fuel your most earnest prayers.

You'll notice that many people have let their hopes go wandering—turning casual hopes into precious hopes and turning genuinely precious hopes into critical or ultimate hopes. The person who commits suicide because a loved one chose another has taken a precious hope and made it the outcome of their very being.

When a precious hope is dashed, it can really break your heart. It may usher in fear and anxiety. You may not recover for a week or five years, depending on the loss and the other resources of your life.

If you put your hope in something that cannot possibly come through for you, you will be constantly let down. It was never meant to play that role. Only God knows the depths of your desires. Only he can come through and meet your needs.

Jesus—rescue my heart and all my dashed hopes. You are the Healer; come and heal every lost hope in me. Resurrect hope, Lord.

YOUR ULTIMATE HOPE

My soul is in deep anguish. How long, LORD,
how long? Turn, LORD, and deliver me; save
me because of your unfailing love.

PSALM 6:3–4

When your casual hopes are suddenly in question, they elicit worry, but nothing more. Precious hopes in question can usher in fear and anxiety. But our ultimate hopes lie in the deepest parts of our soul—our life-and-death hopes. When ultimate hopes suddenly seem uncertain, they can shake the soul to its core. I would suggest that the only things that belong in the category of ultimate hopes are the things that will destroy your heart and soul if they are not fulfilled. "I hope God can forgive me." "I hope somehow my mistakes can be redeemed." "I hope I will see you again."

And I will be forthright with you—very few things deserve the place in your heart made for ultimate hopes, because when an ultimate hope goes unanswered, the result is devastation from which you will feel you will never recover.

It's easy to let your heart go wandering, but by aligning your heart to what matters most, your first hope—the hope in the renewal of all things—you can overcome.

I align my deepest, ultimate hopes with you, Lord. I give my heart of hearts over to your return, and the renewal of all things. Nothing else will do.

AWAKENED BY EXTRAVAGANCE

Through him all things were made; without him nothing was made that has been made.

JOHN 1:3

Remember—an artist is revealed in the work he or she creates, and in the abundance of the work created.

Think of the ocean. Imagine sitting on the beach watching the swells roll in toward you. Each wave builds as it approaches, ascending, taking shape, deep greens below sweeping upward into translucent aquamarine. A sculpture in motion, curling forth like shavings from a jade carving. The sheer elegance is enough to take your breath away.

Hear the breakers thundering on the reef a hundred yards out, and beyond that is the open ocean. What does this tell you about Jesus? What words come to mind? *Majestic, powerful, wild, dangerous.* Yes, *tempestuous*, like the clearing of the temple. But also gently playful as the water laps at your feet, swirling round your toes, pulling the sand away from beneath you.

If all this is the work of an artist's hand, what does it tell you about the artist? Creation is epic and intimate. *He* is epic and intimate.

Can you name the places in your life where your heart feels awakened because of Jesus' extravagant generosity? *Jesus—open my eyes to your generosity again.*

HE LONGS FOR YOU

*"Those who accept my commandments and obey
them are the ones who love me. And because
they love me, my Father will love them. And I will
love them and reveal myself to each of them."*

JOHN 14:21 NLT

What is it that God wants from you? He wants the same thing that you want. He wants to be loved. He wants to be known as only lovers can know each other. He wants intimacy with you. Yes, yes, he wants your obedience, but only when it flows out of a heart filled with love for him. Following hard after Jesus is the heart's natural response when it has been captured and has fallen deeply in love with him, a place only he can fill. Likewise, there is a place in God's heart that only you alone can fill. You. He longs for *you*.

God wants to live this life together with you, to share in your days and decisions, your desires and disappointments. He wants intimacy with you in the midst of the madness and mundane, the meetings and memos, the laundry and lists, the projects and pain. He wants to pour his love into your heart, and he longs to have you pour yours into his. He wants your deep heart, that center place within that is the truest *you*. He is not interested in intimacy with the person you think you are supposed to be. He wants intimacy with the real you—who you are now.

Pause, and reflect—what is it that you have been thinking God wants from you?

THE INTEGRITY TRAP

*Thanks be to God that, though you used to be slaves
to sin, you come to obey from your heart.*

ROMANS 6:17

There are traps that over time can replace the simple priority of loving Jesus. Here is a very surprising one—the trap of integrity. What I mean by this is when your attention turns to maintaining personal righteousness. This seems noble and right. Jesus told us to keep his commands. But this can be a trap because most Christians *interpret this* as "Try harder; do your best."

And this is what most Christians experience as the Christian life: try harder; feel worse.

I find myself slipping back into this weekly. A handful of symptoms tips me off. Exhaustion, for one. I'll just find myself wrung out again. Or an unnamed internal distress; my insides all twisted up. Discouragement, that old nagging cloud of "I'm totally blowing it" comes back over me. Irritation with needy people. These symptoms—and a host of others—are the collateral damage that results from trying my best.

They let me know I've fallen back to thinking that to love Jesus is to give my very best in living for him. And this is a sticky business. Because on the one hand, that's true—to love him is to obey. But out of what resources? From the fountain of inner strength? Or out of obeying from my heart?

Jesus—your yoke is easy and your burden light. I give you now every burden of trying to please you. I choose to simply rest in your love.

HIS TRANSFORMATION OF YOU

"I am the vine; you are the branches. Those who remain in me, and I in them, will produce much fruit. For apart from me you can do nothing."

JOHN 15:5 NLT

Let me tell you, few things can mess you up as badly as trying to do your best. For the tender heart, the earnest heart, it is *so* discouraging to give everything to do what you *think* Jesus would have you do, then find yourself falling short at every turn. Discouragement and shame will settle in like a long Seattle rain.

When I fall into "trying my best," I can be fooled into thinking it's out of my faithfulness. My integrity. A willingness to sacrifice. Of course your choices matter. But didn't Jesus also say, "Apart from me you can do nothing"? The good news is this—you were never meant to imitate Christ. Not if by that you mean doing your best to live as he did. It ought to come as a great relief. Because without understanding that *I was never meant to do my best*, it's easy to lose heart.

The secret of Christianity is something else altogether—the life of Christ *in* you. Allowing his life to become your life. His revolution is not self-transformation, but his transformation of you, from the inside out, as you receive his life and allow him to live through you. Vine, branch. Anything else is madness.

Jesus—I return my life to you. I give this "branch" back to you, the Vine. Fill my life with your glorious life!

THE ALLURE OF HOLINESS

*[He] climbed up in a sycamore tree so he
could see Jesus when he came by.*

LUKE 19:4 THE MESSAGE

We are entering a period of great trial upon the earth. You've seen the news; you've watched your friends suffering. The spiritual war is heating up. It is going to take a supernatural life to withstand these trials. Holiness, friends, is the strength of your condition.

Zacchaeus was desperate to see Jesus. God wants people to be desperate for him. He wants folks climbing sycamores of this world to get a glimpse of Jesus. Don't you? Now, God has arranged this story in such a way that it is largely through *your* life that others get a glimpse of Jesus.

If you want to turn your children off to Jesus, ignore holiness (or choose the technical rule-keeping impostor). Be a jerk and then insist the family pray at mealtimes; let them see you lie to your boss or your parents and then insist you all go to church. Want to turn your neighbors off to Christianity? Let them see you yell at your dog, then head off all dressed up for Sunday service. It is the lack of holiness that has clouded our "witness" in this world. Thank God the opposite holds true as well: the beauty of your life as God's dearest friend is the sweetest and most winsome argument for Jesus there could ever be.

Ask yourself today: *When it comes to my life, what is the Jesus people see?* Sit in prayer with Jesus and ask him, *Jesus, give me your life. Give me your holiness.*

FORGETFULNESS

Don't forget anything of what you've seen. Don't let
your heart wander off. Stay vigilant as long as you live.
DEUTERONOMY 4:9 THE MESSAGE

We're warned about forgetfulness in Scripture. In the Old Testament, the pattern is so predictable it becomes expected. God delivers his people from the cruel whips of Egypt by a stunning display of his power and care. The Israelites celebrate with singing and dancing. Three days later, they are complaining about the water supply.

They let it slip from their hearts. All of it. This becomes the pattern for the entire history of Israel. God shows up; he does amazing things; the people rejoice. They fall under calamity and cry out for deliverance. God shows up; he does amazing things; the people rejoice—you get the picture.

Things aren't changed much in the New Testament, but the contrast is greater, and the stakes are even higher. God shows up *in person,* and before he leaves, he gives us the sacraments along with this plea: *do this to remember me.*

They don't remember him. It happens to the best of us. Of all the enemies your heart must face, this may be the worst because forgetfulness is subtle. But the distance it causes between your heart and your God can be harmful.

I am forgetful, Lord; forgive me all my wandering. I come back to you now, to be one with you. To stay with you. Restore my life in union with yours, Lord.

I AM GOD'S; HE IS MINE

Despite all these things, overwhelming victory is ours through Christ, who loved us. And I am convinced that nothing can ever separate us from God's love.

ROMANS 8:37–38 NLT

Hearing from God *flows out* of your relationship with him, and that relationship was established by Jesus Christ. "Therefore, since we have been justified [made right with God] through faith, we have peace with God through our Lord Jesus Christ, through whom we have gained access by faith into this grace in which we now stand" (Romans 5:1–2). Whatever you might be feeling, you *do* have relationship with God now, because you belong to him. And your relationship is secure.

I am God's. He is mine.

Because you have relationship with God secured by Jesus Christ and all he has done, you can now grow in *developing* that relationship. You can, on the basis of what is objectively true, move into an experience of God in your life that deepens over time. And that includes learning to hear his voice. Praying to him not as a one-sided conversation, but as the act of talking to and hearing from God. A two-sided conversation. It is a rich inheritance you have.

Taking the journey toward an intimacy with God that includes conversational intimacy is a beautiful thing, and you will be filled with surprises and gifts from him.

I want a deeper friendship with you, God. I want to hear you speaking to me. Open my ears to hear your loving voice.

SELECTIVE MORALITY

"You should tithe, yes, but do not neglect
the more important things."
MATTHEW 23:23 NLT

I knew a man who was fired from his job at a Christian high school because one of the church elders saw him purchasing cigarettes. They smugly canned him even though he was the best teacher they had. What is even more diabolical is the pleasure these Pharisees had in firing him. Their judgment was swift and severe; their self-righteous was far sicker than any cigarette.

The poison of technical rule-keeping is that it shifts the focus from serious issues to ridiculous peccadilloes, thus allowing the legalist to live what he believes is a "righteous life" when in fact he is failing at the very things God majors in. Take as an example a man who resents his wife, but has never committed adultery; he is "faithful." He prides himself on his selective morality—keeping the letter of the law while ignoring massive problems in his heart. Is this holiness?

Holiness isn't the same thing as morality. You can be a moral person and not love God. You can keep the laws and hate your neighbor. Jesus is not trying to produce Pharisees; he is trying to restore your humanity by giving you the beauty of his holiness, make you whole and holy by his love.

I want to be made whole and holy by your love, Jesus. I don't want a legalistic life—I want the beauty of your holiness!

THE SPIRIT OF RELIGION

Make sure that you stay free.
GALATIANS 5:1 NLT

The Religious Spirit has turned discipleship into a soul-killing exercise of principles. Most folks don't even know they can hear God's voice. Satan's stigmatized counseling as something only for the sick, so the wounds of the heart never get healed. He's taken healing away almost entirely, so that we sit in pews as broken people feeling guilty because we can't live the life we're *supposed* to.

He's taken the hidden assaults on our hearts and mocks them. Most of the church knows almost nothing about how to set captive hearts free. We're not advancing the kingdom; we're holding car washes—we have surrendered without a fight.

The reason I bring this up is that if you want the real deal, if you want the life and freedom that Jesus offers, then you are going to have to break free of the Religious Spirit in particular. So here's a bottom-line test to expose the Religious Spirit: If it doesn't bring you freedom and it doesn't bring life, it's not Christianity. If it doesn't restore the image of God and rejoice in the heart, it's not Christianity.

Jesus, set me free from every Religious Spirit. Break every "spell" I am living under. I want freedom and restoration! I want you, Lord, not religion.

YOUR EVERYTHING

Their trust should be in God, who richly
gives us all we need for our enjoyment.
1 TIMOTHY 6:17 NLT

Sometimes the sorrows of your life are in part God's weaning process. We give our hearts over to so many things other than God, because we look to so many other things for life. I know I do. Especially the very gifts that God himself gives to us—they become more important to us than he is. That's not the way it is supposed to be. As long as your happiness is tied to the things you can lose, you are vulnerable.

This truth is core to the human condition and to understanding what God is doing in your life. We believe that God's primary reason for being is to provide us with happiness, give us a good life, but it doesn't occur to us that *God* is meant to be our all, and that until he is our all, we aren't living the life he intended for us. The first and greatest command is to love God with our whole being.

Oh friend, there is so much about the world that is good and beautiful even though it is fallen. And there is so much good in the life that God gives you. Make room in your soul for God; he will be your enough.

Is there something God might be "weaning" from your life? Something you need to surrender to him? Have you made some happiness more important to you than God is?

TRAPPED IN THE PRESENT

*"I live in the high and holy places, but also
with the low-spirited, the spirit-crushed."*
ISAIAH 57:15 THE MESSAGE

The Religious Spirit sets out to reduce the wildness of life by constructing a system of promises and rewards. It really doesn't matter what the particular bargain is—doctrinal adherence, moral living—the desire is the same: taming God in order to tame life. Never mind those deep yearnings of the soul; never mind the nagging awareness that God is not cooperating. If the system isn't working, it's because you're not doing it right. There's always something to work on.

Through baseball and politics and music and sex and even church, there is a desperate search for a Larger Story in which to live and find your role. All of these smaller stories offer a taste of meaning, adventure, or connectedness. But none of them offer the real thing; they aren't large enough. The loss of confidence in a Larger Story is the reason immediate gratification is demanded. We need a sense of being alive now, for now is all we have. Without a past that was planned for you and a future that waits for you, you're trapped in the present. There's not enough room for your soul in the present.

What would you say is the "story" you are living in right now? Who is the hero? The villain? What is the plot? How does it compare to the Great Story God is telling?

STAY CLOSE

As you received Christ Jesus as Lord,
continue to live your lives in him.
COLOSSIANS 2:6

Remain in me, and I will remain in you," Jesus said (John 15:4 NLT). A simple command, it seems. And yet we overlook it.

If Jesus must tell us to remain in him, then he seems to be assuming that it's quite possible *not* to remain in him. The common life is, in fact, a life lived separate from him, which is a dangerous place to live. An old saint once said to me that the devil doesn't so much care what particular thing we fall prey to as long as it's outside of Christ, for then we are vulnerable.

I want two things that are mutually opposed—I want to live a nice little life, and I want to play an important role in God's kingdom. And it's in those times that I am trying to live a nice little life that I make decisions and choices that cause me in small and subtle ways to live outside of Jesus.

You cannot enjoy the fellowship of God, or his protection, or all the benefits of his kingdom unless you remain in him—that is, live in him—in your day-to-day life. Vine and branches, Shepherd and sheep. *Stay close. Stay with me*, Jesus is saying.

I come back to you, Lord, from all my wandering and striving. I come back to you now, and I give myself over to you to be one with you in everything. This is where I choose to stay—in you.

DOUBT IS NOT A VIRTUE

"Put your finger here; see my hands.
Reach out your hand and put it into my
side. Stop doubting and believe."
JOHN 20:27

I don't remember the issue my friend and I were talking about—it had something to do with Christianity—but I do remember my friend's response: "Gosh, I'm not really sure," he said. And I thought it a humble and gracious posture to take. Only it's been five years now and he's still saying, "I'm not really sure." I see what happened. He has chosen *doubt*, a posture very honored in our day.

Doubt is "in." We embrace it because it feels "authentic." So doubt, masquerading as humility, has become a virtue, a prerequisite for respect. People of strong conviction are suspect. Many Christians I know have settled for a sort of laid-back doubt, believing it to be a genuine character decision; they think it's a virtue. Now, I appreciate the desire for humility, and the fear of being dogmatic. I think those are good concerns. But friend, conviction is not the enemy. Pride is. Arrogance is. But not conviction.

Enter Jesus (who is always so wonderfully countercultural). There is no question about his sincerity, his humility, or his graciousness. But doubt—this will be a great surprise to many people—is not something Jesus holds in high esteem. Rather he wants you to believe.

❧

Has doubt crept into your life? Have you even made agreements with doubt, because it feels like the humble posture? What does "stop doubting and believe" look like for you?

HOLINESS THROUGH BELIEF

When [Peter] saw the strong wind and the
waves, he was terrified and began to sink.

MATTHEW 14:30 NLT

When Jesus found Peter on the boat, he didn't commend Peter for his authenticity. "Wow, Peter, I love how honest you were with your doubts, sinking in the ocean. So many people will be able to relate to that." No, he rebukes him for doubting.

Not only does doubt make you fit comfortably within the culture, but it also excuses you from having to act. If you were convinced that people actually did go to hell unless they knew Christ as Savior, you would have to be far bolder about sharing your faith—and wouldn't *that* be awkward at work? So take notice just how convenient doubt is for you. Motives are at play here. Doubt is not a virtue nor humility. Doubt is unbelief. Jesus wants you to get past it, not embrace it, for heaven's sake.

I raise this up because it reflects the times. You are urged in Scripture not to let the times infect you. You breathe this present cultural air; you take in its assumptions. But you're after something far more genuine: the beautiful holiness of Jesus.

Jesus, you have my yes! I say yes to you, Lord. I choose to believe. I choose to align with you, Lord!

DESIGNED TO FLOURISH

LORD, all my desire is before You.
PSALM 38:9 NASB

I was thumbing through a catalog that called itself "a catalog for cooks," but really, it's a catalog of the life we wish we had. Everything in it is immaculate—there are no messes. Glancing through its pages, you get a sense of rest. Life is good. *You see,* the images whisper, *it can be done. Life is within your grasp.* And so the quest continues. But, of course, our address used to be Paradise, remember?

And oh, how we yearn for another shot at Eden. Flip with me for a moment through the photo album of your heart, and collect a few of your most treasured memories. Perhaps it's time with a loved one. Or when you first learned to ride a bike, or a treasured vacation.

You were *meant* to live in a world like that—every day. Just as your lungs are made to breathe oxygen, your soul is designed to flourish in an atmosphere rich in love and meaning, security and significance, *intimacy* and *adventure.* But you don't live in that world anymore. So you try to resolve the dilemma by disowning your desire. It doesn't work. It is the soul's equivalent of holding your breath. Eventually you'll find yourself gasping for air. You can't live with ignoring your desire. Eventually something comes along and touches those essential places in you, to awaken the more you were meant for.

Recall a time in your life when you *knew* you were loved. Invite Jesus into the desire awakened in that memory.

SYSTEM OF GUILT

*"Come to me, all you who are weary and
burdened, and I will give you rest."*
MATTHEW 11:28

Jesus spoke to the people about rest and thirst. The Pharisees demanded that they obey religious laws and traditions, chastising them for staggering under the load. They led people in the exact opposite direction from where their salvation lay—in admitting their weariness and fainting. As long as they hoped in their self-sufficiency, they would not call out to God and receive forgiveness, healing, and restoration.

So many of our contemporary churches operate on this same system of guilt. When our people are crying out for communion and rest, we ask them to teach another Sunday school class. When they falter under the load, we admonish them with Scriptures on serving others. Many of us think of spiritual progress as requiring us to do more, even our heart cries out to us to lay our burdens down. One wonders what would happen if all activity motivated by this type of guilt were to cease for six months.

As Jesus talked about thirst and rest, he brought people to the reality of their own hearts. And that reality brings us back to Jesus.

Jesus, I am thirsty. Weary, and thirsty. I give you all my striving, all my weariness. Come into my thirst, Lord. Give me living water.

HOLINESS MEANS HEALING

*Fix your attention on God. You'll be
changed from the inside out.*
ROMANS 12:2 THE MESSAGE

It seems that much of what Christians believe they are called to is a cluster of activities that include regular church attendance, Bible study, giving, and attending the annual retreat. Now—what is all this activity supposed to do in us? If it's not restoring the whole person, it may be completely missing the point of what God is after in our life: to heal us as human beings.

It might help to contrast this with a couple other popular options out there: the self-help movement's goal of getting your life working—helping you with your anxiety or your weight problems. It is right and it is wrong. I believe with all my heart that God wants life for us there. But when we focus on fixing problems, the transformation of our *character is missed.*

Then you have what we'll call *righteousness Christianity,* focusing mostly on "sin" and "the loss of morality." A great deal of energy is spent trying to make people behave. And it is right and it is wrong. Yes, we're supposed to live godly lives, but where's the joy and the intimacy with God?

God is restoring the creation he made. Whatever holiness truly is, the effect of it is healing. That's what it does to a person.

Is the Christianity you are living healing your life? Is it ushering in restoration? If not . . . you might want to ask Jesus if he has something new for you.

LAY DOWN YOUR "DOINGS"

When troubles of any kind come your way,
consider it an opportunity for great joy. For
you know that when your faith is tested,
your endurance has a chance to grow.

JAMES 1:2–3 NLT

It is impossible to live the pure spiritual life because your heart and mind become enemies rather than allies. Neither are you free to love or serve. The problem is not that people aren't important enough to you. It is that they are too important—you seek their approval too much.

God comes to the Israelites in Exodus 23 telling them that he will not drive their enemies from the land in a day because they are not substantive enough to hold the land. They must learn to rest in him, and from that place of abiding *in* him, they will be able to hold on to what is theirs. James tells us that we should count it all joy when we fall into various trials because God will use them to make us substantive. This happens as you learn to trust totally in God rather than yourself, with God as a fallback.

When you hear the phrase "Trust totally in God," you probably hear it as one more requirement that you will never be able to live up to. But instead of seeing it as a requirement, what if you were to listen to your heart, and hear it as a need to lay down your "doings," simply make your needs known to Christ, and rest in him?

O Jesus—I lay down all my "doings." I give everything, and everyone,
to you. Take their place in my heart; come and fill me, Lord.

KEEP YOUR CONFIDENCE

GOD, your God, is above all a compassionate
God. In the end he will not abandon you.

DEUTERONOMY 4:31 THE MESSAGE

The meadowlark has long been my favorite songbird. It's because it evokes so many precious memories. More than anything else, it has become for me a symbol of hope. The meadowlark returns to Colorado in the early spring, which typically means it arrives about the time our snowstorms hit. What courage; if it were me, I'd wait until June when the weather warms up. But they come in spite of the snow, perch on the tops of trees, and begin singing. Hearing a midsummer song almost seems out of place when flurries are whipping about your face. But that is exactly when we need it.

I was listening to two meadowlarks one cold and windy day, calling and responding to each other. God began to speak to me through them. I heard him urging me to keep my own summer song, even though life's winter tries to throw into my spring cold wind and snow. *Do not throw away your confidence,* he said. *Do not budge from your perch, but sing your song, summer confident, sure of my great goodness toward you. You did not bring this spring, dear child; you do not have to arrange for the summer to follow. They come from thy Father's will, and they will come.*

Jesus, where have I lost my "song"? Where have I lost hope that "summer" is coming?

A GREAT RELIEF

*"Enter through the narrow gate. For wide is
the gate and broad is the road that leads to
destruction, and many enter through it."*

MATTHEW 7:13

You live in the age of information, and it can often all feel like drinking from a fire hose and snorkeling through mud. More information doesn't seem to help.

You have been inundated with the promise that *you can do anything.* But a limitless universe of options is not a gift, not even an opportunity to dream; it is overwhelming. Paralyzing. And untrue. You can't do everything. I'm not trying to be a naysayer, but a road as vast as the horizon is no road at all. And when you are honest yourself, you'll find that the horizon is not nearly as vast as you have been told—or as the Internet makes it seem.

The truth is, the options before you are limited *and that is a great relief.* The open ocean is beautiful to look at, but terrifying if you have to navigate it in a small boat. But you are not facing the open ocean. God puts you within a context, with limited gifting and limited resources, and that is immensely kind.

And when you begin to factor in decisions based on reality, opportunity, finances, and the constraints of love, I think you will find the road to life refreshingly narrow—that is, a path you can actually follow.

As you think about decisions or your future, have you felt that paralyzing feeling? Knowing that God has actually set limits around you, out of his kindness, does it now feel like a relief?

FEBRUARY

THE ASSAULT ON DESIRE

Do not let sin reign . . . so that you obey its evil desires.
ROMANS 6:12

The battle of desire isn't something that just takes place within you or even between us. It is also taking place *against* you. Your desire is under constant attack. We look to others to teach us what to desire, for we're intensely imitative creatures. It's how we learn language; it's how we master just about anything in life. It is also how we come to seize upon the objects of our desire.

As an example, at a garage sale I found a table saw at a wonderful price. Another fellow was close, but not particularly interested. I made the fatal error, saying: "Wow, what a great price." Immediately, his nonchalance became intense interest, and *he* drove off with the saw that earlier he didn't give two hoots about.

The constant effort to arouse your desire and capture it can be described only as an assault. From the time you get up to the time you go to bed, you are inundated with one underlying message: *The life you are longing for can be achieved. Only buy this product, take this vacation, join this gym, what have you.* The only disagreement is over the means, but everyone agrees on the end: find life now.

However, once you give over your desire for life to anything other than God, you become ensnared. You become a slave to that which at the outset you thought would serve you.

Where are you currently "looking for life"? What has hijacked your desire these days?

YOU HAVE A CHOICE

*"Do not let your hearts be troubled
and do not be afraid."*
JOHN 14:27

Tucked away at the end of the fourteenth chapter of John, we find Jesus preparing his closest friends (and soon-to-be successors) for his departure. They still don't believe or don't *want* to believe he's leaving. Jesus says to them (and to us): "Do not let your hearts be troubled and do not be afraid."

I find this to be one of the most startling things Jesus says. I thought, *We have a choice? We let our hearts be troubled?* I've always assumed it was the other way around—that trouble strikes in some form or other, and the heart simply responds by being troubled. I'll bet this is how you look at it too. Trouble descends upon you: your house is robbed, your daughter gets pregnant, you lose your job. In that moment are you thinking, *This doesn't have to take me out. I'm not going to let my heart be troubled?* No way. We think "troubled heart" is unavoidable, appropriate even. But Jesus is talking about his coming torture, his death, and, following that, his departure from them. On a scale of personal crises, this is a ten. Yet he says, *Don't let your hearts be troubled.*

Friend, this is important. You have a say in what your heart gives way to.

Oh, Jesus, rescue me. Forgive me when my heart gives way to panic. Remind me that I have a choice to turn my troubled heart and eyes to you, God. May I rejoice and trust in you alone.

FAMISHED CRAVING

The eyes of the LORD are on those who fear him,
on those whose hope is in his unfailing love.

PSALM 33:18

We are by nature ravenous creatures; a famished craving haunts every one of us. We were created for utter happiness, joy, and life. But ever since we lost Eden, we have never known a day of total fullness. People are like cut flowers—we appear to be well, but we are severed from the Vine, desperately looking to anything that'll numb the ache. We are ravenous beings.

We don't trust anyone or anything anymore. Every institution that once provided psychological and moral stability is crumbling—families, communities, church allegiances are breaking down—adding a kind of unchecked desperation to the ravenous hunger.

Then the world stands in the way of our famished craving. People don't treat us as we long to be treated, and when somebody gets in the way of our desperate hunger, they'll feel the fury of our rage.

This is the current condition—ravenous and increasingly desperate. And there appears to be nothing to stop the slide into chaos. Something is happening to the human heart; we have clearly lost hope. We need to understand this if we want to make sense of our desperate need for his promised hope.

Have you noticed an impatience in yourself lately? Perhaps a growing anger? Is something standing in the way of your "famished craving"?

YOU ARE DESIRE

The unfailing love of the LORD fills the earth.
PSALM 33:5 NLT

You *are* desire. It is the essence of the human soul, the secret of your existence. Absolutely nothing of human greatness is ever accomplished without it. Not a symphony has been written, a mountain climbed, an injustice fought, or a love sustained apart from desire. Desire fuels our search for the life we prize. Your desire, if you will listen to it, will save you from the sacrifice of your heart on the altar of "getting by." The same old thing is not enough. It never will be.

Life as usual is not the life you truly want. It is not the life you truly need. It is not the life you were made for. If you would only listen to your heart.

You will find the meaning of your life is revealed through experiences you wish would never end. Those timeless experiences you want to last forever whisper to you that they were *meant* to. My friend, you were made to live in a world of beauty and wonder, intimacy and adventure all your days, and what your heart responds to there you will find is God pursuing the deepest places of your soul.

God is pursuing your heart through the things you love—is that a new thought to you?

BATTLE AND JOURNEY

*Treasure my commandments within
you, make your ear attentive to wisdom,
incline your heart to understanding.*

PROVERBS 2:1–2 NASB

Life is now a battle and a journey. It's not that there isn't joy and beauty, love and adventure now—there are. The invasion of the kingdom has begun. But life in its fullness has yet to come. So you must take seriously the care of your heart. You must watch over your desire with a fierce love and vigilance, as if you were protecting your most precious possession. You must do battle with the enemies of your heart—those sirens that would seduce and shipwreck your desire and those arrows that aim to kill it outright. And you must journey forward, toward God, toward the Great Restoration and the adventures to come.

So let me say it again: life is now a battle and a journey. This is the truest explanation for what is going on, the only way to rightly understand your experience. Life is not a game of striving and indulgence. It is not a long march of duty and obligation. Life is a desperate quest through dangerous country to a destination that is, beyond all your wildest hopes, indescribably good. You see, different roads lead to different places. To find the Land of Desire, you must take the journey of desire. You've got to get your heart back . . . which means getting your desire back.

Jesus—restore me to my heart's true desires. Restore me to the True Story—that this life is a fight and a journey to find my way home.

SEEKING LIFE

This day is holy to God. Don't feel bad.
The joy of GOD is your strength!
NEHEMIAH 8:10 THE MESSAGE

God knows the danger of ignoring our hearts, and so he reawakens desire. You see a photo in a magazine, and find yourself pausing. You're channel surfing one night and see someone doing the very thing you always dreamed you would do—the runner breaking the tape, the woman enjoying herself immensely as she teaches her cooking class. Sometimes all it takes is seeing people enjoying themselves doing anything, and your heart says, *I want that too.*

God does this to reawaken desire, to stir your heart up from the depths you sent it to. He does it so that you don't fall prey to some substitute that looks like life but will instead become a type of addiction.

He awakens your desire so that you will seek the life you were meant to seek. Isn't this just what happens to the prodigal son? He wakes one day to say, "All those farmhands working for my father sit down to three meals a day, and here I am starving" (Luke 15:17 THE MESSAGE). *Look at their lives,* he says. And is stirred to head for home. To seek life. Dear friend, where you find God stirring your heart, you will find that is the place where he is calling you home.

So—where is God stirring your heart? Is it through longing? Something you have seen? Perhaps even through disappointments?

A CHOICE

"I . . . am the one who takes care of your sins—
that's what I do. I don't keep a list of your sins."

ISAIAH 43:25 THE MESSAGE

The time will come to forgive those who have wounded you. Paul warns us that unforgiveness and bitterness can wreck our lives and the lives of others: "See to it that no one falls short of the grace of God and that no bitter root grows up to cause trouble and defile many" (Hebrews 12:15). As someone has said, forgiveness is setting a prisoner free and then discovering the prisoner was you. When my friend experienced forgiving his father, he told me, "I began to think of him not as someone who had deprived me of love or attention or companionship, but as someone who himself had been deprived, by his parents and by the culture."

Now you must understand: forgiveness is a choice. It is not a feeling, but an act of the will. It will happen as you allow God to bring the hurt up from your past. Acknowledge that it hurt, that it mattered, and choose to extend forgiveness. Dear friend, this is *not* saying, "It didn't really matter." Forgiveness says, "It was wrong, it mattered, and I release you." And then ask God to father you, and love you the way he created you to know love. Out of a heart that has been set free.

I know—this is a hard thing to face. But perhaps there is someone in your life right now you need to forgive. Simply start there.

REAWAKENED

*Remember his covenant forever—the commitment
he made to a thousand generations.*

1 CHRONICLES 16:15 NLT

We live in a world at war. But there is a part of human nature we must understand—we just don't want to face all that. Instead we want to find some way to numb ourselves out of the present reality and re-create some level of the pleasures of Eden. We just want life to be good.

This is why we are commanded, hundreds and hundreds of times throughout the Bible, to remember. We must continually be reawakened from our sleepwalking.

Remembering brings you back to reality; it breaks the spell of "I just want life to be good." It invites us up into the Story of God, invites us to take our role in a much greater purpose, to join him in his battle against evil and in bringing Jesus Christ—the only solution to this broken planet. Soon a day will come when life will be good. Till then, we must remember, or we'll be numbed by forgetfulness and sedated by that baser part of our nature that just doesn't want to face reality.

Jesus said nothing about pillows and comfortable retirement. He launched the invasion of the kingdom of God into a world held by darkness. He invites you to join him in living in that startling, dangerous, and beautiful Story.

❧

Dear Jesus, help me remember what is true about life. Help me see, understand, repent, forgive, heal, and become. Jesus, I give you access to all of my heart; bring me back to your Story.

YOUR TRANSFORMATION

GOD alone led him; there was not a foreign god in sight.
DEUTERONOMY 32:12 THE MESSAGE

Jesus says that as your Good Shepherd, he is leading you. What an encouraging thought. I can feel something in my heart loosening even now as I consider this. *I don't have to make life happen on my own.* Now, if Christ takes it upon himself to lead, then your part is to follow. And you'll find that it helps in your following if you know what God is up to. True, you may not know *exactly* what God is up to. Sometimes we can get clarity, and sometimes we can't.

But whatever else is going on, you can know this: God is always up to your transformation.

God has something in mind. He is deeply and personally committed to restoring humanity. Restoring you. He had a specific man or woman in mind when he made you. By bringing you back to himself through the work of Jesus Christ, he has established relationship with you. And now, what he is up to is restoring you. He does that by shaping your life. By shaping you into the image of Jesus. You can be confident of this. It's a given. Whatever else might be going on in your life, God always has his eye on your transformation.

Jesus—show me what you are working on in me, with me, these days. I want to cooperate with you. With my transformation.

SPIRITUAL SURRENDER

*"Father, if You are willing, remove this cup from
Me; yet not My will, but Yours be done."*
L U K E   2 2 : 4 2   N A S B

Think of Jesus in the Garden of Gethsemane as he prayed the night before his crucifixion. His face is lost in the shadows so that you can't even see his lips, and before all the powers on earth or heaven he is powerless.

Christ is weeping freely; his prayers are marked by loud cries and tears. He makes it very, very clear what he desires. Not once but three times he begs his Father to remove this awful cup from him: "Yet not my will, but Yours be done" (NASB). He surrenders with desire, in desire. Making himself poor, he opens up to us the treasures of heaven. We see in that moment, Christ surrenders his will.

You see, friend, true surrender is not an easy out, calling it quits early in the game. This kind of surrender comes only *after* the night of wrestling. It comes only after you open your heart to care deeply. Then you choose to surrender, or give over, your deepest desires to God. And with them you give over your heart, your deepest self. You will find that the freedom and beauty and rest that follow are among the greatest of all surprises.

Pause, and give this a moment . . . what do you need to surrender today?

DISRUPTIVE HONESTY

My honesty will testify for me.
GENESIS 30:33

Most people go through their entire lives without anyone ever speaking honest, loving, direct words to the most damaging issues in their lives. Let's be honest—it will cost you dearly if you're more honest with others. John the Baptist got his head handed to him on a platter for telling it like it is. Kill the messenger. You don't want to pay that bill. If you speak as honestly as Jesus does, or even venture that direction, it's going to make the relationship messy to say the least.

And so the collective silence—carefully justified as being polite or not wanting to be judgmental or whatever—the silence dooms us. Jesus is the boy in the tale of "The Emperor's New Clothes"—while everyone else fawns and feigns, pretending, looking the other way, he says, "Excuse me, but did you know that you are buck naked?" I'm not stunned by Jesus' words of honesty. I'm stunned by the courage and love this takes.

The man shoots straight. Sometimes he's playful; sometimes he's fierce; the next moment he's generous. This is the beauty of his disruptive honesty—you can count on Jesus to tell you the truth in the best possible way for you to hear it.

Count the times someone has spoken honest words to you in a loving but direct way. Better yet, count the times you have offered this to someone you love.

A SHARED LONELINESS

"Stay here and keep watch with me."
MATTHEW 26:38 NLT

Jesus enjoyed people. Not everyone does, you know. Many stories find him feasting with a rowdy crowd. He invited twelve men to spend day and night with him for three years. Yet, as you read in Matthew, his longing for companionship intensifies to a crescendo in Gethsemane. *Don't leave me alone, not now.* How urgently human. Yes, Jesus knew loneliness. He who created love and friendship longed for it.

This is no superhero, steeled and impervious to the human condition. Far from it. Loneliness is something we all share with him. To be misunderstood and judged unfairly. To go on for years unappreciated, even unknown by those closest to you. Imagine living your entire life in a world where the people closest to you don't get you. Oh . . . you do live in that world. And Jesus understands.

Now, I don't believe that Jesus was always lonely. There are moments of remarkable tenderness recorded in the Gospels. Mary washing his feet with tears, all that time walking the roads with the fellas, all those campfires. However, his loneliness didn't define him, as it can many of us. Jesus is an essentially happy man. He loves life. How could the joy of the Lord be our strength if the Lord is not essentially joyful?

Has loneliness taken your joy away? Does knowing that Jesus completely understands help? Can you invite Christ into your deepest loneliness?

LOVE JESUS IN YOUR PAIN

We love, because He first loved us.
1 JOHN 4:19 NASB

There is nothing like suffering to wreak havoc in your relationship with God. The damage pain does to our relationship with Jesus is often far, far worse than the pain itself.

During one episode of heartache, every time I turned to Jesus, the first thing he would say was, "Love me." At first it surprised me—*Aren't* you *supposed to say you love* me? *I'm the one who's hurting here.* But somehow, instinctively, I knew what he was after. "Love me now, in this—not *for* this, but *in* this." Those words have been a rescue.

Pain causes you to pull away from God when you need him most. Your soul withdraws, like a snail into its shell. Then you not only have the heartache, you have "lost" God for a while too. Desolation on top of suffering. Sometimes it takes months, even years to recover the relationship. Jesus was rescuing me from that cycle by telling me to love him now, right in the midst of the pain.

When I love God in this place, it opens my heart and soul back up to him right where I need him most, right in the center of the pain. Too often what we cry out for is understanding—"Why, God?" But I've learned over the years that when you are in the midst of the suffering, you don't often get understanding, and frankly, you don't need understanding—you need God.

Where are you hurting right now? Can you turn to Jesus in the midst of that pain? When you can, it will open your heart back up to him.

AN ANCHOR FOR THE SOUL

Three things will last forever—faith, hope, and love.
1 CORINTHIANS 13:13 NLT

When God says faith, hope, and love last forever, he names them as immortal powers. A life without faith has no meaning; a life without love isn't worth living; a life without hope is a dark cavern from which you cannot escape. These things aren't simply "virtues." Faith, hope, and love are mighty forces meant to carry your life forward, upward; they are your wings and the strength to use them.

I believe hope plays the critical role. You'll find it pretty hard to love when you've lost hope; hopelessness collapses into *Who cares?* And what does it matter that we have faith if we have no hope? Faith is just a rigid doctrine with nothing to look forward to. Hope is the wind in your sails, the spring in your step. Hope is so essential to your being that Scripture calls it "an anchor for the soul" (Hebrews 6:19).

In an untethered world, we need a hope that can anchor us.

Hope is unique; hope looks forward, anticipating the good that is coming. Hope reaches into the future to take hold of something we do not yet have, may not yet even see. Strong hope seizes the future that is not yet; it is the confident expectation of goodness coming to us.

Pause and ask yourself, *How is my hope these days? Where is my hope these days?*

ETERNAL LIFE

*"I came so they can have real and eternal life,
more and better life than they ever dreamed of."*
JOHN 10:10 THE MESSAGE

Eternal life—you tend to think of it in terms of existence that never comes to an end. And the existence it seems to imply—a sort of religious experience in the sky—leaves you wondering if you would want it to go on forever. But Jesus is quite clear that when he speaks of eternal life, what he means is life that is absolutely wonderful and can never be diminished or stolen from you. He says, "I have come that they may have life, and have it to the full" (John 10:10). Not "I have come to threaten you into line," or "I have come to exhaust you with a long list of demands." Not even "I have come primarily to forgive you." But simply, *My purpose is to bring you life in all its fullness.*

In other words, eternal life is not primarily duration but quality of life, "life to the limit."[3] It cannot be stolen from you, and so it does go on. But the focus is on the life itself. "In him was life," the apostle John said of Jesus, "and that life was the light of mankind" (John 1:4).

O Jesus, dear Jesus—I need Life! Come and fill me with your life today! I give my life to you to be filled with your life!

GOD THWARTS YOUR IMPOSTOR

*My dear child, don't shrug off God's discipline, but
don't be crushed by it either. It's the child he loves that
he disciplines; the child he embraces, he also corrects.*

HEBREWS 12:5–6 THE MESSAGE

It is a very dangerous moment when you feel that God is set against everything that has meant life to you. Satan spies his opportunity, and leaps to accuse God in your heart. *You see*, he says, *God is angry, and disappointed in you. If he loved you he would make things smoother.* The enemy tempts you back toward control, to recover and rebuild your false self. So you must remember that it is out of love that God thwarts your impostor. As Hebrews reminds you, it is the son whom God disciplines, therefore do not lose heart.

God thwarts you to save you. You think it will destroy you, but the opposite is true—you must be saved from what really will destroy you. If you would walk with him in your journey, you must walk away from your false self and give it up willingly.

If you have no clue as to what your false self may be, a starting point would be to ask those you live with and work with, "What is my effect on you? What am I like to live with (or work with)? What *don't* you feel free to bring up with me?"

Do you know what your false self is? Can you name the "fig leaf" you use to keep yourself from being rejected, or to get some praise, or to control your world?

YOUR SOURCE OF STRENGTH

*Let the peace of Christ keep you in tune with each other,
in step with each other. . . . And cultivate thankfulness.*
COLOSSIANS 3:15 THE MESSAGE

Your emptiness and woundedness can be a tremendous source of shame. But it need not be. From the very beginning, back before the Fall, yours was meant to be a dependent existence. Like a tree and its branches, explains Christ. He's not berating you here, thinking: *I wish they'd pull it together and stop needing me so much.* No. You are *made* to depend on God; you are made for union with him and nothing about you works right without it.

This is where your sin and culture have kept you in bondage, preventing the healing of your wound. Your sin is that stubborn part inside that is fiercely committed to living independent from anyone—especially God. You come to believe deep in your heart that needing others is a weakness, and a setup for heartbreak.

Why is this important? Because so many of us live with a deep misunderstanding of Christianity. It's seen as a "second chance" to get your act together. You've been forgiven, but now see it as needing to get with the program. You're trying to finish the marathon with a broken leg. But the deeper reality is this: your *true* essence of strength is passed to you from God *through your union with him.* Just as Jesus lived: "The Father and I are one" (John 10:30 NLT).

Yes, God—I need union with you. I need oneness. I give my brokenness to you to be united with you.

TOO EASILY PLEASED

My heart, my heart—I writhe in pain! My
heart pounds within me! I cannot be still.

JEREMIAH 4:19 NLT

The middle years of the Christian life are often thought of as a time of acquiring better habits and accompanying virtues. But inviting Jesus into what Oswald Chambers called the "aching abyss" of your heart perhaps has more to do with holding your heart hopefully in partial emptiness in a way that allows desire to be rekindled. There comes a place on your spiritual journey where renewed religious activity is of no use whatsoever. It is the place where God holds out his hand and asks you to give up your lovers and come and live with him in a much more personal way.

You are both drawn to it and fear it. Part of you would rather return to Scripture memorization, or Bible study, or service—anything that would save you from the unknowns of walking with God. You are partly convinced your life is elsewhere. You are deceived.

The desire God has placed within you is longing to pursue the One who is unknown. Its capacity and drive is so powerful that it can only be captured momentarily in moments of deep soul communion. And when the moment has passed, you can only hold it as an ache, flashes of a remembrance of innocence known and lost and, if you have begun to pass into the life of the Beloved, a hope of ecstasies yet to come.

Jesus—I invite you into the aching abyss of my heart. I give over my
idols to you, to be filled by you and you alone.

YOUR WOUND, YOUR GLORY

When Christ (your real life, remember)
shows up again on this earth, you'll show
up, too—the real you, the glorious you.
COLOSSIANS 3:4 THE MESSAGE

True strength does not come out of bravado. Until you are broken, your life will be self-centered, self-reliant; your strength will be your own. What will you need God for?

Only when you enter your wound will you discover your true glory. There are two reasons for this. First, the wound was given in the place of your true strength, as an effort to take you out. Until you go there you are still posing, offering something more shallow and insubstantial. And therefore, second, it is out of your brokenness that you discover what you have to offer the community.

Your false self is never wholly false. Those gifts you've been using are often quite true about you, but you've used them to hide behind. The power is in *your true self*. When you begin to offer not merely your gifts but your true self, that is when you become powerful. That is the place God can come in and heal, and the glory of your creation will shine.

Jesus longs to heal your heart. Take some time with him today. Ask him to reveal to you a defining wound received from your father or your mother. What happened? Friend, it matters to be very specific and intentional about healing your heart.

A HOPEFUL TRUTH

*We do not make requests of you because we are
righteous, but because of your great mercy.*

DANIEL 9:18

How someone prays reveals what they really think about Jesus. Does God sound near, or does the prayer make him seem far away? Does it sound as though Jesus might be someone we're bothering with our requests? Is it formal, and religious, or "Good morning, Papa"?

Dear friend, we interpret Jesus through our brokenness. A painful truth, but also a hopeful truth, because maybe it can open up doors you didn't know were closed.

For as long as I can remember, I've been haunted by the feeling that "it's never good enough." It doesn't particularly matter what "it" is—a project, a friendship. It's just never good enough. This began way before I met Jesus. When I became a Christian with this belief already deeply rooted in my psyche, what happened was, it got attached to Jesus as well. Nothing ever really feels good enough for him. *I'm not doing enough, I'm not loving him enough, I'm not . . .* you get the picture.

But this has absolutely nothing to do with who Jesus really is. What you bring to Jesus is enough, and when you choose to move toward him, he will have access to your heart and the veils will fall.

*O Jesus—show me the ways I am misunderstanding you. Show me
through my own prayers what I believe about you.*

YOUR HEART IS GOOD

Those who belong to Christ Jesus have nailed
the passions and desires of their sinful nature
to his cross and crucified them there.

GALATIANS 5:24 NLT

The idea that we are ready to sin at a moment's notice, incapable of goodness, and far from any glory is a common mind-set. It's also unbiblical.

The passage people think they are referring to is Romans 7:18, where Paul says, "For I know that in me (that is, in my flesh,) dwelleth no good thing" (KJV). Notice the distinction he makes. He does *not* say, "There is nothing good in me. Period." What he says is that "*in my flesh* dwelleth no good thing." The flesh is the old nature, the old life, crucified with Christ. The flesh is the very thing God removed from our hearts when he circumcised them by his Spirit, as Paul explains in Galatians.

Yes, you will still battle with sin. You have to *choose* to live from the new heart, and your old nature doesn't go down without a fight. But the question on the table is: Does the Bible teach that Christians are nothing but sinners—that there is nothing good in us? The answer is *no!* Christ lives in you. You have a new heart. Your heart is good, and that good heart is what is true about who you are.

Which version do you believe—that your heart is simply wicked, or now that Jesus Christ lives in your heart, God is giving you his holiness?

HONOR WOUNDS

"The kingdom of heaven suffers violence,
and violent men take it by force."
MATTHEW 11:12 NASB

You will be wounded. Just because this battle is spiritual doesn't mean it's not real; it is, and the wounds you can take are in some ways more ugly than those that come in a firefight. To lose a limb is nothing compared to losing heart; to be crippled by shrapnel need not destroy your soul, but to be crippled by shame and guilt may. You will be wounded by the enemy. He knows the wounds of your past, and he will try to wound you again in the same place. But these wounds are different; these are honor-wounds.

We have no equivalent now for a Purple Heart of spiritual warfare, but it will come. One of the noblest moments that awaits you will come at the wedding feast of the Lamb. Our Lord will rise and begin to call those forward who were wounded in battle for his name's sake and you will be honored, your courage rewarded.

When Jesus says, "The kingdom of heaven suffers violence," do you feel that is a good thing or a bad thing? Contrast it with this: "The kingdom of heaven is open to passive, wimpy souls who enter it by lying on the couch watching TV." If you are going to live in God's kingdom, Jesus says, it's going to take every ounce of passion and forcefulness you've got. Things are going to get fierce; that's why you were given a passionate heart.

Notice how your heart responds to this reading—does it shrink back in fear, or rise with passion to be part of the Lord's fight?

A DEEPER WORK

He Himself is our peace, who made both groups into one and broke down the barrier of the dividing wall.

EPHESIANS 2:14 NASB

Resignation is not just the sigh that groans with something gone wrong. Resignation is acceptance of a loss as final. It is the condition in which you choose to see good as no longer startling in its beauty and boldness, but simply as "nice." Evil is no longer surprising; it is normal.

It is from this place of heart resignation where perhaps all of us at one time or another, having suffered under the storms of life's arrows, give up on the Sacred Romance. But your heart will not totally forsake the intimacy and adventure you were made for and so you compromise.

But this side of Eden, even relationship with God brings you to a place where a deeper work in your heart is called for if you are to be able to continue your spiritual journey. It is in this desert experience of the heart, where you are stripped of the protective clothing of the roles you have played in your smaller stories, that the wounds are resurfaced. Healing and faith are called for in ways you have not known previously. At this place on your journey, you face a wide and deep chasm that refuses you passage through self-effort. And it is God's intention to use this place to eradicate the final heart walls and obstacles that separate you from him.

Jesus—you have my permission. Break down the walls that separate us. Only do it as gently as you can, Lord.

WARFARE OF OTHERS

The world has been crucified to me, and I to the world.
GALATIANS 6:14

Spiritual warfare often tries to work like a computer virus—it loves to transfer around to as many people as it can, infecting whole households or even churches. You will step into certain fellowships and immediately feel an arrogant attitude, or perhaps something that feels very "religious" and stifling; perhaps there is a sense of guilt overwhelming the group. You've seen the same thing in family systems—how a particular sin or brokenness will play out down through a family line, such as divorce, infidelity, alcoholism, violence, poverty. Somebody's sin opened the door, and because the spiritual realm works on authority, the enemy will seize the opportunity of the sin and will try to oppress all those within the "system."

Once again, the cross is your rescue, to which you are crucified to all that is ungodly; the mass of mankind alienated from God. You are crucified to that controlling mother or your angry boss.

The beauty is, the cross never prevents love from passing between you, never prevents the Spirit of God from coming between you. The cross only cuts off unhealthy things, so there is never any fear in bringing it between you and others.

It is helpful to pray: *I bring the cross of my Lord Jesus Christ between me and* [name your issue]. *By the cross I break all unhealthy ties and every unholy bond with them. I allow only the love of God, the Spirit of God, and the kingdom of God between us. In Jesus' mighty name, and by his authority. Amen.*

RULED BY OTHERS' DESIRE

Awake, sleeper, and arise from the dead,
and Christ will shine on you.
EPHESIANS 5:14 NASB

I love what I do for a living. But it hasn't always been so. Several years ago I worked in D.C. While I didn't really want to go there, I had come to a point where I didn't know what I wanted in life. My real passion had been the theater, and for many years I pursued that dream with great joy. But through a series of what felt like betrayals, I left the theater and just went off to find a job. The D.C. offer came up, and although my heart wasn't in it, I let the opinions of others dictate my course. Without a deep and burning desire of our own, we will be ruled by the desires of others.

I have met many others in the same position. Every one of us in some way has buried our heart to seek a safer life.

The damage of disowning your desire is a life lost unto itself. Millions of souls drifting through life, without an inner compass to give them direction, unable to distinguish real life from a tempting imitation. You'll find you take your cues from others and live out scripts from someone else's life. It's a high price to pay. You can feel it's a taste of the life you were meant for, but often, it is no life at all.

"What do you want to be when you grow up?" is a playful question for kindergarteners. But the truth is, that question matters more as we mature. So consider: What are your disowned desires?

WILL YOU COME WITH ME?

*"Anyone who intends to come with me has
to let me lead. . . . Don't run from suffering;
embrace it. Follow me and I'll show you how."*
LUKE 9:23 THE MESSAGE

It helps to understand why Jesus keeps introducing "new frontiers" to you. Just when you think you've got a pretty good grasp on your inner world, Jesus shows you something else that needs healing. And have you wondered why things are always changing—why does God arrange for new frontiers to always be cropping up in your life? Because *God is growing you up.*

God is growing me up changes your expectations. When you show up at the gym, you are not surprised or irritated that the trainer pushes you into a drenching sweat; it's what you came for. Bilbo hesitates leaving the Shire; he's not sure he wants this new frontier being offered him. I think we can all relate. And that is why Jesus asks: *Will you come with me?*

God almost always has some "new frontier" for you—something he is inviting you into, new ground he wants you to take, or a new realm of understanding; maybe a move in your external world, or a shift in your internal world; might be a new "spiritual" frontier. Sometimes those new frontiers are thrust upon you; sometimes you choose them willingly. Either way, God is taking you into new frontiers because he is growing you up. *Will you come with me?*

Where has Jesus been inviting you into *more*? Have you asked him? Maybe he's already put it on your heart. What new realm would you like to grow into?

OUR DIFFERENCES

*I pray that your love will overflow more and
more, and that you will keep on growing
in knowledge and understanding.*

P H I L I P P I A N S 1 : 9 N L T

The biggest fear of men is failure, and the biggest fear of women is abandonment. This is so important to know about your heart. Though we all put our best foot forward, we are wearing different shoes. Guys do it so they don't look like a fool, and women do it so they won't be rejected. Start with your core fears, and you will learn a lot about the internal world of men and women.

Some people fear that admitting these deep differences between men and women will hurl us back into 1950s discrimination. I believe it opens the door for us to better love one another. The same folks who cringe at the mention of gender distinctions will tell you the next moment how arrogant it is for you to assume that your friend from Palestine looks at the world the way you do. Poetry translated from one language to another always loses something essential; if you want to experience what the poet meant, learn the language he or she was writing in. This is humility, not discrimination.

If we approach our differences from the viewpoint of wanting to understand one another, I think we can avoid stepping on landmines. We learn about the differences in order to be better lovers.

&

Jesus—I want to be a better lover. Where am I misunderstanding the men/women in my life?

MARCH

YOUR DEEPEST CONVICTIONS

It is with your heart that you believe.
ROMANS 10:10

The purpose of this thing called the Christian life is that your heart might be restored and set free. That's what Jesus came to do. Jesus wants Life for you, Life with a capital *L*, and that Life comes to you through your heart. But restoring and releasing the heart is no easy project. God doesn't just throw a switch and *poof*—it's done. He sends his Counselor to walk with you instead. That tells you it's going to be a *process*. All sorts of damage has been done to your heart over the years by your enemy, who seeks to steal and kill and destroy you, the image bearer of God.

You're told to "trust in the LORD with all your heart" (Proverbs 3:5), but frankly, it can be hard to do. Does trust come easily for you? I would *love* to trust God wholeheartedly. Why is it almost second nature to worry about things? Why is it so easy to grow indifferent toward the very people you once loved? The answers lie down in the heart. Your deepest convictions—the ones that really shape your life—are somewhere in the depths of your heart. As God restores more of your story and broken heart, you will be able to live in the fullness of God's promise, the promise of a life set free.

Jesus—I need you to come and uncover for me the deeper convictions of my heart. I want my whole heart free, free to love you.

YOU ARE FEARED

*You will be a crown of splendor in the LORD's
hand, a royal diadem in the hand of your God.*

ISAIAH 62:3

Your wounded heart is real and it matters. And you won't understand the long and sustained assault on your life until you see it as part of something larger.

The evil one had a hand in all that has happened to you. If he didn't arrange for the assault directly—and certainly human sin has a large enough role to play—then he made sure he drove the message of the wounds home into your heart. He is the one who has dogged your heels with shame and self-doubt and accusation. He is the one who offers the false comforters to you in order to deepen your bondage. He is the one who has done these things in order to prevent your restoration. For that is what he fears. He fears who you are; what you are; what you might become. He fears what you offer.

You really won't understand your life until you understand this: You are passionately loved by the God of the universe. You are passionately hated by his enemy.

And so, take heart, God is pursuing your restoration. For there is One greater than your enemy. One who has sought you out from the beginning of time. He has come to heal your broken heart and restore your soul. He is after you.

Do you believe that, really? That the God of the universe is "after you," to bring about your restoration? How would you live differently if you *did* believe it?

GOD IS YOUR DELIVERER

Instead of trusting in our own strength . . . [God]
rescued us. . . . And he'll do it again, rescuing
us as many times as we need rescuing. You and
your prayers are part of the rescue operation.
2 CORINTHIANS 1:8–10 THE MESSAGE

I was thinking about the name of Jesus. How it means "God saves," or "God is your deliverer, your salvation."

Which got me to thinking about the idea of God as Deliverer, as opposed to, say, the preferred idea of God as Preventer. It made me realize how much I want God to be my Preventer more than my Deliverer, meaning, I want him to prevent bad things from happening in my life. To *prevent* means that "it" will never happen to me. To *deliver* means I am in deep trouble and need God to rescue me. I think we all prefer the notion of God as Preventer so that we can live happy lives.

And yet God is so much more often presented in the Bible as Deliverer. My goodness, just read the Psalms. "Arise, O LORD! Deliver me" (3:7). "Deliver my life from the sword" (22:20). "For he will deliver the needy who cry out" (72:12). And just think about the history of God's people; it is one deliverance after another. Paul's life is as well, which causes him to say, "On him we have set our hope that he will continue to deliver us" (2 Corinthians 1:10).

Not prevent. Deliver. It is a very different view of life with God.

How have you been perceiving God—as Preventer or as Deliverer?

GOD IS YOUR SHIELD

Trust the LORD! He is your helper and your shield.
PSALM 115:9 NLT

God is your Deliverer, yes, but I also believe God is your Preventer at times. Scripture presents him as your shield. And you have no idea all that he has shielded you from. Which is actually my point. You don't notice God as Preventer, or shield, because you don't know what was going to happen to you since God shielded you from it. All you experience are those things where you need God to rescue you, to be your Deliverer.

But it would be helpful to come to terms with how much we'd all prefer God to be our Preventer. Because when you hold fast to this view, you experience a lot of turmoil with all those things that don't get prevented. *Why did God not . . . ? How come this? Did I not . . . ?* You know how this works. Notice when he doesn't prevent bad things from happening, you get shaken. You go to doubt, or some sort of self-accusation and blame. It causes a lot of distress.

But when you realize God is more your Deliverer, it helps you not be thrown by the fact that you sometimes find yourself thrown into the furnace. God has not abandoned you. You have not blown it. You understand God is far more Deliverer than Preventer, and you can then cry out with confidence, "O God, deliver me" and wait with hopeful and confident expectation that he loves you more than anything, and he will deliver.

O Jesus, I may not be fully convinced yet, but still I cry out—deliver me, Lord! Come to my rescue, God!

TWO-WAY COMMUNICATION

Today when you hear his voice,
don't harden your hearts.

HEBREWS 3:15 NLT

Prayer is entering into conversational intimacy with God. Father to son or daughter, friend to friend, essential prayer is conversational. It involves a give-and-take.

Hearing the voice of God is one of the lost treasures of Christianity—an intimate, conversational relationship with God is available, and is meant to be normal. In the gospel of John, Jesus is describing his relationship with us, how he is the Good Shepherd and we are the sheep in his care. Lovingly, tenderly, and yet firmly Jesus is urging us—don't just wander off looking for pasture, looking for the life you seek. Stay close. Listen for his voice. Let him lead.

I realize that many dear followers of Christ have been taught that God only speaks to his sons and daughters through the Bible. But the Scriptures are filled with stories of God speaking to his people—intimately, personally. Adam and Eve spoke with God. As did Abraham, Moses, and Elijah.

If you hear his voice and open the door of your life to him, Jesus will come closer, become even more intimate with you. For this very intimacy you were created! And it is a rescue, a comfort, a source of a thousand blessings.

Have you been taught that God still speaks to his people? Would you like to develop the ability to hear his voice? Ask him!

GENUINE GOODNESS

Worship the LORD in the splendor of his holiness.

1 CHRONICLES 16:29

A certain kind of "goodness" is actually hip these days. It is human nature: to find a morality that is comfortable and convenient and let it suffice for holiness. But it does not. So you ride your bike to work, or drive a hybrid car—but you have hatred in your heart.

I think the culture of popular goodness has confused a lot of young people who are sincere about pursuing holiness. Recycling is just not on a scale with loving Jesus or telling other people *about* Jesus.

Clearly, Jesus believes that some commands are weightier than others. So why is it that loving God isn't one of the categories you think about first? Churches tend to think in moral categories of "They are faithful attendees; they tithe every week. They're *good people*." But do they love God? We have churches filled with people who don't really love God as the central mission of their lives; yet they are faithful, so we think, *Wow, that's great, they're neat people.* But they're flunking Holiness 101.

It's easy to fall into this trap. It's easy to try to be good without allowing Jesus to make us holy. But it is in him we find both life and holiness, and out of that can flow genuine goodness.

O God—help me make first things first. Help me make loving you top of my list!

FIERCE INTENTION

He rescued us from the domain of darkness, and transferred us to the kingdom of His beloved Son.
COLOSSIANS 1:13 NASB

We forget that Jesus was operating in enemy territory. We project into the gospel stories a backdrop with the charm of a Middle Eastern travel brochure. We forget the context of his life and mission. His story begins with *genocide*—Herod's attempt to murder Jesus by ordering the execution of all young boys around Bethlehem. I've *never* seen this included in any crèche scene.

The Father's strategy is intriguing—surely God could have simply taken Herod out. Why must they run for their lives? It makes you think twice about how God orchestrates his plans. But he is intentional.

Surely you see that Jesus was a *hunted* man? You'll see this across the pages of the Gospels. But is it not more true to say that he is the Hunter?

When Jesus steps into the task set before him, both men and demons begin to feel his fierce intention. Most of us wouldn't walk into a dark alley if we could avoid it. Jesus walks right up to people in full-blown demonic possession and confronts the ancient spirits very intentionally and quite fierce.

Friends, it is with *this* intention he is after *your* heart.

Have you seen Jesus as a Great Warrior, or only as the Gentle Shepherd?

A MAN ON A MISSION

Jesus called in a loud voice, "Lazarus, come out!"
JOHN 11:43

Oh, to have heard Jesus' command, heard the mightiness in his voice. John uses the word *loud* to describe it; he uses this very same word to describe the ferocity of a storm that nearly sank their boat. Apparently, Jesus' command here reminded John of the intensity of a storm. Jesus doesn't ask Lazarus to come out; he doesn't suggest he do it. He commands him to life with the rumble of thunder and the crack of lightning.

This is a man on his mission. The same man who could be so playful is also a man on fire. If you would know Jesus, you must know that this—his fierce intentionality—is essential to his personality.

Nature bears witness. Picture an African lion, stalking through tall grass, closing in on its prey—the ruthless focus, the vigilant keenness. How about a mother brown bear when her cubs are threatened? Six hundred pounds of unrelenting fury. Now imagine you are watching one of these scenes not on the nature channel but from thirty feet away. Oh, yes, we find a very fierce intentionality in nature—reflecting the personality of the Artist.

Knowing this—*delighting* in this—will help you delight in his highly provocative actions. There is nothing like arrogant religious falsehood to arouse Jesus' intention.

Jesus—I keep putting you back in a religious box. And you want to keep breaking out. Come and be yourself with me; come and reveal who you truly are.

TO RECAPTURE YOUR HEART

The LORD longs to be gracious to you, and therefore
He waits on high to have compassion on you.

ISAIAH 30:18 NASB

God's pursuit of humanity is a long story. Satan wanted center stage, and his plan now is to ruin your relationship with God by telling you that *you are the point.* You can see how humanity goes along with this. Cain murders Abel; Lamech threatens to murder everyone else. Humanity grows worse and worse until God says in pain, "I'm sorry I ever made them." But he doesn't give up. First with Noah, then Abraham, then Israel, we see God pursuing a people whose hearts will be for him, with whom he can share the joy of the Larger Story. But their faithfulness lasts about as long as the morning dew.

What is *God's* heart experiencing through all of this? His heart is broken, but he keeps pursuing you. To bring his children back, the king clothes himself as a beggar and renounces his throne in order to win your hand. The incarnation, the life and the death of Jesus, answers once and for all the question, "What is God's heart toward me?" This is why Paul says in Romans 5, "Look here, at the cross. Here is the demonstration of God's heart." You don't have to wait for the incarnation to see God as a character in the story and learn something of his motives. But after the incarnation there can be no doubt.

Let your heart simply answer this question without the pressure to say the right thing: What do you believe God's heart toward you is really like? Do your actions support this?

TO LEAVE WINTER BEHIND

*In his great mercy he has given us
new birth into a living hope.*

1 PETER 1:3

Of course you aspire to happiness you can enjoy now. Your heart has no place else to go. You have made a nothing of eternity. If I told you that vacation you've wanted is just around the corner, you'd be excited. The future would look promising. It seems possible, desirable. But your ideas of heaven, while possible, aren't all that desirable. Nearly every Christian I've spoken with has some idea that eternity is an unending church service, settling on an image of the never-ending sing-along in the sky, one great hymn after another, forever and ever, amen.

Forever and ever? That's the "good news"? And then you sigh and feel guilty that you're not more "spiritual." You lose heart, and you turn once more to the present to find what life you can now. Eternity feels like the *end* of the search for life.

Remember, *you can only hope for what you desire.* How can the church service that never ends be more desirable than the richest experiences of life here? Remember, eternity has been set in your heart (Ecclesiastes 3:11). Where in your heart? In your *desires.*

Friend, how have you pictured eternity? What do you think it would be like? The promise that "spring" is about to come around, bringing with it the restoration of all things—if you let that be true for just a few moments, what do you feel taking place in your soul?

YOUR FIRST LOVE

"'Love the Lord your God with all your heart and with all your soul and with all your strength and with all your mind'; and, 'Love your neighbor as yourself.'"

LUKE 10:27

I always felt it strange that God needed to command us to love him. (It is the first and greatest of all the commandments.) Now I see better. When God calls us to love him as our "first love," it is not only because he deserves to hold that place in our hearts, but also because he knows what pain will come when we get that out of order. If you give the part of your soul that is meant for God to lesser things, they will break your heart because they cannot possibly come through for you in the ways God can. Only he will never leave you or forsake you. The command is a rescue from disaster.

Maybe you have begun to discover the joy and freedom that loving God brings to the rest of your life. Keeping God as our first love, we are not destroyed when others fail to love us well; we are able to weather criticism, loneliness, and rejection. Our other loves are able to find their whole and wholesome expression, and we are able to flourish as human beings. Anchored in True Love, our hearts can go on to love. Because we have first things first, as the saying goes.

God, thank you for loving me and choosing me before you made the world. I turn my heart fully to you today and ask that you take the place in my life that you truly deserve as my first love. Help me to be anchored in your True Love today, walking in step with you.

HE GOES AHEAD OF YOU

*"He goes on ahead of them, and his sheep
follow him because they know his voice."*

JOHN 10:4

Today I'm struck by the phrase "He goes on ahead of them." It's almost as if I'd never given it my heart's attention. Jesus goes ahead of us. That is so reassuring, and that is *such* a different view than the one with which I approach each day.

Do you really, Jesus? Do you really go on ahead of me?

That is such a better view of God, a view where he is engaged with us and intimately involved in the world and in our lives. As I think about it now, I think I have been something of an unconscious deist. God is there, but I'm doing my darnedest down here while he is sort of smiling down on me, not really engaged in the details. That view is not true of him, and it is an awful way to live.

The question is, will you follow God, as opposed to just going on your way into each day? That is the transition to a better life. To be asking him where he is headed and what he is doing *throughout* the day. So that while he *is* going on ahead of you, you are following.

Will you let Jesus lead you in a practical way—day by day? Will you pause long enough to ask his opinion on things? And obey?

TURN YOUR GAZE TOWARD GOD

Why am I discouraged? Why is my heart so sad? I will put my hope in God! I will praise him again.

PSALM 42:5 NLT

The child who cries out in the dark feels very differently when mother comes in and switches on a light. What felt so real and inevitable vanishes. Be careful you don't embrace the pain in such a way that you forbid God to turn on the light and draw near.

I appreciate how David in the Psalms admits the storms of his soul, pouring out with raw honesty, *but he does not allow himself to stay there.* He reminds his own soul that things have not always been like this—and isn't that where your heart begins to make the fatal shift? When you are in the darkness, you begin to feel like you have always been there. *But it is not true.* God has been faithful in the past; God will be faithful again. David urges himself to put his hope in God, because the morning *will* come.

You'll see how David escapes the shipwreck of the soul: he turns his attention from the debris of his life in a much healthier direction; he turns his gaze toward *God.* Where is the gaze of your soul placed?

When praying, be aware of making agreements while you give yourself permission to have a full emotional life with God. "I *feel* forsaken!" is very, very different from, "I *am* forsaken!" "I *feel* overcome" is much different from "I *am* overcome."

THE RELIEF OF HOLINESS

May God himself, the God who makes everything
holy and whole, make you holy and whole, put
you together—spirit, soul, and body. . . . The One
who called you is completely dependable.
1 THESSALONIANS 5:23–24 THE MESSAGE

The hope of Christianity is that you get to live life like Jesus. That beautiful goodness can be yours. He can heal what has gone wrong deep inside you. The way he does this is to give you his goodness; impart it to you, almost like a blood transfusion. You get to live his life—that is, live each day by the power of his life within you. He makes you whole by making you holy. He makes you holy by making you whole. Friend, the pursuit of a deep and genuine holiness is worth whatever it costs you.

Think of how you feel when you commit some offense— yell at your kids, harbor resentment or bitterness toward a friend. Whatever your regrets may be, think of how you feel when you commit these acts repeatedly, when you vow never to do it again and find yourself doing it moments later. And think of what an utter relief it would be to be free from the whole entangled nightmare. I mean to be so free that you simply don't struggle with whatever it is that haunts you; it's not an issue.

That's the utter relief of holiness. That's what happens when the life of Jesus invades your life.

Jesus, give me your holiness. Invade my life, my every breath. I ask you to come.

WILL YOU GET CLOSE?

"While he was still a long way off, his father saw him coming. Filled with love and compassion, he ran to his son, embraced him, and kissed him."

LUKE 15:20 NLT

When Jesus died, that most holiest of curtains was ripped in half. Torn, top to bottom. And who was it that did that? Surely not the priests. It was God himself. He took that veil and ripped it in two.

So why do we insist on stitching it back up? Much of what passes for worship, sacrament, and instruction in Christian circles is trying to hang that veil again. Done in the same spirit that says, "God is too holy for us to approach." *We must not be too familiar with God. Do not presume to come too close.*

They're trying to re-create the Holy of Holies in the name of reverence. Except it was God who ripped that curtain forever with his own two hands. It's clearly over. Understanding this truth will open up new realms for you in relating to Jesus, enabling your heart to love him.

Do you recall the parable he told about the prodigal son? Jesus explains how God wants to relate with us. By using the phrase "embraced him and kissed him," he meant that *he embraced him and kissed him.* Does this sound like the hymns you sing, the prayers spoken, the way God is approached in your church? I hope so.

Jesus, thank you for loving me. Draw me close to you today. I need you. I need your love and your embrace. I let you draw near.

WORTH FIGHTING FOR

The LORD himself will fight for you.
EXODUS 14:14 NLT

Your God is a Warrior because there are certain things in life worth fighting for, that must be fought for. He makes you a warrior in his own image because he intends for you to join him in that battle.

One day the young man Moses, prince of Egypt, went out to see for himself the oppression of his kinsmen. When he witnessed firsthand an Egyptian taskmaster beating a Hebrew slave, he couldn't bear it, and killed the man. A rash act, for which he becomes a fugitive, but you see something of the warrior emerging in him. Years later, God sends him back to set all his people free, and, I might add, it is one intense fight to win that freedom.

There are certain things worth fighting for. A marriage, for example, or the institution of marriage as a whole. Children, whether they are yours or not. Friendships will have to be fought for, as you've discovered by now, and churches too, which seem bent on destroying themselves if they are not first destroyed by the enemy who hates them. Many people feel that earth itself is worth fighting for. Doctors fight for the lives of their patients, and teachers for the hearts and futures of their students. Take anything good, true, or beautiful upon this earth and ask yourself, *Can this be protected without a fight?*

What in your life right now needs fighting for? Ask Jesus to give you his courage and passion to get in the fight—and to fight alongside you, for you.

INVITE HIM IN

*"I stand at the door. I knock. If you hear me
call and open the door, I'll come right in."*
REVELATION 3:20 THE MESSAGE

This is a famous passage of Scripture that many people have heard in the context of an invitation to know Christ as Savior. He does not force himself upon you. He knocks, and waits for you to ask him in. The first step of this is salvation. We hear Christ knocking and we open our hearts to him as Savior. It is the first turning, but the principle remains throughout your Christian life.

You see, we all pretty much handle our brokenness in the same way—it's mishandled. It hurts too much to go there. So you shut that door in your heart, and you throw away the key. But that does not bring healing. Perhaps relief—for a while. But never healing. The best thing is to open the door and invite Jesus in to find you in those hurting places.

It might feel surprising that Christ asks your permission to come in and heal, but he is kind, and the door is shut from the inside, and healing never comes against your will. In order to experience his healing, you must also give him permission to come in to the places you've shut to anyone. *Will you let me heal you?* Jesus knocks through your loneliness, your sorrows, a betrayal, rejection. He knocks through many things, waiting for you to give him permission to enter in.

Yes, Jesus, yes. I do invite you in. Come to my heart in my shattered places. Come to me and I willingly open the door of my heart. I give you permission to heal my wounded places. Come for me there.

YOU CAN MOVE MOUNTAINS

*"Truly I tell you, if you have faith as small as
a mustard seed, you can say to this mountain,
'Move from here to there,' and it will move.
Nothing will be impossible for you."*

MATTHEW 17:20

Prayer sets up a terrible dilemma. You want to pray; it's in your nature. You desperately want to believe that God will come through. But then he doesn't seem to, and where does that leave you?

I believe God is in the dilemma; I believe he wants you to push through to real answers, solid answers. We hold dangerously incomplete understandings of our situation, such as, *God is all-powerful. He did not intervene. So it must not be his will to intervene.*

Yes—God is sovereign. And in his sovereignty he created a world in which the choices of men and angels matter. Tremendously. Your choices have enormous consequences. Friend, prayer is not as simple as, "I asked; God didn't come. I guess he doesn't want to."

You have embarked on the most exciting story possible, filled with danger, adventure, and wonders. There is nothing more hopeful than the thought that things can be different, you can move mountains, and you have some role in bringing that change about.

Pause—have you been looking at prayer as, *I asked; God didn't come. I guess he doesn't want to*? What has been the fruit of that—faith, hope, and love, or profound discouragement? Jesus said, we will know things by their fruit.

PROFOUND TRUST

When they hurled their insults at him, he did not
retaliate; when he suffered, he made no threats.
Instead, he entrusted himself to him who judges justly.

1 PETER 2:23

The reason you fear to step out is because you know that it might not go well (is that an understatement?). You have a history of wounds screaming at you to play it safe. You feel so deeply that if it doesn't go well, if you're not received well, others' reactions become the verdict on your life, on your heart. You fear that your deepest doubts will be confirmed. Again. That you will hear the message of your wounds, the piercing negative answers to your question. That is why you can *only* risk stepping out when you are resting in the love of God. When you believe *his* verdict on your life—that you are chosen and dearly loved. Then you are free to offer.

People did not respond very well to Jesus' love, to his stepping out in faith and playing the role that was his alone to play. And that would be a ridiculous understatement. The very people Jesus died for hurled insults at him, mocked him, spat at him, then crucified him. Jesus had to trust his Father *profoundly*, with his very being. Peter uses him as our example, saying, "He entrusted himself" to God.

Jesus lived a life of love, and he invites you to do the same. Regardless of the response.

O Jesus—show me where I am self-protecting. Show me where I need to step out in courage, regardless of how it goes.

DON'T LIMIT JESUS

*We look forward with hope to that wonderful
day when the glory of our great God and
Savior, Jesus Christ, will be revealed.*

TITUS 2:13 NLT

Your experience of Jesus is limited most often by the limits you put on him! A painful truth, but also a hopeful one. Let's take down some of those barriers.

Most of the limits you put on Jesus happen unconsciously. Though Jesus has been vandalized by both religion and the world, he is still alive and very much himself. He's still the same beautiful outlaw, with the same personality—though it does require removing some debris nowadays to know him as he truly is.

Step one to a deeper experience of Jesus is knowing what to look for. That's why it matters to look at his personality. If you can hang on to this, an entire new world will open up for you. This is a Jesus you can actually love because this is who he is.

Step two involves removing some of the debris that has been in the way. For example, if you believe for whatever reason that *Jesus doesn't really love me*, then it will be awfully hard to experience the love of Jesus. Are you following me?

It is a stunning realization: you will find Jesus pretty much as you expect to.

Jesus, I renounce every limit I have ever placed on you. I break all limitations, renounce them, revoke them. Jesus, forgive me for restraining you in my life. I give you full permission to be yourself with me. Come in, Lord, and reveal yourself to me.

WHAT YOU ARE MEANT FOR

We proclaim to you the one who existed from
the beginning, whom we have heard and seen.
We saw him with our own eyes and touched him
with our own hands. He is the Word of life.

1 JOHN 1:1 NLT

What if you could have Jesus the way Peter and John had him? The way Mary and Lazarus did?

You get to.

You are *meant* to have this Jesus, more than you have each new day, more than you have your next breath. For heaven's sake—he *is* your next day, your next breath. You are meant to share life with him—not just a glimpse now and then at church, not just a rare sighting. And you are meant to live his life. The purpose of his life, death, and resurrection was to ransom you from your sin, deliver you from the clutches of evil, restore you to God—so that his personality and his life could heal and fill your personality, your humanity, and your life. This is the reason he came.

Anything else is religion.

Sadly, for too many people, the Christ they know is too religious to love, too distant to experience, and too rigid to be a source of life. It explains the abject poverty of the church. But hear this—Jesus hasn't changed one bit. He is still quite himself. This is still how he acts. The Scriptures assure us that Jesus is the same yesterday, today, and forever. God is better than you thought. Much better than you feared. Better even than you dared to believe.

❧

You get to know Jesus like his closest friends. How do you respond?

THERE IS A LARGER STORY

*God has now revealed to us his mysterious plan
regarding Christ, a plan to fulfill his own good
pleasure. And this is the plan: At the right time he will
bring everything together under the authority of Christ.*

EPHESIANS 1:9–10 NLT

Walk into any large mall, museum, amusement park, university, or hospital, and you will typically meet at once a very large map with the famous red star and the encouraging words *You are here.* These maps are offered to visitors as ways to orient themselves to their situation, get some perspective on things. This is the Big Picture. This is where you are in that picture. Hopefully you now know where to go. You have your bearings.

Oh, that you had something like this for your life, such as: *This is the Story in which you have found yourself. Here is how it got started. Here is where it went wrong. Here is what will happen next. Now this—this is the role you've been given. If you want to fulfill your destiny, this is what you must do. These are your cues. And here is how things are going to turn out in the end.*

You can.

You can discover *the* Story. Maybe not with perfect clarity, maybe not in the detail that you would like, but in greater clarity than you now have, and that would be worth the price of admission. I mean, to have some clarity would be gold right now. Wouldn't it?

Jesus—I would love some clarity right now. Show me the Bigger Picture. Open the eyes of my heart to your Great Story.

HEAVEN ON EARTH

*Heaven must receive him until the time comes
for God to restore everything, as he promised
long ago through his holy prophets.*

ACTS 3:21

Jesus is in heaven, along with your Father, the Holy Spirit, and the angels. Which makes it a breathtaking place! Heaven is absolutely real and precious far beyond words. It is the "rest of" the kingdom of God, the "Paradise" Jesus referred to. The city of God is currently there.

For the time being. Remember—Peter explained in his sermon in Acts 3 that Jesus remains in heaven *until* his return, when all things are made new.

Until—so much gravity and excitement contained in that word, such patient anticipation. When the time comes for God to restore everything, Jesus leaves heaven and comes to earth. To stay. The heavenly Jerusalem comes to earth, and "God's dwelling place is now among the people" (Revelation 21:3). Heaven is not the eternal dwelling place of the people of God. The new earth is, just as Revelation says. Just as the entire promise of the renewal of all things says. Just as Jesus explained, and the Bible declares.

Better said, you get heaven *and* earth; both realms of God's great kingdom come together at the renewal of all things. Then will you truly say, "It's heaven on earth." For it will be.

Did you know this—that heaven comes to earth? That God is going to restore the earth any day now, and with it all your special places?

HOW HAVE YOU LEARNED CHRIST?

You have the words of real life, eternal life. . . . You are the Holy One of God.
JOHN 6:68–69 THE MESSAGE

It is very helpful to realize that words and phrases carry a certain meaning and spirit to us, because they open up our hearts to the meaning God intended, while others close our hearts to his meaning.

Peter said of Jesus that he had the words of eternal life. This is a good test. Ask, *Does what I have heard in fact bring life?* If not, perhaps you have not yet found the words that convey the spirit of his teaching to your heart in particular. I am not saying that we are always going to like what Jesus said, or is saying, to us. Surely his words sometimes bring conviction and cut to the quick. But even then, when the conviction of God comes, is there not life in it? To be known, to be found out, is in some sense a great relief—if the spirit in which it comes also offers to us, as God is constantly offering, a way out through repentance and forgiveness.

That is the beauty of asking God what his word to you is, personally. We do not worship language, we worship the *living* God, who assures us that his word to us is full of the Spirit and life (John 6:63).

Jesus—open my ears to hear your voice. I want to hear you more clearly. Speak to me your words of life. Give me the faith to believe I am hearing you.

SHOWERS OF GENEROSITY

God can point to us in all future ages as examples of the
incredible wealth of his grace and kindness toward us.
EPHESIANS 2:7 NLT

Late into the night, early in the morning, walking down the road, in the middle of his supper, at home, abroad, Jesus offers. His time, his words, his touch, flowing like the wine at Cana. To appreciate the reality of it all, remember his loneliness, his weariness, his humanity. This is utterly remarkable—this is a man on a life-or-death mission, yet he is lavish with himself.

And that's the key, right there—that giving of himself. That is what is so precious. Moses offered leadership, and tirelessly. Solomon handed out the rarest of wisdom free of charge. Jesus gives *himself*. This is, after all, what he came to give.

He has come to share his life with you. And if you look around, creation is pulsing with life. It is the life of Jesus, given generously for the life of all things.

This is the life he offers you; this is the extravagance with which he offers it. Jesus doesn't only give his life *for* mankind, he also gives his life *to* mankind. It is showered upon you daily like manna.

The man was generous. Extravagant. He still is.

O Jesus—forgive me for seeing you as stingy. You are generous.
Extravagant. I open my heart to your extravagant offer of yourself.

BELIEVE MY LOVE

We have come to know and have believed the love
which God has for us. God is love, and the one who
abides in love abides in God, and God abides in him.

1 JOHN 4:16 NASB

I bought a new journal this week because my old one had filled up. I always feel strange writing on the first page of a new journal. It feels momentous, like a new beginning. What will unfold? And what should I put on the first page? After all, it's the opening page of a new book in my life, the next chapter with God. It deserves something significant.

Looking down at the blank page, I ask God in my heart, *What needs to go here?* You know what he said? *My love.*

So that's what I write down. Two words. "My love." It is more than enough. Whatever else gets written in this journal, let it all come under *His love.* I sit there and let it sink in. I am turning my heart toward his love. Letting it be true. Letting it be life to me.

What else, Lord?

Believe my love.

Yes, I do. I believe your love.

And something in me shifts. I am coming to believe it more than I ever have. It is changing me. I feel less driven. Less compulsive. And less empty. I feel like I want to stay here. To live in his love.

And you—are you coming to believe his love more than ever? Is something in the way? Can you take that to Jesus, invite him into it?

THE FULLNESS OF GOD

*I pray that out of his glorious riches he may
strengthen you with power through his Spirit in your
inner being, so that Christ may dwell in your hearts
through faith. And I pray that you, being rooted and
established in love, may have power, together with all
the Lord's holy people, to grasp how wide and long
and high and deep is the love of Christ, and to know
this love that surpasses knowledge—that you may
be filled to the measure of all the fullness of God.*

EPHESIANS 3:16–19 THE MESSAGE

Paul is praying something you desperately need:
That God your Father would strengthen you with power
through his Spirit in your inmost being. That Jesus might really
fill and dwell in your heart. (*Yes, God! Fill my heart with the presence of Jesus!*) That you might be rooted and grounded in love.
(*Incredible! Who do you even know that is rooted and grounded in
love? Weariness and unsettledness cause me to need more of God.*)
That you might have power to grasp the full breadth of Jesus' love.
(*Oh yes, Father—I need this! I believe it would transform my life.*)
Paul prays that you would *know* this love (experience it—deep, personal knowing). That you might be filled to all the fullness of God!

What a treasure this is for you. What a rescue. A path is laid
out for you—one given by God himself. He *wants* you to find fullness in him.

Try this—pray through this progression for yourself. Chase this.
Stay in this for a while. The fruit will be wonderful.

AWAITING JESUS

With minds that are alert and fully sober, set
your hope on the grace to be brought to you
when Jesus Christ is revealed at his coming.

1 PETER 1:13

Whenever the church is wrestling to understand or recover some treasure of the faith, it's always a good idea to return to what Jesus himself had to say about the matter. After all, this is his story. It is his teaching on hope for the renewal of all things. This promise, this greatest hope, has set us out on our wondrous journey. Where exactly does Jesus want us to fix our future hopes?

Jesus wants us to interpret the story from the vantage point of his return.

Heaven is very, very precious. Heaven is the paradise of God. But—and I say this reverently, carefully—heaven is not the great anticipated event the writers of the New Testament look forward to. Rather it is the return of Jesus. "And we are eagerly waiting for him to return" (Philippians 3:20 NLT).

The great hope and expectation of the Christian faith is focused on one dramatic, startling event, sudden as a bolt of lightning, sharp as the tip of a sword: the bodily return of Jesus Christ, and with that, the renewal of all things. The two are united, as surely as God the Father and God the Son are united—the renewal of all things awaits the coming of our Lord, and the coming of our Lord ushers in the renewal of all things.

Have you made your great hope and expectation the imminent return of Jesus? If not, why not?

WHAT JESUS WEEPS OVER

"I am the way and the truth and the life. No one comes to the Father except through me."

JOHN 14:6

To make sure you understand what Jesus is saying, it's that he alone is the means to heaven. No one comes to the one true God except through him. Offensive as the claim may be, it still needs to be dealt with. Either it is arrogant, or it is true.

God does not want to lose a single human soul. In fact, those hellfires weren't even created for man. They were created for the devil and his demons (Matthew 25:41). Jesus doesn't want *anyone* there.

Jesus' heart of love is not diminished by the fact that some people will actually choose hell over surrendering to God. He weeps over it. He warns, urges, pleads, performs miracles. As they nail him to the timbers, he says, "Father, forgive them, for they don't know what they are doing" (Luke 23:34 NLT). Because if they *don't* find forgiveness, it is going to be a mighty black day of reckoning. Jesus prays for them, prays they will find mercy.

Most attempts to convince the world that Jesus was a "really great guy, not mean and dogmatic," carry their task all the way to the point of hiding or eliminating this exclusivity of Jesus. "Well, yes, but he didn't *mean* all that." Jesus said it very clearly; he speaks the truth in love because he doesn't want to lose anyone.

What about you—have you sort of "hidden" the unpopular side of our faith, that it is only by Christ a person can be saved? What would it look like for you to speak the truth in love?

CHERISHED IDOLS

Looking at the man, Jesus felt genuine love for him. "There is still one thing you haven't done," he told him. "Go and sell all your possessions."

MARK 10:21 NLT

This "rich young ruler" has idols he is clutching in his heart. They are his secret love; you know from his reaction. Jesus knew by looking into his heart. We have come to interpret this passage as poverty being a requisite for following Christ. But that misses the point entirely. God tells us often about idolatry, that if anyone set up an idol in their heart, God would set himself against them. But oh, it's difficult to topple a cherished idol.

Can you imagine how devastating this was for the young leader who thought he had lived a righteous life? And in one comment, said like an afterthought, Jesus yanks this man off balance, and in the same moment extends his hand to catch him: "Let this go. Then come, join me. I want you to join me." What an invitation.

But the thought of giving his precious treasure away—his life-source, his security and status—it is too much for the earnest young man. He walks away, head cast down in sorrow. Exposed and captive to his false god. Again, wealth is not the point. The idol is.

Ask God to expose what false idol you have currently set up in your heart. It could be anything—your job, power, family, even church. It may not be easy to have this revealed, but he feels genuine love for you, and he wants you to join him, still.

GROWING UP

. . . Until we all reach unity in the faith and in the
knowledge of the Son of God and become mature.

EPHESIANS 4:13

Teaching our sons to drive was a hair-raising endeavor—merging into traffic felt like Han Solo pushing the *Millennium Falcon* into light speed; sudden braking seemed certain to send me through the windshield. It was terrifying, but I was delighted with their efforts. Of course, I would be disappointed if their driving was the same years later.

So it is with God—he is utterly delighted with your attempts at prayer; he loves your simple prayers. And he is calling you upward to grow into the maturity you were destined for.

But here is the problem—most of us don't quite share God's fervent passion for our maturity. Really, now, if you stopped ten people at random on their way to church next Sunday and polled them, I doubt that you would find one in ten who said, "Oh, my first and greatest commitment this afternoon is to mature!" Our natural investments lie in other things—lunch, the game, our general comfort, including getting others to cooperate with our agenda.

It is gracious and really helpful to remember we are all at different stages in our spiritual journeys. And God is absolutely committed to growing us up.

Where is God trying to grow you up? Do you even know? Can you see it through the trials you are currently facing? Are you embracing the growing-up process or fighting it?

APRIL

HEAVENLY LAUGHTER

*"The time is coming when you're going
to hear laughter and celebration."*
JEREMIAH 33:10–11 THE MESSAGE

Have you ever wondered if God laughs? To even have to think about it shows how far we have strayed from his heart. His personality. Does Jesus have a sense of humor? Well, he created laughter. And think of the crowd he dined with. This was a wild group, and surely such a crowd got rolling in laughter from time to time, if only from the joy they were experiencing being with Jesus. Now, surely the Creator of these colorful characters didn't sit there frowning, looking pious, Mr. Killjoy, Mr. I'm-Above-All-This. Imagine his own happiness at having these very lost sheep back at his side.

Laughter is from God. This one quality alone might save you from the religious veil that forever tries to come in and cloud your perception of Jesus.

After all—it was God who gave you a sense of humor. Do you really think Jesus came to take it away?

Perhaps if you allow Jesus the playfulness you see in his creation, you can then see him at play in the Gospels. Perhaps it will help you unlock some of these otherwise perplexing stories that are meant to show you the stunning character of the One who loves you the most.

Did you know God has a sense of humor? That Jesus loves to be playful? Would you like to see his playfulness with you? Ask him!

RISK OPENING YOUR HEART

*Come and listen to my counsel. I'll share
my heart with you and make you wise.*
PROVERBS 1:23 NLT

You aren't meant to figure life out on your own. You know this in your core. And God's offer is to father you. The truth is, he has been for a long time—you just haven't had the eyes to see it. He wants to walk with you much more intimately, but you have to be in a posture to receive it. What that involves is a new way of seeing, a fundamental reorientation of how you look at life, and your situation in it.

First, you allow that you are an unfinished son or daughter. Actually still quite young inside, and you need the love your Father is offering. In many, many ways.

So you turn from your independence and all the ways you either charge at life or shrink from it; this may be one of the most basic and the most crucial ways you repent. I say "repent" because I imagine your approach to life is based on the conviction that God, for the most part, doesn't show up much. I understand where the conviction came from, battle it constantly myself, but still—it's faithless, is it not? You must be willing to take an enormous risk, and open your heart to the possibility that God is present—even in the very things in which you thought he'd abandoned you. You open yourself up to being fathered.

We all have an approach to life based on the conviction that God, for the most part, doesn't show up much. Can you see how that is operating in your choices and ways of living?

YOU CAN WALK AWAY

"Everything is possible with God."
MARK 10:27 NLT

Jesus knows the sincerity of the rich young man of Mark 10—something about him made Jesus love him. Jesus pulled the *one* thread that will unravel the whole fabric of this man's life, and Jesus knows it worked. He watches the man walking away. Jesus nods. "With man this is impossible." But he sees what you do not, sees the internal revolution already taking place, "but not with God; all things are possible with God." With a smile and a wink it's as if he says, "He'll be back." Then he turns and walks out of town.

Wow, is Jesus good.

He is advancing against the prince of darkness in a bid for the human heart. Some hearts have been snared through abuse, some through seduction, others by means of religion. Oh, how hard it is to rescue the human heart, to dislodge people from their chosen means of survival without toppling them into resignation, despair, or defensiveness.

Jesus doesn't force us to follow him. He never overwhelms our will. He woos, he confronts, he heals, and he shoots straight. He lives out before us the most compelling view of God, shows us an incredibly attractive holiness while shattering the religious glaze. But still, he lets us walk away if we choose.

O Jesus—I don't want to walk away. I know my heart is entangled in so many places; I know I have my own idols. But come and set me free, Jesus. Come and free my heart to be yours.

HOLY GRACE

God did not call us to be impure, but to live a holy life.
1 THESSALONIANS 4:7

Now, I know many will protest that it is the cross of Jesus Christ alone that opens the way to heaven. No amount of personal righteousness could ever suffice. I believe this. It is grace alone—the unmerited and undeserved forgiveness of God—that opens the way for you to know God, let alone come into his kingdom. Thank God for that.

However, you also find in Jesus and throughout the Scriptures a pretty serious call to a holy life.

In fact, one of the most stunning things about Jesus is how such a gracious, kind, patient, and forgiving man holds—without so much as wavering—such a high standard of holiness. On the one hand, you have the beautiful story of a woman caught in the act of adultery. The mob drags her before Jesus, ready to stone her.

But then, the town square is deserted; only the woman—wrapped in nothing but a bedsheet and shame—and Jesus remain. He rescued her from a terrible death, and then forgives her. But Jesus has one more word for her: "Go and sin no more" (John 8:11 NLT).

Yes, grace reigns in the kingdom of God. But right there alongside it is an unflinching call to holiness.

We keep falling into one of two traps—everything is just grace, or we are always trying to "clean up our act." You *do* live under grace. Now, from that secure place, where is God saying to you, "Go and sin no more"?

ALL IS FORGIVEN

*If we confess our sins to him, he is faithful
and just to forgive us our sins and to
cleanse us from all wickedness.*

1 JOHN 1:9 NLT

God's promise to you is total forgiveness if you will come to him and ask for it.

This offer is for you and for me. You cannot begin to truly face your life in the light of God's goodness until you know that you are under grace, that all is forgiven. Think of the difference between these two scenarios: someone you love pulls you aside and says, "Can I talk to you about something I see in your life?" Versus this: someone you know who doesn't even *like* you calls you into his office to say, "I need to talk to you about your life." Your internal reaction is totally different. You don't want to be exposed. Think of how you act in elevators: you hide. But in the case of love, you can face your life because you know there is no condemnation. This is how it is meant to be between you and Jesus.

Whatever it is you need to face about yourself, it has already been forgiven. You can go there because though the exposure may be painful—you are under grace. It is hard to face sin. The whole thing is booby-trapped with shame, fear, condemnation, and all manner of false conviction. The only way through the slough of despond is this: All is forgiven. Everything. By grace.

Jesus, I choose to live in your love. I know you accept me, and love me. Now show me where you are working in my life.

AN UNFATHOMABLE HONOR

"The goal is for all of them to become one heart and mind—just as you, Father, are in me and I in you."
JOHN 17:22 THE MESSAGE

We've all heard the story and missed the miracle—God begins his greatest work by including us. Even though it was bungled so badly the first time, back in Eden. Once again he shares in the excitement. Come with me, you have a part in this—the re-creation of the world.

Everyone who hears about Jesus hears about "the Twelve," and can probably name Peter, Matthew, James and John, certainly Judas. Jesus and "his disciples" go hand in hand.

And once chosen, Jesus then needs to *disciple* these fishermen, tax collectors, and political revolutionaries who dropped their careers to follow him. I'm not sure you've understood the ramifications of his decision. You just think, *Oh, yeah, the disciples,* and forget what was actually required for them to *become* apostles. It would take a lot of patience and long-suffering to train this group.

But right from the start, Jesus acts like it's not all about him. He shares the stage, shares the spotlight. He shares his glory. He even shares his suffering. The crown of thorns, the cross—is this not the noblest part of his whole life, the very thing you most worship him for? It is an honor I cannot begin to fathom.

The humility of this is so . . . humbling. It just takes my breath away.

Did you know that you have a part to play in Jesus' mission on the earth? Have you asked him what it is?

WHERE IS YOUR HOPE?

*Let us hold fast the confession of our hope without
wavering, for He who promised is faithful.*

HEBREWS 10:23 NASB

To shepherd your first hope for the treasure it is, you need to be
aware of what you are currently doing with hope right now.
Have you attached it to just about anything?

Several years ago I had a dream come true to bow hunt moose
in the Yukon. We were remote in the wilderness and our guide told
us the wildlife would probably never have seen a human. Wolves.
Bears. Moose standing eight feet at the shoulder. It was breathtaking, and I had *so* much hope set on it. But like so many things
in this life, the reality fell short of my expectations. The weather
wasn't good; we didn't sleep well; the moose weren't around.

The emotional roller coaster was miserable: hope and despair
every day. Back at camp the night of day six, cold and dejected, I
finally prayed, *Jesus, you've got to catch my heart.* The verse from
1 Peter came to my heart: "Put all your hope in the gracious salvation that will come to you when Jesus Christ is revealed" (1:13
NLT). It was not what I wanted to hear; I wanted to hear, *Your moose
is coming!* But Jesus knew exactly what I needed. *Set my hope fully
on his return?* At the moment my hopes weren't even set partially
there. I gave my kingdom heart to that dream trip; I keep putting
my ultimate hopes in places they shouldn't be.

Right now, today, where are your hopes set? Do you even think
about Jesus' return? If not, does that reveal to you that your hopes
are, for all practical purposes, set on something here?

MY FRIEND, YOU HAVE AN ENEMY

For the LORD takes delight in his people;
he crowns the humble with victory.
PSALM 149:4

I am staggered by the level of naïveté that most people live with regarding evil. They don't take it seriously. They don't live as though the Story has a villain—the incarnation of the very worst of every enemy they've ever met. Life is very confusing if you do not take into account that there is a villain.

Satan mounted his rebellion through the power of an idea: *God is holding out on us.* After the angels' insurrection was squelched, they were hurled from the high walls of heaven. "Satan, who deceives the whole world; he was thrown down to the earth, and his angels were thrown down with him" (Revelation 12:9 NASB).

Yes, God and his angels won. Through force of arms. But power is not the same thing as Goodness. Just because God won, doesn't mean our hearts can easily trust, because evil has entered our story in dreadful form. But oh friend. This is a battle for your freedom. And the victory is God's. If only you will trust him. He has fought for you, and triumphed.

Is this how you see the world? In the past, who have you blamed for the pain and sorrows of life? Doesn't it make a difference to know it was not God, not primarily people, but your enemy?

O Jesus—open my eyes to the ways the enemy is coming against my heart these days. Expose his lies, Lord.

PARADISE LOST

*When the Woman saw that the tree looked like good
eating and realized what she would get out of it—
she'd know everything!—she took and ate the fruit
and then gave some to her husband, and he ate.*

GENESIS 3:6 THE MESSAGE

Y ou know this story. Evil was lurking in that Garden. The
mighty angel, beautiful and powerful beyond compare. But
he rebelled against his Creator, and was banished but not destroyed.
He waited in the shadows for an opportunity to take his revenge.

You must understand: the evil one hates God, hates anything
that reminds him of the glory of God. Unable to overthrow the
Mighty One, he turned his sights on the ones who bore his image.

Satan came into the Garden and whispered to Adam and Eve—
and in them, to you—"You cannot trust the heart of God . . . you've
got to take matters under your control." He sowed the seed of mistrust in your heart; he tempted you to seize control.

The evil one lied to you about where true life was found and
you believe him still: *Trusting God is way too risky. Rewrite the
story. Give yourself a better part. Arrange for your own happiness.*

God gave you the wondrous world as your playground, and he
told you to enjoy it fully and freely. Yet despite his extravagant generosity, the one forbidden thing was reached for. In that moment
your heart shifted. You reached, and in the reaching you fell.

*Jesus—expose the ways my enemy has used my wounds to shape my
view of life; even of you, Lord. Expose the agreements I have made
with the enemy's lies.*

ACTUALLY, IT'S NOT JUST YOU

Take up the shield of faith, with which you can
extinguish all the flaming arrows of the evil one.
EPHESIANS 6:16

S atan's purpose is to convince you that you need to create your own story. One that does not admit the deep wounds of your heart—the rejection and hurt, the shame and sorrow, the anger and rage—exist. In turn, these rooms of your heart become darkened, and the enemy sets up shop there as his playground of accusation.

I am not just speaking metaphorically when I refer to the enemy accusing you. It may just feel like you're speaking to yourself in your head. But this is the enemy's deception: "I am not here. It's just your struggles." This feels so defeating. And indeed, deep in your heart, the shame and self-contempt you feel *are* like the attack of a roaring lion. You hide the lion's roar because the enemy has convinced you that it is *just you.*

When the adversary is involved, the intensity of feelings provoked by everyday occurrences of life can be compared to gasoline poured on a fire. The fire would burn and hurt you even without the gasoline, but its additional fuel totally consumes the kindling of your soul in an inferno of shame and contempt for yourself, but also scornful of the people who have "caused" you such pain. Meanwhile, the real enemy who caused this conflagration sits unnoticed in the background, full of glee.

Satan loves to keep his presence hidden: "I'm not here; this is just you." Do you live each day with an awareness that you have an enemy?

A JOY TO LIVE

*Beloved, do not be surprised at the fiery
ordeal among you . . . keep on rejoicing.*

1 PETER 4:12–13 NASB

No discussion of holiness is true or helpful without a healthy appreciation for how earnestly Satan wants to destroy us. Satan lured Adam and Eve to compromise one single act, one slip of holiness, and from there he has brought unspeakable carnage to the human race and to the earth. Friend, he hasn't stopped his war against us.

After years of ignoring this reality and paying for my ignorance (which is often in us a *chosen* naïveté), followed by decades taking up sword and shield and fighting the good fight, I have come to adore something Jesus says shortly before Gethsemane and the cross. He urges us not to let our hearts be afraid. Then he says to his close companions, "I will not say much more to you, for the prince of this world is coming. He has no hold over me, but he comes so that the world may learn that I love the Father and do exactly what my Father has commanded me" (John 14:30–31).

He has no hold on me?! Do you have any idea what a relief this would be? Just imagine for a moment if you were fortressed to all the ploys, accusations, temptations, snares, assaults, and deceptions of the enemy. What would it be like if they had no effect on you? Your life would be a joy to live.

Jesus—I can hardly imagine it. But I long for the freedom and the joy this would be. Breathe your holiness into me, Lord. I want the enemy to have "no hold on me" too!

THE SELF-LIFE

Why do you look with envy, O rugged mountains,
at Mount Zion, where God has chosen to live,
where the LORD himself will live forever?
PSALM 68:16 NLT

When mankind chose against God at the Fall, we exalted self in the place of God. You'll notice how seriously Jesus takes the matter when he said we must daily die to self if we would be his followers, if we would be the sons and daughters of God. We don't particularly like that part of the Christian invitation; notice the absence of any best-selling book entitled *Die to Yourself Every Day!* It's the self-life, by the way, that doesn't like the subject.

Now to be clear, what I mean by "the self-life" is the part of us that during a conversation is waiting for our moment to be asked how we're doing; waiting to tell *our* story. It's that part of us that finds it difficult to rejoice when others rejoice. That part of us that is so easily offended when we feel we have even been slightly wronged. The self-life is the breeding ground for envy.

Dorothy Sayers wrote, "It begins by asking, plausibly, 'Why should I not enjoy what others enjoy?' and it ends by demanding, 'Why should others enjoy what I may not?' Envy is the great leveler, if it cannot level things up, it will level them down."[4]

Jesus—I don't want to live with offense. I don't want to live with envy.
How is this operating in my life, Lord?

CHOOSE LOVE

*"'Your brother came home. Your father has
ordered a feast . . . because he has him home
safe and sound.' The older brother stalked off
in an angry sulk and refused to join in."*

LUKE 15:27–28 THE MESSAGE

Envy is a destroyer, and your enemy uses the open door of it as an occasion to come and steal the good things of your life.

What has happened to our culture is that we have lost the ability to admire anything that is greater than ourselves. But friend, admiration is the language of the kingdom of God. You celebrate that family, writer, leader, or athlete simply because of the glory of God that is reflected in them. You rejoice with those who rejoice. (Notice the difficulty of the older brother in the parable when he sees the father's lavish grace on his prodigal brother.)

Envy cannot admire.

Spiritual envy—envying the giftedness of another—is doing all sorts of damage in your soul, in the church, and in the Christian communities. It "partners" with the enemy to allow in division. Our culture has embraced the very toxic idea that everyone should look and feel and have exactly what everyone else has. That is not how the kingdom of God works! And boy oh boy is it a breeding ground for offense—the offended self. You can choose something so much better—you can choose love!

Jesus, show me the people I can begin to celebrate. I want to choose to admire and celebrate other people's gifting, blessing, talent, success. Show me where to begin.

YOUR HAPPILY EVER AFTER

God has moved into the neighborhood, making his home with men and women! They're his people, he's their God. He'll wipe every tear from their eyes.
REVELATION 21:3–4 THE MESSAGE

Friend, every story has an ending. Including yours. Have you ever faced this? Even if you do manage to find a little taste of Eden in this life, you cannot hang on to it. You know this. Your health cannot hold out forever. One by one your friends and loved ones will slip from your hand.

And then what? If that is the end, this Story is a tragedy.

Our enemy is a thief, and of everything he's stolen from your heart, his worst act of treachery was stealing all the promise and wonder of your happily ever after. Very few of us live with hope. To those without faith, he has whispered, "Your story ends and then . . . there is nothing. This is as good as it gets."

Small wonder people drink and eat too much, watch too much TV, basically check out. If they allow themselves to feel the depth of their actual longing for life and love and happiness, but have no hope that life will ever come . . . it's just too much to bear.

God has set eternity in your heart. Scripture bears witness that, in fact, the best of those stories are very close indeed to what is about to happen in *your* story. It's full of hope, and it will take your breath away.

To awaken this hope, think back to movies and stories that you love. Think about a few of your favorite endings. What hope is awakened there for your story?

UNIQUE TO YOU

*Keep me as the apple of your eye; hide
me in the shadow of your wings.*

PSALM 17:8

The enemy's one central purpose is to separate you from the Father. He uses assaults that are unique to your story. The enemy uses a story of neglect to whisper, *You see—no one cares. You're not worth caring about.* He uses a sudden loss of innocence to whisper, *This is a dangerous world, and you are alone. You've been abandoned.* And in this way he makes it very hard to come home to the Father's heart toward you. The details of your story are unique to you, but the effect is always a wound in the soul, and with it separation from and suspicion of the Father.

It's been very effective.

But God is not willing to simply let that be the end of your story. Filled with compassion, our Father God will come like a loving Father, and take you close to his heart. He will also take you back to heal the wounds to finish things that didn't get finished. He will come for the young, hurting place in you, no matter how old you might now be, and make you his Beloved. You *are* his Beloved, dear friend. He has come so that you will have life to the fullest, together, in union with him.

Have you ever asked the Father to "father" you? To come close, and be your Father each day? Can you do so now?

A BID FOR THE HUMAN HEART

The Messiah would experience
suffering, followed by glory.
1 PETER 1:11 THE MESSAGE

Satan has an ace up his sleeve—even if his captives want out of the POW camp, he has a legal claim to them. These prisoners can be ransomed, but only at a terrible price.

It appears the evil one doesn't understand Jesus' next move. He sees an opportunity to finish what he started back in the massacre of the innocents. The authorities grab Jesus at night, bring him in under false charges, bribe witnesses, then get a cynical Roman puppet to execute him because the mob is about to riot. Jesus seems to have run out of options. Yet this plays right into his plan—his secret plot to overthrow the rule of the evil one on earth.

Apparently, Satan did *not* know that by sacrificing Jesus he would pull the one pin that would crumble his entire kingdom, fall into the very scheme God the Father had ever so carefully arranged for the undoing of evil: "No, the wisdom we speak of is the mystery of God—his plan that was previously hidden, even though he made it for our ultimate glory before the world began. But the rulers of this world have not understood it; if they had, they would not have crucified our glorious Lord" (1 Corinthians 2:7–8 NLT). It ruined everything—from a certain point of view.

Jesus—thank you for rescuing me! For ransoming me! Thank you for the greatest rescue of all time!

YOUR HEART'S DEVOTION

Impress these words of mine on your heart and on your soul; and you shall bind them as a sign on your hand.

DEUTERONOMY 11:18 NASB

God and Satan each have a plan to capture your heart's devotion. The desire for intimacy, beauty, and adventure are placed and nurtured in the deepest longings of your heart by God himself. God's grand strategy, birthed in his grace toward you in Christ, is to release you into the redeemed life of your heart, knowing it will lead you back to him even as the North Star guides a ship across the vast unknown surface of the ocean.

If you were to find yourself living with total freedom, you would find yourself loving God with all of your heart and "you will know the truth [me], and the truth will make you free" (John 8:32 NASB).

The enemy's strategy to capture you is the opposite: to disconnect you from your heart *and* the heart of God toward you by any means possible. His grand tactic in separating you from your heart is to sneak in as the storyteller through your fears and the wounds you've received, accusing you through the words of parents and friends and God himself. He calls good evil and evil good and always helps you question whether God has anything good in mind in his plans for you. He has stolen your innocence and replaced it with distrust.

Did you think about your life this way—that God and the devil are both trying to capture your heart's devotion? Who is currently winning?

ASSAULT ON YOUR HEART

> *The Spirit of GOD . . . anointed me. He sent*
> *me to preach good news to the poor, heal the*
> *heartbroken, announce freedom to all captives.*
> ISAIAH 61:1 THE MESSAGE

This is the heart of Jesus' mission and why the glory of God is man fully alive: *to heal your heart.* It's what he said he came to do. So it's downright evil that your heart has been so misunderstood, maligned, feared, and dismissed. But there is your clue. The war you are in would explain so great a loss. This is the last thing the enemy wants you to know. His plan from the beginning was to assault the heart, just as the Wicked Witch did to the Tin Woodman. Make you so busy, you ignore the heart. Wound you so deeply, you don't want a heart. Twist your theology, so you despise your heart. Take away your courage. Destroy your creativity. Make intimacy with God impossible for you.

Of course your heart would be the object of a great and fierce battle. It is your most precious possession. Without your heart you cannot have God. Without your heart you cannot have love. Without your heart you cannot have faith. Without your heart you cannot find the work you were meant to do. In other words, without your heart you cannot have *life.*

The question is, did Jesus keep his promise? What has he done for your heart?

The answer is more than you can ever imagine.

The heart is central; to find our lives, we must make it central again. Do you believe this?

TRIUMPH AND VICTORY

The Devil is poised to pounce. . . . Keep your guard up.
1 PETER 5:8–9 THE MESSAGE

Warfare prayer is not a backup when all else fails. It is not a specialty form of prayer for the uniquely called or gifted. We are all called to preach the gospel; we are called to resist the enemy. We are living out our daily lives in the context of war. The men and women who choose to equip themselves and become practiced in warfare prayer are the ones who enjoy the greatest freedom and breakthrough.

In fact, by choosing to rule in this category of reality, you will discover a wonderful surprise—all those passages in Scripture that shout with praises of triumph and victory will make sense to you. It's like discovering the missing chapters to your story.

Now, I do not mean to minimize the difficulty of the enemy's attacks. By saying this is typically a simple and effective form of prayer, I do not mean it's always simple. But it is *always* effective, especially as you operate as a son or daughter, seated with Christ in authority. Freedom is your right. For as Paul urged in Galatians, "It is for freedom that Christ has set us free. . . . Do not let yourselves be burdened again by a yoke of slavery" (5:1). Do not "let"—the choice is up to you.

Jesus—I choose to take my stand in you, with you. I renounce the enemy and his lies in my life. I claim your victory against my every foe. I reject the ways the enemy is trying to "yoke" me again. In Jesus' name!

THE THIEF WANTS IT ALL

Keep a firm grip on the faith. The
suffering won't last forever.
1 PETER 5:9–10 THE MESSAGE

Any movement toward freedom and life, any movement toward God or others, *will be opposed.* Marriage, friendship, beauty, rest—the thief wants it all. A. W. Tozer wrote, "So, it becomes the devil's business to keep the Christian's spirit imprisoned. Satan works to keep us bound and gagged and imprisoned in our own grave clothes. He knows that if we continue in this kind of bondage . . . we are not much better off than when we were spiritually dead."[5]

Sadly, many of these accusations will actually be spoken by Christians. Having dismissed a warfare worldview, they don't know who's stirring them to say certain things. These words will come from anywhere; be careful what you are agreeing with.

When you agree with those words, it becomes a kind of permission you give the enemy, sort of like a contract. Some foul spirit whispers, *I'm such a stupid idiot*, and you'll agree with it; then it'll take months and years trying to sort through feelings of insignificance. You can end your agony if you'll treat it for the warfare it is, break the agreement you've made, and send the enemy packing.

Learning to break agreements with the enemy is a wonderfully freeing thing. So—what do you say to yourself when you mess up some project, conversation, event? What do you say to yourself when things aren't going well? Most often, those are agreements. Now that you can name them, renounce them! Right now!

REJECT THE FALSE VERDICT

*May the Lᴏʀᴅ bless you and protect you. May the
Lᴏʀᴅ smile on you and be gracious to you.*
Nᴜᴍʙᴇʀs 6:24–25 ɴʟᴛ

Your wounds brought messages with them: "You're worthless."
"You're too much . . . and not enough." "You're a disappointment." "You are repulsive." Because they were delivered with such
pain, they *felt* true. They pierced your heart. So you accepted the
messages as fact. You embraced them as the verdict on you.

The vows you made as a child act like a deep-seated agreement with the messages of your wounds. "Fine. If that's how it is,
then I'll live my life in the following way. . . ." Those childhood
vows are very dangerous things. You must reject the messages of
your wounds. It's a way of unlocking the door to Jesus. Agreements
lock the door from the inside. Renoucing the agreements unlocks
the door to him.

Friend, sit with Jesus and ask for forgiveness for embracing
these lies. Renounce them. He calls you his Beloved. His friend.
He sees you and will keep pursuing you. Make an agreement with
his truth.

You might have done this after yesterday's reading, but
friend, breaking agreements often takes some repetition and
"stubbornness" on our part. So pray again, *Jesus, I renounce the
agreements I've been making with these messages all these years.
Bring the truth here, O Spirit of truth.*

IT'S A DANGEROUS WORLD

*"Stay alert. This is hazardous work I'm
assigning you. You're going to be like
sheep running through a wolf pack."*
MATTHEW 10:16 THE MESSAGE

Many of us are interpreting reality like this: *The world is a broken but still pretty decent place, and while awful things happen, for the most part I'm going to be okay because God can help me find a life worth living. If he cooperates.*

To give you a vivid contrast, Jesus says to his dearest friends: "I am sending you out like sheep among wolves" (Matthew 10:16). I'm sure the illustration was chosen to shake their assumptions. But since most of us have never lived with sheep nor seen a wolf, let me attempt a translation: *I am sending you out like puppies on a freeway.*

Let it sink in. Jesus assumes a dangerous world. Not an unpredictable one, but clearly a world in which you find yourself in battle with evil. God *is* your ally, but not primarily to find you a simple life. Your story is not one of abandonment—another reason for unbelief—but rather a clear illustration that this is a world in a brutal war and you must live like it.

Jesus—I don't want to be naïve. I want to live close to you, aligned with you. So I take my refuge in you today, and every day. You are my Refuge and my Fortress; I choose to live in you!

BELIEF CHANGES EVERYTHING

*Why are you looking among the dead
for someone who is alive?*

LUKE 24:5 NLT

Jesus *will* return. Swiftly, unexpectedly. Any moment. His return will usher in the renewal of all things. That includes the execution of justice, rewards, the feast, your "estates," your appointed role in his great kingdom—along with the restoration of everything you love. This has some pretty staggering implications.

For one thing, it ought to radically transform your attitude toward death. Far too often Christians experience the death of a loved one as devastation. But if you think about it, heaven does not leave room for devastation.

Yes, losing someone you love is an earthquake; it is traumatic. Because what you experience is the massive sudden and ongoing loss, death is filled with tragedy and mockery. It seems to have the last word. You do not yet see the resurrection; you do not yet see the renewal of all things, and so you are vulnerable to massive agreements with loss, even with grief. But the moment you allow life to win, the moment you accept Jesus' "I'm just going away for a bit," it will change everything.

How does the coming return of Jesus transform your attitude toward death? Whom are you looking forward to seeing again at the renewal of all things?

INTERPRET YOUR SUFFERING

*The more we suffer for Christ, the more God will
shower us with his comfort through Christ.*

2 CORINTHIANS 1:5 NLT

Suffering will try to separate you from Jesus. You must not let it. The worst part of suffering is the damage it can do to your view of God, your relationship with him. Feelings of abandonment creep in: *Why did he let this happen?* Anger. A loss of hope. Mistrust. At the very time you need him most, you will feel most compelled to pull away from Jesus, or feel that he's pulled away from you.

There is a popular theology out there that says a Christian can avoid suffering. (Most of us have unknowingly embraced it—simply notice your reaction when life turns on you.) It is a devastating heresy because suffering will come, and then what will you do? It shakes your faith in God because you thought it wouldn't come, shouldn't come.

Be very careful and pay attention to how you *interpret* your suffering. Beware of the agreements you make. This is where the enemy can destroy you. Agreements such as *God has abandoned me*; *It's my fault*; and a host of others. If you've been making these agreements, you will want to break them. They allow a chasm to form between you and your Jesus.

Too many Christians simply fold under hardship and give way to the feelings of abandonment. Instead, protect your heart and your relationship with God by inviting Jesus into your suffering. Where do you need to do that today?

BEYOND YOUR SADNESS

*The LORD is close to the brokenhearted; he
rescues those whose spirits are crushed.*

PSALM 34:18 NLT

I want you to know there is something beyond your sadness. I'm keenly aware how easy it is when you're hurting to make agreements. This is the time you've really got to "watch over your heart with all diligence, for from it flow the springs of life" (Proverbs 4:23 NASB). It's far too easy to go from the immediate pain, which is real, to something sweeping like, "Life is just loss." Or "I hate change." Or "What is there to look forward to now?" Pain can so quickly open the door to other things you don't want to let in—like despair, or hopelessness, or resignation.

You actually have a choice whether you will let Jesus comfort you in this. Really.

Pain can feel so "true," so "real," that you actually push the comfort of God away because you feel you need to stay in the pain to honor it, or because it might be the most you've felt anything in a long time, or because those subtle agreements have begun to creep in and you've given place to pain as what is most true about life. I don't want to do that. You don't want to do that. No agreements. No pushing Jesus away. Whatever the loss may be.

Have you been resisting the comfort of Jesus because it isn't the comfort you wanted? Maybe what you wanted was relief, or an answer to prayer, and meanwhile Jesus is trying to offer you himself. Can you let him in?

YOU ARE ALIVE TO GOD

When Jesus died, he took sin down with him,
but alive he brings God down to us.
ROMANS 6:8 THE MESSAGE

I am deep in the jungle of the assault, and the only verse I can even remember to hang on to is "Count yourselves dead to sin but alive to God in Christ Jesus" (Romans 6:11). I repeat it to myself. Over and over. It gives me strength to fight the contempt and judgment.

Through the repetition, the enemy seems to be weakening.

It's important to remember this: the issue is never the presenting sin, but the surrender, however subtle, of our hearts. What follows is the enemy's real goal—our separation from God and from our true selves. I think most Christians never see the battle. They think they crave evil things, and they embrace the resulting contempt for their own hearts as true conviction. Then they assume that, of course, God is going to be distant and they live under all of that for years. They think that's the Christian life.

But it's not.

Or at least, it doesn't have to be. Sin isn't your true heart—it is your enemy. You can fight back. You must guard your heart. The assault will lift, if you hold fast. God is fighting for the victory with you.

What verses and truths do you use to hold on to when you are feeling "hard-pressed"? If the answer is, *I can't really think of one,* maybe you ought to find a few! "I am dead to sin and alive to God" is a good beginning.

LONGING TO BELONG

"Let us make human beings in our image, to be like us."
GENESIS 1:26 NLT

You'll find that the heart of all things is, in fact, just that—a Heart. A personality. Or better, a fellowship of hearts. Community. Trinity. In other words, reality is relational to its core.

You simply have to look at people to find this to be true. Aren't the greatest joys and memories of your life associated with family, friendship, or falling in love? Aren't your deepest wounds somehow connected to some*one* also, to a failure of relationship? That you were loved but are no longer, or that you never have been chosen? Then came agreements of loneliness and abandonment.

One of the deepest of all human longings is the longing to belong, to be a part of things, to be invited in. You desire to be part of the fellowship. Where did *that* come from? You are relational to the core. You are made in the image of God or, better, in the image of the Trinity. From the Heart of the universe come our beating hearts. From this Fellowship spring all of our longings for a friend, a family, a fellowship—for someplace to *belong*.

How have you felt about this longing in your life? Did you realize this longing came from God? Where are you currently taking it?

LONGING FOR LOVE

*Heal me, LORD, and I will be healed; save me and
I will be saved, for you are the one I praise.*

JEREMIAH 17:14

I know I'm not alone in having a hard time believing in the love of God for me (we think he loves everyone else), or letting it catch my heart up into life and joy, or maybe especially, staying there for any reasonable period of time. Now I'm trying to bring my heart back to the love of God, let it heal me, and stay there.

Your story of love is a very tangled story about the most precious thing in your life (your longing for love). It's a hard story to tell for two reasons. For one thing, you're too close to it to often have any clarity at all. Can't see the forest for the trees. More deeply, it's a heartbreaking story, and you're not sure you want to revisit the painful details. That's why we're ambivalent about love. Oh, you yearn for it. Of course, dear friend, you want to be loved. But you hide from it too, building defenses against it, fortressing yourself from being hurt again.

God knows the details of your hurt. And more than anything, he longs for you to let his love in so deep that it heals you. He longs for connection with you. Oh friend, remain in his love.

Jesus—I have very mixed feelings about my longing for love. You know how my story has shaped me. But I pray that you would come into my story of love, and that you would heal love in me. I want your love, Lord. I really do.

STORING UP TO OVERFLOW

"Every teacher of religious law who becomes
a disciple in the Kingdom of Heaven is like a
homeowner who brings from his storeroom
new gems of truth as well as old."

MATTHEW 13:52 NLT

Think of a canal: it runs dry so quickly, shortly after the rains subside. Like a dry streambed in the desert. But a reservoir is a vast and deep reserve of life. You are called to live in a way that you store up reserves in your heart, and then offer from a place of abundance. When Jesus talks about the storeroom, I find myself thinking, *Storeroom? What storeroom?* "A good man brings good things out of the good stored up *in his heart.* . . . For the mouth speaks what the heart is full of" (Luke 6:45, emphasis added).

I'm afraid I can live spiritually like I live financially—I get a little, and go spend it. I live like a canal. I *look* like a reservoir when the rains come, but shortly after, I'm dried up again. (My financially responsible readers have just congratulated themselves on living a more disciplined life. But may I ask, are you using those reserves to do things that nourish your heart? Many a Scrooge has filled his coffers while starving his soul.) One woman deeply involved in ministry wrote to me that she is "burned out to a crackling crunch." She has been a canal. She hasn't cared for her heart. She is not alone.

Make some time to take care of your heart this week. What do you need to fill your reservoir? Better yet, ask God what you need.

LIVING IN YOUR NARRATIVE

All the stages of my life were spread out
before you, the days of my life all prepared
before I'd even lived one day.

PSALM 139:16 THE MESSAGE

Story is the language of your heart. Your soul speaks to the images and emotions of story. Contrast your enthusiasm for studying a textbook with the offer to go to a movie. You'll find the answer to the riddle of your existence in story.

For hundreds of years, our culture has been losing its story. The Enlightenment dismissed the idea that there is an Author but tried to hang on to the idea life could still make sense. Western culture rejected the transcendence of the Middle Ages and placed its confidence in progress and the Age of Reason. The Author was dismissed, and it didn't take long to lose the Larger Story. The central belief of our times is that there is no Story, only the random days of our life. Tragedy still brings you to tears and heroism still lifts your heart, but there is no context for any of it.

So, you create your own story line to bring some meaning to your experiences. Of course, because your heart is made to live in a Larger Story. A story of purpose and walking in union with God. This is why it's important to remember the Author of your story, and the goodness of his heart for you.

Write down your favorite movies. Ask Jesus to show you the parts of his Story that are coming to you through the stories you love.

MAY

LOVE IS CHOSEN

For the Lord is the Spirit, and wherever the
Spirit of the Lord is, there is freedom.
2 CORINTHIANS 3:17 NLT

L ove is chosen. You cannot, in the end, force anyone to love you. So if you are writing a story where love is the meaning, where love is the highest and best of all, where love is the *point*, then you have to allow each person a choice. You have to allow freedom. You cannot force love. God gives you the dignity of freedom, to choose for or against him (and friend, to ignore him is to choose against him).

But why would a kind and loving God create a world where evil is possible? Doesn't he care about our happiness? Isn't he good? Indeed, he does and he is. He cares so much for your happiness that he endows you with the capacity to love and to be loved, which is the greatest happiness of all.

For this creator God is no puppeteer.

God says to us in Genesis, "I have given the entire earth to you, for your joy. Explore it; awaken it; take care of it for me. And I have given you one another, for love and romance and friendship. You shall be my intimate allies. But you must trust me. Trust that my heart for you is good."

O Jesus—I want to be your intimate ally. Thank you for giving me the capacity to choose love. I choose love. I choose love.

YOUR GLORY BESTOWED

In that day the LORD of hosts will become
a beautiful crown and a glorious diadem
to the remnant of His people.
ISAIAH 28:5 NASB

Earlier in the Story, back in the beginning of our time on earth, a great glory was bestowed upon us. All of us—men and women—were created in the image of God. Fearfully and wonderfully made, as the saying goes. Living icons of the living God. Those who have ever stood before *him* fall to their knees without even thinking, as you find yourself breathless before the Grand Canyon or a sunrise. That glory was shared with us. All that you ever wished you could be, you were—and more. We were glorious.

I dare say we've heard a bit about original sin, but not nearly enough about original glory, which comes *before* sin and is deeper to our nature. We were crowned with glory and honor. Why does a woman long to be beautiful? Why does a man hope to be found brave? Because we remember, if only faintly, that we were once more than we are now.

God created you in his image, with the ability to reason, to create, to share intimacy, to know joy. He gives you laughter and wonder and imagination. And above all else, he endows you with that one quality for which he is most known. He enables you to love.

Do you think about your story as starting with sin and brokenness—or do you think about your story as beginning with a great glory bestowed on you? A glory Jesus is even now restoring?

KNOW THEIR STORY

Stay on good terms with each other, held
together by love. Be ready with a meal or a bed
when it's needed. Why, some have extended
hospitality to angels without ever knowing it!

HEBREWS 13:1–2 THE MESSAGE

As you get to know people in your close circle of friends, it will be so helpful to know their stories and what has shaped them. You want to know who they really are. Where did they experience shame, and for what? Where did they experience being prized— and for what? Because everything we say and do is being filtered through our way of seeing the world.

Remember—whoever they are, they have a false self too, constructed to avoid rejection and win approval, often flipping from one personality to another based on, *Just tell me who you want me to be, and I'll be it.* The purpose of getting to know someone will show you which is the false self and which is the true self. You were not meant to walk through life alone, so as you pursue friendships, pursue community, you will want to fight for their true selves to come alive, while being careful not to step into the traps of what the false selves offer. You must know the things that have shaped them, and from there, friendships can be forged and community strengthened.

Do you know the stories of those who matter most to you? What makes them *them*?

MYSTERY TOO GREAT TO MENTION

*God created man in His own image, in the image of God
He created him; male and female He created them.*

GENESIS 1:27 NASB

It is a mystery almost too great to mention, but God is the expression of the very thing we seek in each other. For do we not bear God's image? Are we not a living portrait of God? Indeed we are, and in a most surprising place—in our *gender*. Follow me closely now. Gender—masculinity and femininity—is how we bear the image of God.

God wanted to show the world something of his strength. Is he not a great Warrior? Has he not performed the daring rescue of his Beloved? And this is why he gave us the sculpture that is man. Men bear the image of God in their dangerous yet inviting strength. Women too bear the image of God, but in a much different way. Is not God a being of great mystery and beauty? Is there not something tender and alluring about the essence of the divine? And this is why he gave us the sculpture that is woman.

Dear friend, we bear his image as men and women, and God does not have a body. So it must be at the level of the soul—the eternal part of us—that we reflect God.

In this world, gender has been dismantled in nearly every way. But gender was God's original intent: "male and female he created them." You have a dignity in your gender. Embrace it!

HIS CHILD

How happy I was with the world he created;
how I rejoiced with the human family!
PROVERBS 8:31 NLT

God endowed you with a glory when he created you, a glory so deep that all creation pales in comparison. A glory unique to you, just as your fingerprints are unique to you, just as the way you laugh is unique to you. Somewhere down deep inside, we continue to look for that glory. A man wants to know that he's truly a man, that he could be brave; he wonders, *Have I got what it takes?* A woman wants to know that she is truly a woman, that she is beautiful; she wonders, *Do I have a beauty to offer?*

Certainly you will admit that God is glorious. Is there anyone more kind, creative, valiant, or true? Is there anyone more daring, more beautiful, wise, or generous? You are his offspring. His child. His reflection. You bear *his* image. Do remember that though he made the heavens and the earth in all their glory, the desert and the open sea, the meadow and the Milky Way, and said, "It is good," it was only *after* he made you that he said, "It is *very* good" (Genesis 1:31, emphasis added). Think of it: your original glory was greater than anything that's ever taken your breath away in nature.

I know—I find it hard to hold on to myself. Does your self-image include the truth that you are a glorious image-bearer of a glorious God?

INTIMACY WITH GOD

*"I will give them a heart to know me, that I am the
LORD. They will be my people, and I will be their God,
for they will return to me with all their heart."*

JEREMIAH 24:7

Whatever else you might believe about intimacy with God, the truth is that God knows you *very* intimately. He knows what time you went to bed last night. He knows what you dreamed about. He knows where you left your car keys. You are known. Intimately.

But does God seek intimacy *with* us?

Well, start at the beginning. The first man and woman, Adam and Eve, knew God and talked with him. And even after their Fall, God goes looking for them. "They hid from the LORD God among the trees of the garden. But the LORD God called to the man, 'Where are you?'" (Genesis 3:8–9). This beautiful story tells us that even in our sin God still wants us and comes looking for us. The rest of the Bible continues the story of God calling us back to himself.

Intimacy with God is why he created you. Not simply to believe in him, though that's a good beginning. Not only to obey him, though that's a higher life still. God created you for intimate fellowship, and in doing so established the goal of your existence—to know him, love him, and live your life in an intimate relationship with him.

Jesus, I long for this; I was made for this. I ask your Spirit in me to lead me deeper—lead me into deeper intimacy with you.

IN THE KINGDOM

*What a blessing it will be to attend a
banquet in the Kingdom of God!*
LUKE 14:15 NLT

My heart rises in hope to think that one day I'm not only going to see Jesus, I'm going to share life with him!

Amidst renewed heavens, a renewed earth. My friend, we get the entire glorious kingdom back. Sunlight on water; songbirds in a forest; desert sands under moonlight; vineyards just before harvest—Jesus fully intends to restore the glorious world he gave us. Paradise lost; paradise regained. A hundred times over.

This was what was in his own thoughts when he said, as he passed the cup to his brothers in the Upper Room just hours before Gethsemane and the Gestapo, "I'll not be drinking wine from this cup again until that new day when I'll drink with you in the kingdom of my Father" (Matthew 26:29 THE MESSAGE). Jesus knew as sure as he knew anything that a new day was coming and with it a glorious kingdom. And there he knew we would feast again—not merely sing—and raise our glasses, and he would break his fast. Food, drink, laughter, life. The joy set before him.

So until then, my friend, make a practice of loving Jesus. Let him be himself with you. Let his life fill yours.

Pause, let this sink in: you are going to have Jesus, and the entire new creation, yours to enjoy any day now. Just let that into your heart.

PART OF SOMETHING BIG

I know, dear God, that you care nothing for the
surface—you want us, our true selves—and so I
have given from the heart, honestly and happily.
1 CHRONICLES 29:17 THE MESSAGE

D eep in your marrow lies a passion to be part of something big. And why did God give you such a heart? Was that placed in you simply to be killed? Never! I know "older" folks can look down at the "younger" generation and say something dismissive about "the idealism of youth" and how it's high time you settle down to real life, but that is not a helpful opinion. I don't believe it's God's opinion either. That counsel comes from folks who have killed their hearts and souls in order to "get along" in the world. God gave you that heart in order that you might discover both the joy of being part of his revolution and your own unique place within it.

There is a lot of wrong to be set right in the world. Everywhere you look, the planet is bleeding, children are trafficked, and truth itself has all but shattered. This is a time for revolution, and one of the great wonders of Christianity is the idea that you are born into the time you were. What could be more exciting? Frederick Buechner wrote, "The place God calls you to is the place where your deep gladness and the world's deep hunger meet."[6] What could be more hopeful?

Do you resonate with this—the longing for purpose and meaning in your life, and to be a part of something bigger? What passions rise within you? Don't ask, "But how?" Just let the desire surface.

WILD SPIRITUALITY

God saw all that he had made, and it was very good.
GENESIS 1:31

Much of your story is ultimately spiritual. The tests and challenges, the joys and adventures are all designed to awaken your soul, draw you into contact with your true self, into relationships, and to God. Any adventure—rightly framed—can be a powerful experience of God. And prayer or Bible study—rightly framed—is meant to be the same. There's a shared perception that God is found in church, and that the rest of life is . . . just the rest of life. The tragedy of this is that the rest of life seems far more attractive than church, and thus God seems removed, even opposed to the things that make you come alive.

But God embraces the physical world; he loves creation as you do. He speaks through it and uses it to teach you many things. We've lost many hearts from the church because it offers a boring spirituality, implying God is most interested in things like hymnals and whispering. And yet most of the stories of men encountering God in the Bible do not take place in church(!). In the desert Moses meets God in a burning bush. Jacob wrestles with God in the wilderness in the dead of night. David wrote most of his psalms under the stars. And most of the stories of Jesus with his disciples don't take place in church. Not even indoors.

God is in the things you love—music, starlight, coffee, running, reading. He is in all creation, and you can find him there. Do something you love this week, and enjoy the presence of God in it!

THE TRUE YOU

*All a person's ways seem pure to them, but
motives are weighed by the LORD.*

PROVERBS 16:2

What do people think of me?" is a *very* powerful motivator. It is still shaping you more than you'd like to admit. It shapes your theology, your politics, your values.

Can you go through one entire day being utterly true no matter how many different environments you move through? Do you even know the true you? *Is* there a true you? Whether it is born of fear or longing or uncertainty or cunning or wickedness, it is so natural to shape yourself according to the moment you scarcely notice how much you do it. Now, toss in the promise of reward— wealth, power, success, the adoration of others—and boy oh boy is it hard to be true.

Friend—surely you are aware that your personality has a *motive* behind it. Only when you have taken an honest look inside yourself, and seen what really fuels the things you do, will you appreciate how utterly remarkable it is to be *true*. And how utterly desirable. We are given the story of Jesus' wilderness trial to help us understand that Jesus has been tried—and proven true. Remember now, it was a genuine test of his character, so profoundly terrible to be seduced by the evil one himself, that Jesus needed angels to minister to him afterward.

Did you know that your personality actually has a motive behind it? If you are brutally honest, can you name that motive? Is it to be liked? To be safe? To get ahead?

GOD'S CREATIVE INVITE

*Let every created thing give praise to the LORD, for
he issued his command, and they came into being.*
PSALM 148:5 NLT

The right opportunity reveals your creative nature. It's precisely what happens when God shares with mankind his own artistic capacity and then sets them down in a paradise of unlimited potential. It is an act of creative *invitation*, like providing Monet with a studio for the summer, stocked full of brushes and oils and empty canvases. Or like setting Martha Stewart loose in a gourmet kitchen on a snowy winter weekend, just before the holidays. You needn't provide instructions or motivation; all you have to do is release them to be who they are, and remarkable things will result.

Oh, how you long for this—for a great endeavor that draws upon your every faculty, a great "life's work" that you could throw yourself into. Your creative nature is essential to who you are as a human being—as an image bearer—and it brings your heart great joy to live it out with freedom and skill. Even if it's a simple act like working on your photo albums or puttering in the garden—these too are how you have a taste of what was meant to rule over a small part of God's great kingdom, and live in the trueness through the story of your life.

If you could rewrite your story starting today, what would you love to do with your life? Again—don't ask, "How could that happen?" Just let your heart's desires surface. What would you long to do? What would you love to be great at?

FULL GLORY

*Early in the morning, Jesus stood on the shore, but
the disciples did not realize that it was Jesus. He
called out to them, "Friends, haven't you any fish?"*

JOHN 21:4–5

As you think about Jesus meeting his disciples on the beach after his resurrection in John 21, consider this: You're the Son of God. You've just accomplished the greatest work of your life, the stunning rescue of mankind. You rose from the dead. What would you do next? Have a cookout with a few friends? It so *ordinary*. Do you see that eternal life does not become something totally "other," but rather that life goes on—only as it should be?

Jesus did not vanish into a mystical spirituality, becoming one with the cosmic vibration. Jesus has a body, and it's *his* body. His wounds have been healed, but the scars remain—not gruesome, but lovely, a remembrance of all he did for us. His friends recognize him. They share a bite to eat. This is our future as well—our lives will be healed and we shall go on, never to taste death again.

His creation groans for this day, the day when we—the sons and daughters of God—are revealed for who we truly are. How wondrous it will be! Creation can be so breathtaking now. Can you imagine what it shall be like when it is released to its full glory?

What is your soul "groaning for" these days? If your life could take a wonderful turn, what would that look like?

A STORY WORTH TELLING

*Let no man's heart fail on account of
him; your servant will go and fight.*
1 SAMUEL 17:32 NASB

I was watching a remarkable documentary on the Dorobo hunters in southern Kenya. Their bows simply aren't strong enough to bring down big game, so they steal the kill off lions. In a stunning display of courage and cunning, they walk right up to a pride devouring a wildebeest; their unwavering confidence causes the lions to run off. In the next scene the men are roasting wildebeest flank over an open fire, talking, and laughing. One of them says, "But not everybody fights lions; some people are cowards." That is the campfire you want to be at—the feast of the daring.

This is going to take courage, because fear is the number one reason you give up. It will take perseverance because nothing worth having comes without some kind of fight. It will take cunning because most of us move into the world with a childish naïveté. You have a number of lions to slay—fear is one. Despair is another. Entitlement is yet another. Either you kill them or they eat you and your dreams for dinner.

Courage, perseverance, cunning—that's how you kill lions. Live that and you will have a story worth telling.

What fears are keeping you from living? From risking? Even from a more daring life with God? Name them; write them down even. And then invite Jesus himself right into the center of those fears.

INVITE JESUS TO HEAL

He cast out the spirits with a word,
and healed all who were ill.

MATTHEW 8:16 NASB

I share this story to show you how Jesus can come into your story to heal. When I was around twelve, I had a summer of nightmares.

Forty years later I came to an older saint who was remarkably gifted in prayer for the healing of the soul. He invited Jesus' presence to bring his healing ministry and asked, "Where's this distress coming from, Lord?" Immediately I was taken back to a memory I had long forgotten—the nightmares.

Jesus lovingly took me back there, to reveal where fear had gotten in. "What is the lie that took root there, Lord?" the old sage asked. My heart answered: *I am alone and unprotected.* "And what are you saying to John to do with that?" Jesus responded, *Banish the fear, in my name.* We commanded the spirit of fear to leave and never return. *Now invite my healing love there.* We did, and it was as if I could feel Jesus' presence in my soul. Jesus entered into the memory and made it his own, comforting that twelve-year-old part of me.

A door was closed to fear that day, and I have enjoyed the relief of it since.

Yesterday I encouraged you to name your fears, and invite Jesus in. Stay with that again today (maybe all week). Keep inviting Jesus in; ask his love to heal your heart where the fear got in. He's great at that.

A TANGIBLE CONNECTION

Every part of Scripture is God-breathed and useful one way or another. . . . Through the Word we are put together and shaped up for the tasks God has for us.

2 TIMOTHY 3:16–17 THE MESSAGE

God speaks to you through the Bible. And what is said there has more authority than anything else in your life. It is the bedrock of your faith and a living connection to the heart and mind of God—when you approach it with the help of the Spirit of God. I add that qualifier because we do well to remember that the Pharisees read and studied the Bible, "but their minds were made dull, for to this day the same veil remains when the old covenant is read. It has not been removed, because only in Christ is it taken away" (2 Corinthians 3:14). How very sad. They read it, but they didn't get it.

The Bible is not a magic book. It doesn't make you holy simply because you hold it in high esteem. Dear friend, you need the Bible and all it has to say to you. You also need the Spirit of God to guide you in your reading and study.

The Bible is meant to be read in fellowship with God. The more you know the Scriptures and the more they become a part of you, the more you'll find that you can walk with God and you'll give the Holy Spirit a library within you to draw upon.

What role does Scripture play in your life? Most people respect it, but rarely read it. Create a few minutes each day simply to let the written Word of God into your life.

WORTH FIGHTING FOR

Behold, how good and how pleasant it is,
for brothers to dwell together in unity!
PSALM 133:1 NASB

A true community is something you will have to fight for. Fight for it like you bail out a life raft during a storm at sea. You *need* this thing to work. Don't ditch it and jump back on the cruise ship. This *is* the church; this is all you have. Without it, you'll go down. Or back to prison.

Suddenly all those "one anothers" in Scripture make sense. *Love one another. Bear one another's burdens. Forgive one another.* Acts of kindness become deeply meaningful because you know you are at war. We know full well that we're all facing battles of our own, giving each other the benefit of the doubt. That's why you must know each other's stories, know how to "read" one another.

A word of encouragement can heal a wound; a choice to forgive can destroy a stronghold. You never knew your simple acts were so *weighty*. It's what we've come to call "lifestyle warfare."

Community is no substitute for God. Others aren't meant to fill the aching void in your heart. You need community, but you also need to be away with God, alone. You first go to God alone, so that you have something to bring back to your community.

O Jesus, lead me to the community you have for me. Show me who and where and how I could join or help form a fellowship of the heart. I give you my fears about it. My doubts and resignation.

CHRIST IN YOU

*I ask him to strengthen you by his Spirit—not a brute
strength but a glorious inner strength—that Christ
will live in you as you open the door and invite him in.*

EPHESIANS 3:16–17 THE MESSAGE

Jesus longs to come into the most vulnerable places of your
story. It is a treasure too many people have not experienced—
possibly because they did not know it is available. But the fruit is a
deeper love of Jesus because of the encounter with his personality.
First consider, where does Jesus Christ now reside in your life as a
believer? Inside you; more precisely, in your heart. So you should
expect to experience Christ within you.

Second, is there any aspect of your personal history that is
beyond the reach of Jesus Christ? Never. "You saw me before I
was born. Every day of my life was recorded in your book. Every
moment was laid out before a single day had passed" (Psalm 139:16
NLT). Would the faculty of your memory be a realm beyond the
understanding of Jesus Christ, or—more important—beyond his
access? No. So, Jesus within you is also Lord of your memory.

Finally, if your relationship with Christ or your witness for him
in this world is being hindered because a part of your soul is not
yet fully under his loving rule, would Jesus want to address that?
Of course he would. Remember his fierce intention over your life.

It begins with simply opening the door, and inviting him in—to a
memory, a secret sin, a place of regret, or heartache. Just open the
door to that part of your soul, and invite Jesus in.

BY WISDOM

They saw that the wisdom of God was in him.
1 Kings 3:28 NASB

A personal walk with God comes to us through wisdom and revelation. You will soon discover that we need both.

If you know the story of *The Last Battle*, you know that King Tirian of C. S. Lewis's Narnia has a good heart. But he also has an unwise heart—an untrained heart. I'd say that's true for most of us. Your heart has been made good by the work of Christ, but you haven't learned how to live fully from it. Young and naive it remains. It's as though you've been handed a golden harp or a shining sword. Even the most gifted musician still has to take lessons; even the bravest of warriors must be trained. You are unfamiliar, unpracticed with the ways of the heart.

This is actually a very dangerous part of the journey. Launching out with an untrained heart can bring much hurt and ruin. Your heart isn't bad; it's just young and unwise.

Notice that when the apostles needed the help of some good men to shepherd the exploding new church, they chose men "full of the Spirit and wisdom" (Acts 6:3). The two go together; you need them both. You need to walk by the inspiration of the Spirit, and you need wisdom as well. Wisdom and revelation.

Do you tend to live more by wisdom, or by the guidance of the Holy Spirit? You need both. Whichever one hasn't had much of a chance in your life, there is the place you need to grow.

GOD THE PURSUER

I am my beloved's, and his desire is for me.
SONG OF SOLOMON 7:10 NASB

You were created for intimacy with God, and for this you were rescued from sin and death. In Ephesians, Paul lets us in on a little secret: you've been more than noticed. God has pursued you from farther than space and longer ago than time. God has had you in mind since before the foundations of the world. And he loved you before the beginning of time, has come for you, and now calls you to journey toward him, with him, for the consummation of your love.

Who am I, really? The answer to that question is found in the answer to another: *What is God's heart toward me*, or *How do I affect him?* If God is the Pursuer, the Lover, then there has to be a Beloved, one who is the Pursued. This is your role in your story.

In the end, all you ever really wanted is to be loved, and God is love. You don't have to get God to love you by doing something right—even loving him. "This is love: not that we loved God but that he loved us and sent his Son as an atoning sacrifice for our sins" (1 John 4:10). Someone has noticed you; Someone has taken the initiative. There is nothing you need to do to keep it up, because his love for you is not based on what you've done, but on who you are.

Jesus, I need a fresh revelation of your heart toward me. Do you like me? What do I mean to you? Give me a revelation of this truth, Lord.

HOW GOD RESTORES US

We're a free people—free of penalties and
punishments chalked up by all our misdeeds.
E P H E S I A N S 1 : 7 T H E M E S S A G E

Whether you are aware of it or not, in the depth of your being, you ache for goodness. We all do. Our souls long for a sense of wholeness, and goodness is essential for wholeness. We are made for goodness like we are made to breathe, like we are made to love.

Friend, you are going to need a deep and profound goodness for all that is coming at you like a freight train. And there is a way to be good again. It comes to us from such a surprising direction—as almost all of the answers to our deepest needs do—that we'd best begin with a question: What is Christianity supposed to *do* to a person?

We exercise because we want to grow stronger; we travel for adventure; we work in the hope of prospering; we love partly in the hope of being loved. So why Christianity? What is the *effect* Christianity is intended to have upon a person who becomes a Christian, seeks to live as a Christian?

The way you answer this one question will shape your thoughts about church and community, service and justice, prayer and worship. It is currently shaping the way you interpret your experiences and your beliefs about your relationship with God.

This would be a very good thing to put some words to. How would *you* answer the question, "What is Christianity supposed to *do* to a person?"

FORK IN THE ROAD

Jesus' refusal was curt: "Beat it, Satan!" He backed
his rebuke with a third quotation from Deuteronomy:
"Worship the Lord your God, and only him.
Serve him with absolute single-heartedness."
MATTHEW 4:10–11 THE MESSAGE

You will face many forks in the road as you journey through life—each choice determining what kind of life you're going to live. Will you sell out for money? Will you pursue love and continue to fight for the relationship? Will you risk for your dreams, or succumb to fear and resignation? Will you let your health go? But this one—Will you face evil? Will you, as a son or daughter of the King, become the warrior he has called you to be?—this choice will have dramatic repercussions for the rest of your life, because everything you want in life you will have to fight for.

This is the fork in the road.

You are exposed to video games and movies that so clearly portray a world at war, great evil powers that must be fought. While a number of church leaders wrote essays denouncing these, I find myself wondering—perhaps this is God's way of preparing us to understand and accept the reality all around us.

Learn to fight not only for yourself, but on behalf of others. The world is a little short on courageous people right now.

How would you live differently if life were as epic, mythic, and urgent as the movies and video games depicting a great battle that must be fought?

A COSMIC DRAMA

God is love, and all who live in love live in God.
1 JOHN 4:16 NLT

The things that have happened to you often suggest that the real script of the play you're living in is "God is indifferent." Deep down in your heart, in the place where the story is formed, this experience of *God as indifferent* drives you to write your own script. Job apparently lived with this anxiety about God even before his tribulations (Job 3:25).

Job was a God-fearing man and yet something in him suspected that faith in God did not necessarily translate into peace and safety. Of course, Job had no inkling of the discussion going on in heaven between God and Satan. Astonishingly, God was placing the perception of his own integrity, as well as the reputation of his whole kingdom, on the genuineness of Job's heart.

Indeed, when we consider how central a part Job was given in the drama God was directing, we are confronted with the reality that we too could be in the same position. It seems that the part God has written for us is much too big and certainly too dangerous. Every human being is of great significance to God, but those whom God has drawn to believe in him are center stage in a drama of cosmic proportions.

You need to believe this truth often before you ever feel it. Our age has lost all belief, and with it, nothing seems epic. Certainly not our lives. Start today with, *My life is part of something very epic.*

YOUR NEXT CHAPTER

*You have caused them to become a Kingdom of
priests for our God. And they will reign on the earth.*
REVELATION 5:10 NLT

The next chapter of your story is precisely that—the chapter that follows all the chapters before and fits them perfectly. God is still telling your story; the next chapter is not disconnected from the rest. (I know it feels totally disconnected, but it is not.) If you will look at your future in light of the Story God has been telling, it will banish the fog like a strong summer sun.

In the next chapter, your powerful and creative Father re-creates you and the earth. He then tells you to do exactly what he told Adam and Eve to do: *reign*. Do you see the exciting connection? You are glorious once again, and given a glorious world in order to do the very things it is in your nature to do. Only this time around with far greater powers, magnificent even. You have within you a latent potency, talents and gifts unrealized, soon to be made new; the renewed earth will be even more responsive to your leadership than the first time around.

What will you do in the coming kingdom? The simple, stunning answer is, you will do everything you were born to do.

So—what do you want to do for the rest of your unending life? Dream a little—what would you love to do?

THIS IS YOUR FUTURE

*While they still did not believe it because
of joy and amazement, he asked them,
"Do you have anything here to eat?"*

LUKE 24:41

As I think again of the happiest endings to the best stories, I realize that what brings me to tears is the recovery of the relationships—the ones you have come to love are brought home again. After he laid down his life for us, Jesus was laid in a tomb. He was buried just like any other dead person. Family and friends mourned. Enemies rejoiced. And most of the world went on with business as usual, clueless to the Epic around them.

Then, after three days, his story took a sudden and dramatic turn: "As they entered the tomb, they saw a young man dressed in a white robe sitting on the right side. . . . 'You are looking for Jesus the Nazarene, who was crucified. He has risen! He is not here'" (Mark 16:5–6).

Jesus came back and was restored to them. He walked into the house where they gathered to comfort one another in their grief and asked if they had anything to eat. It was the most stunning, unbelievable, happiest ending to a story you could possibly imagine. And it is also yours.

While we really pay attention to this story only around Easter, it is the story of hope for every day. Jesus is the Forerunner. You too will rise, and carry on with your friends, just as he did. Is that how you've been envisioning your future?

YOU ARE NEEDED

*Behold, a white horse, and he who sat on it
had a bow; and a crown was given to him, and
he went out conquering and to conquer.*

REVELATION 6:2 NASB

Yours is a Love Story, set in the midst of a life-and-death battle. Just look around you at the casualties strewn across the field. The lost souls, the broken hearts. Friend, you must take this seriously. This is no child's game. This is war—a battle for your heart, and many others.

And you have a crucial role to play.

That is the truth spoken about every great story, and it happens to be the one we most desperately need if we are ever to understand our days. Frodo of *The Lord of the Rings* underestimated who he was. As did Peter, James, and John. It is a dangerous thing to underestimate your role in the Story. You will lose heart, and you will miss your cues.

This is our most desperate hour. You are needed. The moment has come where you must find your courage and rise up to recover your heart and fight for the hearts of others.

Jesus calls to you to be his intimate ally. There are great things to be done and great sacrifices to be made. You won't lose heart if you know what's really going on here. This is the gospel. This is the Story you are living in.

Jesus, forgive me for living in such small stories. I get caught up in such small dramas. I give my heart and my life back to you, Lord, to live from the heart in your Story—to fight for the hearts of others.

HAVE YOU ASKED HIS OPINION?

Come near to God and he will come near to you.
JAMES 4:8

Paralysis (masquerading as "confusion") can haunt every person when a looming decision will require a lot of us. Make note of that; don't let it keep you from seeing the light in front of you. God is here to help us with our fears, but only once we name them as fears and don't hide behind "I just don't know what to do."

You are friends with the brightest person in the universe—have you asked his opinion on the matter? This seems so obvious, but you'd be surprised at the number of Christians who don't ask God or give him more than a day to respond.

Learning to hear the voice of God, learning to recognize his counsel, is something we grow into. But my goodness—take the time to cultivate this in your life. It can be frustrating at times, waiting for his guidance—don't sabotage this wait with impatience.

I was driving home one day, angry and impatient with the car in front of me. I made a move to pass; my action nearly caused an accident. Sixty seconds later I saw a road sign that said Do Not Pass. It had a holy weight to it; I felt busted.

God speaks in all sorts of creative and playful ways. The real issue is, are you willing to listen?

Practice hearing God's voice today. Start by asking him what he thinks of you and believe that the kind words you hear are from your loving Father. Give it time, and you'll be amazed by what he says.

LONGING FOR LIFE

"Keep on asking, and you will receive what you ask for."
MATTHEW 7:7 NLT

We all share the same dilemma—we long for life and we're not sure where to find it, and if we ever do, can we make it last? The longing for life within you seems incongruent with the life you find around you. You must journey to find the life you prize. And the guide you have been given is the desire set deep within, the desire often mistaken for something else.

One of our greatest tragedies is giving up the search. There's nothing of greater importance than the life of your deep heart. To lose heart is to lose everything. And if you're to bring your heart along in your life's journey, you simply cannot abandon this desire.

The clue as to who you really are and why you are here comes to you through your heart's desire—awakened through whispers from God himself. But it comes in surprising ways, and often goes unnoticed or is misunderstood. Once in a while life comes together for you in a way that feels good and right and what you've been waiting for. The moments in your life that you wish could go on forever. They aren't necessarily all the great celebrations. More often God brings it in unexpected ways—like a glorious sunrise or coffee with a friend—as if to sneak up on you.

Think of times in your life that made you wish you could make time stand still. Were they not moments of love, moments of joy? Simple moments of rest and quiet when all seems to be well. Something in your heart says, *Finally—it has come. This is what I was made for!*

QUESTIONS OF YOUR HEART

Give me understanding and I will obey
your instructions; I will put them into
practice with all my heart.

PSALM 119:34 NLT

It's possible to recover the lost life of your heart and with it the intimacy, beauty, and adventure of life with God. But you must leave what is familiar and comfortable. Your journey first takes you on a pilgrimage of the heart to those secret places and times when your heart was still with you. God will help you remember what engaged you in deep ways when you were a child.

Continue to explore the hidden questions of your heart, remembering the stories of your life. By entering into those places you will begin to see how your story is interwoven with all God has been telling since before the dawn of time. It is on this pilgrimage that you begin to see that it was created specifically with you in mind. God will continue to show you all that is set within your heart, which you have known, longed for since you were a child.

Your journey begins by asking questions, putting words to the movements of your heart. *What does the spiritual life have to do with the rest of my life? What does it have to do with God? Did I stop listening? When did his voice first call to me, and how?*

Bring these questions to God; listen to what he is wanting to reveal: *What is this restlessness and emptiness I feel? What is at the core of that, God? What is set so deeply in my heart that no longer feels alive? How have you been speaking to me all along? Let me hear and know your voice, God.*

GOD DOES TALK TO YOU

"His sheep follow him because they know his voice."
JOHN 10:4

You are meant to hear the voice of God. An intimate, conversational relationship with God is available, and is meant to be normal. In the gospel of John, Jesus describes his relationship with you, how he is the Good Shepherd and you are in his care. He warns you that you live in dangerous country. There are wolves and a thief who comes to steal, kill, and destroy your life. Lovingly, tenderly, and yet firmly Jesus is urging you—don't just wander off looking for greener pasture, looking for the life you seek. Stay close. Listen for his voice. Let him lead.

I realize that many dear followers of Christ have been taught that God only speaks through the Bible. The irony of that theology is, that's not what the Bible teaches! Scriptures are filled with stories of God speaking to his people—intimately, personally. Adam and Eve spoke with God. As did Abraham, Moses, and Elijah. Again and again, the Scriptures provide doctrine and examples that show we are meant to hear God's voice.

If you hear his voice and open the door of your life to him, Jesus will come closer. For this very intimacy we were created! And it is a rescue, a comfort, a source of a thousand blessings.

Let's keep practicing this—what do you need to hear from Jesus today? What issue or question do you need him to speak to? Pause, and ask. Listen. Look for how he is speaking to you through the day.

HEARING HIS VOICE

Samuel said, "Speak, for your servant is listening."
1 SAMUEL 3:10

I find it nearly impossible to hear from God under immense pressure, as in, *I have to hear and hear now!* It's the spiritual equivalent of saying to yourself: *I simply* must *get a good night's sleep tonight!* You know the result of that.

As you grow in your intimacy with God, your ability to hear his voice grows. To help develop your conversational intimacy, start with yes or no questions. Pull away to a quiet place. Keep your heart open to whatever answer he has for you. (This is a beautiful part of learning to listen. Being open deepens your holiness and deepens your intimacy with God.) Repeat the question as you pray and listen—that keeps you focused. Bring your heart into a place of surrender, which prepares you to hear.

Another helpful practice is to first ask God a question you know the biblical answer to. For example, ask him, "Do you love me, Jesus?" The Scriptures have answered that—*yes*—beyond all doubt he does. Jesus will immediately say, *Of course I do.* It will help you and God go to the core of your relationship. He loves you. From there, you'll be confident with more specific questions.

Take some time to hear the voice of God. Quiet yourself. Ask a simple, but perhaps vulnerable, question. Listen to his answer. Let his answer be the anchor of your soul today.

YOUR INMOST BEING

What you're after is truth from the inside out.
Enter me, then; conceive a new, true life.
PSALM 51:6 THE MESSAGE

Most of us simply try and put things behind us, to forget the pain as quickly as we can. Really—denial is a favorite method of coping. But not with Jesus. He wants truth in the inmost being, and to get it there he's got to *take you into* your inmost being.

Christ will open the wound, not just bandage it. Sometimes he'll take us there by having an event repeat itself, years later, only with new characters in our current situation. We find ourselves overlooked for a job, just as we were overlooked by our parents. Or we experience fear again, just as we felt those lonely nights in our room upstairs. These are all invitations to go with him into the deep waters of our hearts and bring in truth that will set us free. Don't ignore it; ask God what he is wanting to speak to; he has something to say.

Is something happening in your life these days that might in fact be God, opening a part of your heart from the past? What is difficult right now? What is hard? How does it remind you of something from your past? Invite Jesus in; ask him to show you what he is trying to reveal. It might be an old agreement. It might be a wound or memory he wants access to. Let him in.

JUNE

GOD'S VOICE ALL AROUND YOU

God's glory is on tour in the skies, God-
craft on exhibit across the horizon.

PSALM 19:1 THE MESSAGE

God speaks through nature. Creation is no accident—it is a proclamation. A wild, bold declaration. Every day, sunrise and sunset remember Eden's glory and prophesy Eden's return.

Allow me a story: I'd just spent two very long days in the hospital with a friend. Hospitals are melancholy places. The corridors are filled with hushed tones. It felt like that's all there was in the world: monitors going off, staff, hallway conversations, the IV and cold rooms and artificial everything. I left to go grab us some dinner, and as I stepped outside I was literally hit with a wave of a summer evening. It was wonderfully warm. The cumulus clouds were building towers for their evening show. Meadowlarks across the field were singing. I could smell flowers. It was like experiencing the renewal of all things.

Nature is God's rescue from the creepy things you've been taught about heaven. That's why you love it so much. That is why God speaks to your heart through it. You break out the grill and have friends over, laughing late into the starlit evening. In this way you get a good, deep drink of the Great Restoration. Drink it in, friend. Let him speak. All of it is yours, forever. Very soon.

What in nature makes your heart especially come alive? Were you aware that God is speaking to you there? It might be good to return to that part of creation—personally, if you can. In photographs if need be.

EXPECT HIS GOODNESS

He took me in the Spirit to a great, high mountain,
and he showed me the holy city, Jerusalem,
descending out of heaven from God.

REVELATION 21:10 NLT

Ask Jesus to show you his kingdom. Sanctify your imagination to him—he wants to tell you all about it. Ask him to reveal to you pictures of the coming kingdom. Be specific—if you want to see those waterfalls, ask to see them. Be open to being surprised, don't "script" it. I dreamed of ships one night—great, three-masted sailing ships. The day was clear and we were tacking into the trade winds at a wonderful speed. The ocean was aquamarine, I could see marine life below us, keeping pace with us. It helped shatter my lingering religious fears that heaven is going to be boring!

Stay open to surprises; keep asking for glimpses of the kingdom any way God wants to bring them. This is how you can reach into the future to take hold of hope and hear God's promises. The more your imagination seizes upon the reality, the more you will have confident expectation of all the goodness coming to you.

Jesus—I do ask you to show me your kingdom. I sanctify my imagination to you. And I ask you to reveal to me pictures of the coming kingdom. Now keep your eyes open, friend. It may come in many playful ways—something you see in nature; a scene from a movie; a cover of a magazine.

HIS LOVE FOR YOU

*May you experience the love of Christ, though
it is too great to understand fully. Then you
will be made complete with all the fullness
of life and power that comes from God.*

EPHESIANS 3:19 NLT

We need love. God wants us to believe that we are rooted and established by his deep love for us. And that's what I want, to be filled with the fullness of God! The path to this is what surprised me—knowing deeply, knowing truly, in the depth of my being, the *love of God*. Really? This leads to that?

I don't think I'm rooted and grounded in love; at least, not as I need to be. Bad news still throws me; I'm cautious about dreaming; I'm driven; I seem to care just a bit too much about what others think of me; my relationships feel guarded; I still feel guilty about things that are decades old; and my prayers don't seem rock-solid. When I am rooted and grounded in love, I approach life much differently.

I think you would too. You need love.

I wonder just how marvelous this would be—if we could have a personal revelation of the love of God for us, frequently. So let's ask for it! Ask God daily, or as often as you can remember, for a personal revelation of his love for you. *And* for the grace to accept it when he gives it.

O Jesus—I do want this! I ask you for a personal revelation of your love for me. And I ask you for the grace to receive it. Help me receive it, Holy Spirit. I want to be rooted and grounded in love.

WITH ALL YOUR HEART

*If you search for him with all your heart
and soul, you will find him.*
DEUTERONOMY 4:29 NLT

Most Christians forget the part about seeking God with all their heart, and then wonder why God doesn't seem to be more present in their lives. Either you have God or you don't. Either he is your ally, or you are on your own. What you believe about this affects everything else.

If you don't have God—and I mean as an intimate ally, right by your side—you must do your best to figure out a path for your life. This is of course how most live, and much of the entire world has based how it functions upon this assumption—universities, markets, career fields, economies.

"There is a God; he is our Father" changes everything.

Now, when I say "believing in God," I'm not referring to a casual acknowledgment of his existence. If you do have God, you must act like it. For he does not lend his help to those who take him casually—just as you don't offer the treasures of your friendship to those who take you casually. You must seek him with all your heart so that you might discover his help and align yourself with where and how he is moving.

We live in a busy and distracted world. Most people check their mobile devices hundreds of times a day. Where can you clear a little space to begin to be more present to God, to "seek" him? First thing in the morning? Maybe during your lunch break? In the thirty minutes before bedtime?

A DIVINE RELIEF

*"Whoever wants to save their life will lose it, but
whoever loses their life for me will find it."*

MATTHEW 16:25

I was at a dinner party and for some reason my internal world was not in sync with the external. All night I was constantly aware of awful things inside me—wanting to be the center of attention, getting irritated at people for their idiosyncrasies—a nightmare of sin. The next morning, the temptation rushed in to make all sorts of resolutions to be a better person. As I sat down to pray, I felt myself resolving to do this and that, basically trying to kill the unattractive parts and buttress myself to be good.

It was a train wreck waiting to happen.

The Achilles' heel of this sort of "repentance" is that it is based in self-effort. Thank God I saw it and asked Jesus to come and have my life more deeply. The relief was almost immediate. Not in the sense that all those flaws instantly vanished, but rather that first, I was rescued from striving and self-resolve. Second, that the presence of Jesus in me does make those flaws recede into the background—some crucified, others to receive his healing grace. The point being, this time I was able to turn to *Christ in me* as my only hope of transformation, and the fruit of this turning-to is profound relief.

Pray this simple prayer today: *Jesus in me, help me with this. I release my self-determination and repent of my self-resolve. Lord Jesus, I give my life to you today so I can live your life.*

A WHOLE NEW WAY

Jesus, with a loud cry, gave his last breath.
At that moment the Temple curtain
ripped right down the middle.
MARK 15:37–38 THE MESSAGE

What an enormously symbolic and staggering event: the moment Jesus dies on the cross. That curtain separated the rest of the temple from the place called "the Holy of Holies." The presence of God dwelt in that forbidden chamber. It was a very clear message—God is too holy for us to approach. The Jews didn't even dare utter his name.

But you do. You're on a first-name basis. Because Jesus changed everything. Through his cross he paid for your sin, cleansed you, and brought you back to his Abba. Jesus established a whole new way of relating to God. He often reclined at meals with people; he stopped along the road to chat; he touched them, embraced them. He called them by name.

Jesus is always closing the distance. The encounters in the Gospels are intimate. Why do we feel we must help Jesus set that mistake right by pushing him off a bit with reverent language and lofty tones? I understand that much of it is done with good intention, by men and women who want to honor Christ. Just like Peter. But the irony is, this isn't how God chose to relate to you.

Is your "religious" language, practice, or posture keeping God at a distance? Can you let go of all that and just let him draw near? Jesus wants to close the distance! The encounters in the Gospels are *intimate*.

RECEIVE HIS LIFE

*"For a branch cannot produce fruit if it is
severed from the vine, and you cannot be
fruitful unless you remain in me."*

JOHN 15:4 NLT

How do you remain in vital union with Jesus? By loving him, by obeying him, by surrendering more and more and more of yourself to him. This is how Jesus lived. He modeled for you a totally surrendered life, a life lived in union with the Father. He came in part to show you how it's done. All that dynamic life you see coursing through him, he received it as you must—through ongoing love and dependence upon God.

Now, you must give your life over to him in order to receive his life. Not just once, but as a regular practice. Of course there is more to this than saying a prayer. It would take another book to describe the ways you make yourself available to his life. You find those practices that help you receive the life of God. Whether it be prayer, worship, silence, sacrament, or the gift of sunshine, sitting beside a stream, music, adventure—you seek out those things that help you to receive the life of God. You have a personal guide now; ask Jesus what to take up and what to set down, so that you might receive his life.

*Jesus—show me how to receive more of your life today, and this week.
What do I need to let go of, and what do I need to "take up"?*

GUIDANCE AND CLARITY

*We ask God to give you complete knowledge of his will
and to give you spiritual wisdom and understanding.*
COLOSSIANS 1:9 NLT

When seeking clarity through prayer, it's important to ask for the Spirit of wisdom and revelation. Both are needed. Sometimes, wisdom holds the answer. Other times, we need a revelation from God (as did Ananias in Acts 9, when the situation seemed to shout, "Don't go near Saul!").

The key to receiving answers to prayers for guidance is to let go of your constant attempt to "figure things out." Really, it can be almost incessant; I will be in the midst of seeking the God of four hundred billion suns on some issue of guidance, and in the midst of asking him I am thinking through the options, trying to figure it out as I pray. I've been in hundreds of meetings where Christians gathered to seek God's counsel on some matter, but they spent the entire time trying to "figure it out."

Friend, it is fruitless to seek God's counsel while you are privately committed to one course of action over all others. You must surrender your agenda. You must surrender your "best thoughts" on the matter. You must surrender your secret desires. Because when you do this, you are in a much better place to receive God's thoughts on the situation.

Lord, forgive me for trying to figure it out even while I'm seeking your help. I surrender figuring it out; I need your light and your counsel. Shine your light on my life, Jesus.

OUTWARD VERSUS INWARD

The Pharisee was shocked and somewhat offended
when he saw that Jesus didn't wash up before the meal.
LUKE 11:38 THE MESSAGE

J esus has accepted an invitation to dinner. Every guest previously has washed before being seated, observing an orthodox custom unbroken for centuries. Jesus knows this, knows they're watching his every move. Yet he walks past the line at the washbasin and gets comfortable at the table. The Pharisee is speechless. Jesus reads the look on his face and offers an explanation: "Oh—the washing bit," he says as he takes a piece of flatbread. "It completely clouds the issue. Outwardly you look sensational. But inwardly, your heart is full of extortion and evil."

The things Jesus says. Apparently, he's not concerned about being invited back. Jesus' three years of public ministry are one long intervention. That's why he acts the way he does.

Remember, Jesus is on a mission to rescue a people who are so deceived, most don't even want to be rescued. His honesty and severity are precise, according to the amount of self-deception encasing his listener. When a soul is encrusted with pride, bigotry, self-righteousness, and intellectual elitism—as was his dinner host—then that shell needs to be struck hard at times in order to cause a crack that might allow in some light. Jesus strikes with the precision of Michelangelo.

The way Jesus behaves at the dinner—is this how you picture Jesus Christ? Are there some stale, "religious" images of him you need to let go of?

YOUR HEART'S REAL THIRST

"The water I give will be an artesian spring within, gushing fountains of endless life."
JOHN 4:14 THE MESSAGE

This may come as a surprise to you: Christianity is not an invitation to become a moral person, a program for getting you in line or for reforming society. Yes, it has a powerful effect upon your life, but when transformation comes, it's always the *aftereffect* of something else, something at the level of your heart. So at its core, Christianity begins with an invitation for you to *desire.*

Look at how Jesus relates to the Samaritan woman he meets at the well. She's alone in the heat of the day to draw water, so she's less likely to run into anyone. You see, her sexual lifestyle has earned her a "reputation." She's on her sixth lover, so she'd rather bear the scorching heat than face the searing words of the "decent" women in town. She succeeds in avoiding the women, but runs into God instead. What does he choose to talk to her about—her immorality? No, he speaks to her about her *thirst*: "If you knew the generosity of God and who I am, you would be asking *me* for a drink, and I would give you fresh, living water" (John 4:10 THE MESSAGE). Remarkable. He doesn't give a little sermon about purity; he only mentions it briefly. Still, he pursues her, saying in effect, *Let's talk about your heart's real thirst, since the life you've chosen obviously isn't working.*

Have you asked yourself lately, *What is it that I want? Where am I thirsty?* Be still, and just let your soul name its thirst. Then invite Jesus into your thirst!

COOPERATE WITH HOLINESS

God is working in you, giving you the desire
and the power to do what pleases him.
PHILIPPIANS 2:13 NLT

I've tried snowboarding, but never really learned. It was always a hazardous, hesitant affair, and there was never much joy in it for me. My basic problem was hesitancy. You have to commit and lean forward, down slope. If you fight that, you're constantly battling gravity and balance. Good riders just go for it—they commit, lean into it, and off they go. Then comes the joy I've never known.

Surfing is the same dynamic. There is a moment when you have to commit to go with the wave or not. Yes, there's some paddling on your part, but when the wave picks you up, your choice is to accept its power and let it hurl you forward. You don't create the wave; the power is utterly beyond you. Once it has you in its mighty grip, your part is to *cooperate*. Then the beauty comes.

Holiness works the same way. What I mean is this: the power is not yours. The power comes from God, from the presence of the living Jesus Christ inside you. He is the wave. If you think you have to paddle fast enough to create the entire experience, you will end up frustrated and exhausted from all the striving. The name for that is Religion. God offers you something far better: "Let me be the wave."

How much of your spiritual life feels like striving, and how much feels like simply letting Jesus-who-lives-within-you have more of you?

LET HIM IN

Jesus doesn't change—yesterday, today,
tomorrow, he's always totally himself.
HEBREWS 13:8 THE MESSAGE

Maybe the most devastating limit that's been put on Jesus is the idea that *he doesn't act like he did in the Gospels anymore. That was then and this is now and things have changed.* In one fell swoop, this belief shuts down just about everything you could hope to experience with Jesus. It simply slams the door to him and leaves you standing on one side and him on the other.

Jesus desires deep intimacy with you. It clearly wasn't Jesus who shut the door, leaving him on the street. He's asking *you* to let him in.

So let him in.

You can begin opening the door by renouncing the lie that Jesus doesn't act toward you the way he acted toward people in the Gospels. To get a little perspective, it's absurd to hold on one hand that the Gospels are the definitive word on Jesus, while holding on the other that he doesn't behave like that anymore. God gives you his Son, and records for all time in the Gospels, against all other claims, who Jesus is. But then, many Christians have been led to believe, God changed the rules: *That's not available to you now. You can't reach out to him in faith as did the woman with the issue of blood and be healed by his life as she was.* It's blasphemy. He is the same, yesterday, today, and forever.

Jesus, come in. I open the door. I want to experience you like your friends did in the Gospels. Reveal yourself to me.

LOVING JESUS

*"I'm unswervingly loyal to the thousands who
love me and keep my commandments."*

EXODUS 20:6 THE MESSAGE

It's commanded: love God with all your heart and with all your soul and with all your mind. So let's keep this simple: Do you love God? It all starts there. Make a practice of loving God. You may ask: *How?* Well, how do you love anyone? You delight in them, give your heart over to them. You choose them over other things and other people. They hold a special place in your heart. They get your time, your attention, don't they? This is what you do—you give your *whole* heart to God, making him the treasure of your life.

It will be a profound moral rescue. It's difficult to lust after a false idol if in that very moment you start saying, *Jesus, I love you, I love you, I love you.* It's difficult to hold bitterness toward someone if in that moment you start loving God.

Loving God will center you. It's the restoration of your reason for existence. What a relief to love God with all your heart, soul, mind, and strength. What an utter relief. For then, every other relationship falls into place; every other desire finds its appropriate place in your life. Again, this is why mere "morality" can never substitute for true holiness. You can keep all the rules you think are important and not love God. This is where it all begins, truly loving Jesus with all your heart.

When you find yourself struggling, right then and there say, *I love you, Jesus. I love you, I love you.* You'll feel your heart being freed.

THE ENEMY'S PLAN

Do not give the devil a foothold.
EPHESIANS 4:27

The enemy's whole plan is based on agreements. When we agree with the demonic forces suggesting things to us, we come under their influence. Let me give you an example.

We'd been looking for a house for four years—four years of ups and downs and promises and hopes and finally, we found it. Beautiful, private, restful: it was a perfect fit. We wrote up a slam-dunk offer, gave it to the Realtor—then we found out another offer beat ours by twenty minutes.

It felt like a setup. Our hearts were so hopeful, open, vulnerable. Losing the house was a direct wound. It wasn't just about a *house*—it was about our relationship with God.

Suddenly I heard: *God has betrayed you. None of what you believe is true. Why walk with God if you can't trust him?* We were reeling.

Jesus said the thief comes to steal and kill and destroy. The enemy stole the house, then wanted to kill our hearts and destroy our faith. During an assault like that, we must remember: make no agreements. The enemy will suggest, *You see—God doesn't care. You're not worth fighting for. Your heart doesn't matter. You can't trust him.* The enemy's plan is to kill our hearts, destroy the glory of our lives. Whatever you do, make no agreements. We have to start there.

Jesus, make me alert to the enemy's strategies, and give me the strength to refute his lies.

PLEASURE IDOLS

[He] fashions a god and worships it.

ISAIAH 44:15

There's nothing like waking up to what you've done, whether it's too much to drink or eat, or letting your anger fly. The remorse after a flagrant sin often brings a sense of clarity and resolution. But if you keep your indulgence at a moderate level, such clarity never comes. You never see it in black and white, for you're always under its influence. Pleasure isn't nearly so much about true enjoyment as it is about anesthetizing yourself. Think about the relief your idols provide: Is your desire truly and deeply satisfied, or does the relief come more through the temporary *absence* of desire?

I didn't see the entire function of pleasure in my life until I had to face intense grief and loss. I tried every drug I could, and nothing worked. Not food. Not sleep. Not work. Not reading. I could not get away from the pain. And then it occurred to me: If I am trying to use pleasure as a drug in this case, how many of my so-called enjoyments are merely the same thing on a lesser scale? Don't be fooled by the apparent innocence of the object you've chosen. Most of your idols have perfectly legitimate places in your life. Be honest about their function.

There is a legitimate place for our hobbies, our little joys, the things that give us pleasure. The simple test to see if they have become "idols" is this: Try giving them up for a week. Fast from them, so that your heart can be free to love God.

SURRENDER YOUR SELF-DETERMINATION

They weren't in love with themselves;
they were willing to die for Christ.
REVELATION 12:11 THE MESSAGE

Love Jesus. Let him be himself with you. *Every day*, allow his life to fill yours.

Of course, this assumes that you are willing to surrender your self-determination. You'll find it hard to receive his life in any great measure if you, as the branch, keep running off on your own, leaving the Vine behind in order to do life as you please. Honestly, I think this is why we accept such a bland, distant Jesus—he doesn't intrude on our plans. One of the most bizarre realities of the religious church is how loving Jesus is considered optional, extra credit. The same sort of madness has crept in with the idea that you can be a Christian and hold on to your self-determination.

And how is that going, by the way?

If you are not drawing your life from Jesus, it means you are trying to draw it from some other source. I'll guarantee you that it's not working. If you grab for life, it will fall through your fingers like sand; give your life away to God, and you will be a person his life can fill. If you want to experience the generous, unquenchable, unstoppable life of Jesus in you and through you, then surrender your self-determination.

Lord Jesus, I give my life to you today. I give everything, and everyone, to you. I give you permission to fill me with your life. Amen.

WE MUST SLOW DOWN

As for me, I look to the LORD for help. I wait confidently
for God to save me, and my God will certainly hear me.
MICAH 7:7 NLT

We cannot control what God, the Romancer, is up to, but there is a posture we can take that will enable you to recognize and receive his wooing. So let me ask—are you willing to allow for a life that exists beyond the realm of analysis? Coming closer to the heart, are you willing to let passion rise in you, though undoubtedly it may unnerve you? To permit the healing of some of your deepest wounds? Are you willing, at some level, to be undone?

Then we may proceed.

To enter into the Romance you must slow down, or you will miss the wooing. Turn off the news and put on some music. Take a walk. What was it that stirred your heart over the years? *Go and get it back.*

This is hard to do, especially as we're out conquering the world. But remember—what the evil one does is try to bury you with battles. Wear you down. But life is *not* all about the battle. The Romance is always central.

God will come through for you. What you fight for is the freedom and healing that allow you to have the intimacy with God you were created to enjoy. To drink from his river of delights.

It really comes down to such simple choices: Turn off the news, set aside your cell phone, and listen to some music. Go for a walk. What was it that stirred your heart over the years? *Go and get it back.*

THE WARRIOR WITHIN

*Tomorrow I will take my stand on top
of the hill holding God's staff.*
EXODUS 17:9 THE MESSAGE

Son or daughter, you are made in the image of God, who is the Great Warrior. Your convictions constitute a great part of your mission here on earth—to join the Great Warrior in the battle against evil. It is this nature that will enable you to overcome the passivity and paralysis inherited from the Fall. In fact, you regularly side with one or the other—the warrior or the paralyzation—in every decision you make, every day.

There are many ways for your warrior heart to emerge. You don't have to join the military, though that is a noble calling; over the ages the pen has proved mightier than the sword, as the old saying goes.

Regardless of how you stand with the Great Warrior, your warrior heart says, "I will not let evil have its way. There are some things that cannot be endured. I've got to do something. There is freedom to be had." The heart of the warrior says, "I will put myself on the line for you." Your nature is fierce, and brave, ready to confront evil, ready to go into battle. There is a time to stop saying, "Why is life so hard?" Instead you partner with Jesus, taking the hardness as the call to fight, to rise up, take it on. Just as Jesus had to do to fulfill his life's great mission.

O Jesus—forgive me for so much self-protection in my life. I want to be a part of your Great Mission. Show me the place you have for me.

THE HELP OF OTHERS

"The Advocate, the Holy Spirit, whom the Father
will send in my name, will teach you all things and
will remind you of everything I have said to you."

JOHN 14:26

Healing through counseling doesn't come *only* from Christ; it flows through his people as well. Yes, the Spirit was sent to be your Counselor. Yes, Jesus speaks to you personally. But often he works through another human being. The fact is, you're usually too close to your story to see what's going on; you sometimes don't know what's true or false, what's real or imagined. It often takes the eyes of someone to whom you can bare your soul.

In every great story the hero or heroine must turn to someone older or wiser for the answer to some riddle. Dorothy seeks the Wizard; Frodo turns to Gandalf.

Having a doctrine pass before the mind is not what the Bible means by knowing the truth. It's only when it reaches down deep into the heart that the truth begins to set you free, just as a key must penetrate a lock to turn it, or as rainfall must saturate the earth down to the roots in order for your garden to grow.

"Behold, you desire truth in the innermost being" (Psalm 51:6 NASB). With the help of others, you can reach into the deep issues in your heart and open the door to more healing.

O Jesus—come into the deep places of my heart. Search me and know me. Come into the places that have been misunderstood and wounded. Come and be my Counselor, and bring others into my life to help as well.

SAFETY IN DISTANCE

Deep calls to deep.

PSALM 42:7

On the one hand, your soul cries out for Jesus. You yearn for his life in you, his love, his nearness. On a conscious level, you ache for his comfort, his counsel, his friendship.

On the other hand, you keep a safe distance. He is so true, to be near him is unsettling because it reveals in a general sense all that is not true in you. Sometimes in a very specific sense. It doesn't happen in a barrage; he is too gracious for that. It doesn't always begin with perfect clarity. You are simply unsettled by his presence, as you might feel in the presence of a silverback gorilla. You pull back.

This is why false reverence is accepted—like having a relationship with someone out of state. It doesn't intrude into your life too much. There is safety in the distance. You secure yourself against a fuller experience of Jesus' presence because he is so unnerving. There is no faking it in the presence of Jesus; there is no way you can cling to your idols and agendas. You sense this intuitively, and so you keep your distance without really *looking* like you're keeping your distance.

When it comes to experiencing more of Jesus in your life, much depends on what you are *open* to experiencing—what you have been told you can experience, *and* what you are comfortable with. Are you willing to let Jesus be himself with you?

Are you?

BECOMING LIKE HIM

*We are Christ's ambassadors; God is making
his appeal through us. We speak for Christ
when we plead, "Come back to God!"*

2 CORINTHIANS 5:20 NLT

One of the reasons we like our friends is because we like who we are when we are with them. Wow, is this true of Jesus—when he and I are close, I like who I am. When we seem to be distant, I am a disaster. Well dressed, perhaps, putting a good face on things, but lifeless—like a cut flower. A friend once said to me, "When I'm in Christ or he's in me or however you describe that, everything is different—the way I see myself, the way I see you. I am the person I want to be."

As you love Jesus, experience him, and allow his life to fill yours, the personality of Jesus transforms your personality. The timid become bold and the bold become patient and the patient become fierce and the uptight become free and the religious become scandalously good. The disciples, his friends, looked to Jesus and became like him. Loving Jesus will help you to become the human being you were meant to be.

We aren't the only ones who need this desperately; the world needs this to happen in us. Whether we know it or not, whether we like it or not—in all our efforts we are continually portraying the personality of God to the world.

Pause for a few precious moments, and simply turn your heart toward Jesus. Remember what he is like; love him. You will be changed.

WITH ALL YOUR HEART

God has not given us a spirit of fear and timidity,
but of power, love, and self-discipline.

2 TIMOTHY 1:7 NLT

Jesus boiled down the true point of our existence to two things: loving God and loving others. Somewhere down inside you know love is the point.

The heart is the connecting point, the meeting place between any two persons. The kind of deep soul intimacy you crave with God and with others can only be experienced from the heart.

Christians have spent their whole lives mastering all sorts of principles, done their duty, carried on the programs of their church . . . and never known God intimately, heart to heart. "I never knew you" (Matthew 7:23 NLT). They attend a class and take in information, then use that information to change the way they live. None of that will bring them into intimacy with God.

What more can be said, what greater case could be made than this: to find God, you must look with all your heart. To remain present to God, you must remain present to your heart. To hear his voice, you must listen with your heart. To love him, you must love with all your heart. You can only be the person God meant you to be, and live the life he meant you to live, when you live from the heart.

Do you believe this to be true? Are you giving your heart room to be present to God?

JESUS IS YOUR LIFE

*. . . To know this love [of Christ] that surpasses
knowledge—that you may be filled to the
measure of all the fullness of God.*

EPHESIANS 3:19

We need Jesus like we need oxygen. Like we need water. Like the branch needs the vine. Jesus is not merely a figure for devotions. He is the missing essence of our existence. Whether we know it or not, we are desperate for Jesus.

To have his life, joy, love, and presence cannot be compared. To know him as he is, is to come home. A true knowledge of Jesus is our greatest need and our greatest happiness. The purpose of your being here on this planet, at this moment in time, comes down to three things:

1. To love Jesus with all that is within you. This is the first and greatest command. Everything else flows from here.
2. To share your daily life with him—on the beach, at supper, along the road, just as the disciples did.
3. To allow his life to fill yours, to heal and express itself through yours. Otherwise you cannot hope to live as he did and show him to others.

Love Jesus. Let him be himself with you. Allow his life to permeate yours. The fruit of this will be . . . breathtaking.

Just let this reading settle in; sit with it. Let it speak.

THE WAY THINGS WORK

He is always wrestling in prayer for you,
that you may stand firm in all the will
of God, mature and fully assured.
COLOSSIANS 4:12

Some prayers work, and some prayers don't. But why does that surprise and irritate you? Some diets work, but most don't; that's not surprising. You simply keep looking for what works for you. Some investments produce, others don't; you look for the program that works for you. *There is a way things work.*

And so it is with prayer. You just want it to be simple and easy; you want it to go like this: *God is loving and powerful. I need his help. I ask for help, as best I know how. The rest is up to him. After all—he's God. He can do anything.*

The problem is, sometimes he comes through, sometimes not, and we have no idea for the rhyme or reason why. You lose heart, and abandon prayer. (And feel hurt, and justified in doing so.) You abandon the very treasure God has given us for not losing heart, for moving the "mountains" in front of you, for bringing about the changes you so desperately want to see in your world.

The uncomfortable truth is this: that is a very naïve view of prayer. That simple view of prayer has crushed many a dear soul, because it ignores crucial facts. There is a way things work.

We all have mixed stories with prayer—some answered, some unanswered. What is your story with prayer? Do you pray much? Why or why not?

THE CRY OF YOUR HEART

Hear my cry, O God; listen to my prayer.

PSALM 61:1

Some prayers just happen; they are the cry of the heart. No training is needed when it comes to this kind of prayer. I've uttered it thousands of times; I'm confident you have too. Like when the phone rings with bad news and all you can do is say, *Father . . . Father . . . Father,* your heart crying out to God. It's a beautiful expression of prayer, rising from the deep places in you, often unbidden, always welcome to his loving ears.

The cry of the heart just comes, if you'll let it. These are the prayers I find myself already praying as I'm waking up in the morning. "O, God—help. Help me today, Lord." Sometimes it's just one word, repeated in my heart: *Jesus, Jesus, Jesus.* It will just flow for you too if you give it permission. Turn the editor off; let your heart and soul speak. In the Psalms, David is clearly unrestrained. Good grief—he's all over the map. One moment it's "I love you, Lord!" and the next it's "Why have you forsaken me?"

David seems reckless and unstable, yet he is called a man after God's own heart. It was *God* who made him king and canonized his prayers in the Bible. These psalms are given to the church as your prayer primer, and they are beautiful. They assure you that not only can God handle the full span of your emotional life, he *invites* you to bring it to him.

Do you feel comfortable sharing your entire emotional life with God? If not—why not?

WORSHIP: THE HEART'S HEALER

*Exult in his holy name; rejoice, you
who worship the LORD.*
PSALM 105:3 NLT

On counsel for spiritual direction, Mother Teresa suggested: *Spend one hour each day in adoration of your Lord, and never do anything you know is wrong. Follow this, and you'll be fine.* Such simple yet profound advice. Worship is the act of the abandoned heart adoring its God. It is the union that you crave. Desperately. Simply showing up on Sunday is not even close to worship. Neither does singing songs with religious content pass for worship. What counts is *the posture of the soul* involved, the open heart pouring forth its love toward God and communing with him.

Worship occurs when you say to God, with all your heart, "You are the One whom I desire."

I spent a year in the Psalms at the time I was resting from the duty of Sunday morning, praying them from my heart. It gave me a voice for the cry of my soul—the anguish, the weariness, the joy, the sorrow. It's all there. No matter where the poet begins, he almost always ends in worship. It is where your journey must lead you. Your only hope for rest from the incessant craving of your desire is in God, and you united to him. The full union, of course, is coming.

Find a worship song that you love, one that expresses your heart. Play it every day this week.

BOLD AUTHORITY

"You gave them authority over all things." Now when it says "all things," it means nothing is left out. But we have not yet seen all things put under their authority.

HEBREWS 2:8 NLT

Why do we pray "in Jesus' name"? The phrase gets tacked onto the end of many prayers, but I think it has about as much meaning to us as "amen." Amen does not mean "That's it . . . I'm done now," the little period at the end of your prayer. It is a pronouncement, firm and authoritative: "Yes! So be it! Let this be done!" Amen is a declaration; in that sense, it is like a command. Or it once was; now it has the emotional force of "talk to you later" at the end of a phone call.

"In Jesus' name" is even more of a command—far, far more declarative and final, like the drop of a judge's gavel. You are using the authority of the ruler of all galaxies and realms to enforce the power of what you have just prayed. As you look deeper into the spiritual realm of prayer, you'll discover that the whole thing runs on authority. It is the secret to the kingdom of God, and one of the essential secrets to prayer that works.

Remember—there is a way things work. Reality is one of the great tools of God to grow people up. And, as you learn, it can be used to your advantage.

Is this what you understood yourself to be doing when you used Jesus' name in prayer? In what ways might this new perspective add more authority to your prayers?

LEARNING YOUR ROLE

Paying in blood, you bought men and women, bought
them back from all over the earth, bought them back
for God. Then you made them a Kingdom, priests
for our God, priest-kings to rule over the earth.

REVELATION 5:9–10 THE MESSAGE

You will reign, dear one, over glorious kingdoms and realms within the great and glorious kingdom of your Father—a role you certainly need some preparation for. In a favorite Narnia story, *The Horse and His Boy*, the lost prince of Archenland is returned to his father—an orphaned boy, returned to his rightful role, just as you will be. But he has some learning to do, some catching up to do before he can assume full responsibility.

A prince totally unaccustomed to the ways of the kingdom cannot be entrusted with the throne until he has had some preparation—just as you need "educating." You really thought this life was simply about getting a nice little situation going for yourself, and living out the length of your days in happiness. I'm sorry to take that from you, but you and I shall soon be inheriting kingdoms and are almost illiterate when it comes to ruling. So God must prepare you to reign. How does he do this? In exactly the same way he grows you up—he puts you in situations that require you to pray and to learn how to use the authority that has been given to you. How else could it possibly happen?

This is happening right now. What situations currently require you to pray, and learn how to use the authority that has been given to you? Well—there's your training.

THE "ZAP" VIEW OF PRAYER

He prayed, and the heavens gave rain.
JAMES 5:18

You have been told over and over that God is almighty. And indeed he is. You have been told he is sovereign. And indeed he is. Perhaps out of respect, you have adopted the notion that if he is going to act, he is going to act quickly. Bam. Zap. (And to be honest, I think we adopted that perspective because it also relieves us of strenuous prayer.) But is this what is seen in many of the biblical accounts?

Clearly, God does not just zap the promised rain—Elijah had to climb to the top of the mountain, and there he prayed eight rounds of intervening prayer. God didn't just zap Joseph, Mary, and the child Jesus down into safety in Egypt—an angel had to come to them as well; they had to flee in the night.

Are you getting the picture? Prayer is not just asking God to do something and waiting for him to zap it. As those intimate allies of Jesus gathered in the night to intervene for Peter, clearly they didn't believe one simple prayer would do it; a few quick "Our Fathers" would *not* have taken all night.

Intervening prayer often takes time. And it takes repetition, repeatedly intervening and invoking.

Notice your heart's reaction—what are you doing with the truth I've just named?

JESUS, GIVE ME YOUR HOLINESS

It is written, "You shall be holy, for I am holy."
1 PETER 1:16 NASB

God is working within you so that you can receive his holiness. But it *is* a process, and you do have a role. But this is a process that God is committed to. To begin, nothing beats this simple prayer: *Jesus, give me your holiness.*

That's what it's all about. In the day to day, when I need it most, this is what I find myself praying: *Jesus, give me your holiness.*

Friend, he *wants* to give you his holiness. Receiving it begins with *asking* for it. There's more to it than that, but it's never *other* than that. Your journey to holiness is the process whereby you receive more and more of the holiness of Jesus Christ, into more and more of your being.

We are nearly halfway through this journey; how is your heart doing? Where do you still need the beautiful, holy life of Jesus to fill your life? Be very specific—God loves it when we are very specific in prayer. Name those places in you that still need his wonderful life, the places needing holiness or healing or simply comfort. Slowly, deliberately, invite Jesus into each place.

JULY

JUST WARMING UP

"Find a quiet, secluded place so you won't be tempted to role-play before God. Just be there as simply and honestly as you can manage. The focus will shift from you to God, and you will begin to sense his grace."

MATTHEW 6:6 THE MESSAGE

I was once taught, "When you think you are finished praying, you are probably just getting warmed up."

Often when you first turn to prayer you are coming in out of the Matrix—that whirling, suffocating Mardi Gras of this world—and it takes some time to calm down and turn your gaze to Jesus, to *fix* your gaze on him. You begin to tune in and align yourself with God as his partner. That itself takes some time. Much of the early stages of your praying involves not so much interceding but getting yourself back into alignment with God and his kingdom. Once in that place you can begin to be aware of what the Spirit is leading you to pray.

Furthermore, as you "press into" prayer, you are not simply begging God to move, but partnering with him in bringing his kingdom to bear on the need at hand. Enforcing that kingdom often requires much "staying with it," and repetition.

This is so important, and hopeful, because many dear folks have given up on prayer, having concluded it doesn't really work, when in fact *quick* prayers often don't work; simple little prayers aren't sufficient to the needs of this world.

It helps to pick one prayer "target" that you plan to stick with over time. Where do you want to practice "pressing in"?

RUSHING THE FIELD

Out in the open wisdom calls aloud.
PROVERBS 1:20

I had a friend who became a missionary. A beautiful dream, but she rushed to the field unprepared in many ways. I don't mean finances and language skills; I mean in the ways of the heart. Lurking down in her soul were some deep and unresolved issues that in turn gave the devil a playground to set her up for a fall. She was unpracticed in spiritual warfare, ill-equipped for what was thrown at her. She went, got hammered, and came home, defeated.

The disaster could've been avoided. Wisdom was crying out: don't rush the field (Luke 14:31); live as though your life is at stake, and the enemy is waiting to outwit you (Matthew 10:16). God has given you all sorts of counsel and direction in his written Word; thank God we have it written down in black and white. You'd do well to be familiar with it, study it with all intensity. The more that wisdom enters your heart, the more you'll be able to trust your heart in difficult situations. Notice that wisdom is not cramming your head with principles. It's developing a discerning *heart*.

Don't seek wisdom because it's a good idea; seek wisdom because you're dead if you don't.

Jesus, open my ears today to all of the wisdom and revelation you have to awaken my soul. I want to hear your voice, I want you to teach me your truth.

A VITAL ACT OVERLOOKED

*Take your everyday, ordinary life . . . and
place it before God as an offering.*
ROMANS 12:1 THE MESSAGE

In your eagerness to see good happen, it's easy to jump straight into praying, without first pausing and aligning yourself with Jesus—like a trombone player who simply starts playing her part without waiting for the conductor. This might be the number one error made by earnest folk. I'll say it again, dear friend—*there is a way things work*. We are in a collision of kingdoms, and it takes intentionality to bring things under and into the kingdom of God.

The act of consecration is the fresh act of dedicating yourself—or your home, a relationship, a job, your sexuality, whatever needs God's grace—deliberately and intentionally to Jesus, bringing it fully into his kingdom and under his rule. You would be surprised how often this vital step is overlooked.

Trust me, it makes a difference. The Scriptures respect the power of consecration. Anywhere and everywhere you want to experience the fullness of God's protection and provision, the life and goodness of the kingdom of God, it will help you to consecrate whatever is in question.

Jesus, I come to you now to present my life to you in an act of consecration. I consecrate to you. . . . [What is it, friend, that needs consecrating in your life? Your health? Your finances? Your appetites? A relationship?] *I consecrate this to you, Lord; I bring it completely under your rule and under your authority. I surrender it entirely to you. In your name.*

ALIGNING AND ENFORCING

Joshua said to the people, "Consecrate yourselves, for tomorrow the LORD will do wonders among you."

JOSHUA 3:5 NASB

Think of consecration as aligning and enforcing—*aligning* yourself with Jesus and all the laws of his kingdom, then *enforcing* his rule and those laws over the matter in question. The first step is mostly the aligning part. But often the enforcing requires a bit more "oomph," especially if you are having difficulties there. Which brings me to the power of *proclaiming*.

In Acts, when Ananias came to pray over Saul, he proclaimed the Lord's intentions there: "He laid his hands on him and said, 'Brother Saul, the Lord Jesus . . . has sent me so that you might regain your sight and be filled with the Holy Spirit'" (Acts 9:17 NLT). You don't see Ananias pray *to* God for Saul; instead, you see him proclaim God's intentions *over* Saul, and that is sufficient to see them fulfilled.

You enforce by proclaiming what is true over the subject. For example, you proclaim your authority over your home, requiring all things to recognize and yield to that authority, announcing that the authority of Jesus Christ is now in effect *here*. Proclaiming also causes your own spirit to rise up—or the spirit of the person you are praying for. Everything sort of stands at attention when you begin to proclaim the truth.

Do you *proclaim* God's truth over your life? If not, start with something simple like, "I declare that I am a child of God. I am loved. I am chosen."

HEALING IS A JOURNEY

Believing-prayer will heal you, and
Jesus will put you on your feet.
JAMES 5:15 THE MESSAGE

Healing prayer is beautiful and indispensable in your journey toward maturity, toward holiness, toward wholeness. But the journey requires other things as well—often counseling, certainly discipleship. There is no "zap" that suddenly makes a person as whole and beautiful as Jesus Christ. Wholeness is something you grow into as you walk with Jesus through the years of your life. And friend, knowing this actually takes a great deal of pressure off—pressure to find the instant fix or have the "one defining moment." It releases you to walk with God and allow him to personalize your healing journey.

Prayer is partnering with God. You don't pretend it's by your power that healing comes; and yet, God has you get involved. You do your part; he does his. This is so helpful to know and hang on to, because trying hard, straining, and stressing actually gets in the way.

Nothing helps healing prayer more than having some personal experience of seeing it happen. (Faith does play a role in this.) Nothing overcomes unbelief like seeing it happen for yourself; even more so as a result of your own prayers! So present yourself to God; partner with him as you step forward in faith and in prayer.

Be honest now—do you believe God heals? How strong is that belief these days? Maybe you need to ask Jesus to help your unbelief (Mark 9:24).

PRAYING DAILY

Before daybreak the next morning, Jesus got up
and went out to an isolated place to pray.
MARK 1:35 NLT

Proclaiming and enforcing God's kingdom over your life is a daily choice to realign yourself with God the Father, God the Son, and God the Holy Spirit; it is a choice to once again draw upon all the resources of the blood of Christ for you.

Dear friend, now that you have some understanding of the collision of the kingdoms all around you, it is so important to be intentional about "remaining" in daily intimacy and union with Jesus. I think you have a better grasp of why praying intentionally every day is essential. What you need first is *aligning* prayer—bringing yourself fully back into alignment with Jesus, taking your place in him and his kingdom, drawing upon his life and the power of his work for you.

Your time in intimacy with God is not mindless repetition; you must be utterly present to your prayers. E. M. Bounds said: "The entire man must pray. The whole man—life, heart, temper, mind, are all in it . . . it takes a whole heart to do effectual praying."[7] There is a need to keep at it—and not let your mind wander. It can be difficult to not give way to other things. Therefore, coming home to God requires some time and focus.

Try praying Our Daily Prayer, which is located in this book's appendix.

REMEMBERING HIS TRUTH

*"When the rainbow appears in the cloud, I'll
see it and remember the eternal covenant
between God and everything living."*

GENESIS 9:16 THE MESSAGE

It is human nature to look at the problem before us, the crisis that has caused us to pray. But the problem is exactly the thing we should *not* be looking at.

You will want to have something before you that helps you turn your gaze from the wreckage to God. What will help you keep your eyes "fixed" on the truth of God? C. S. Lewis had only one picture on the walls of his bedroom—a photo of the image of Jesus' face from the Shroud of Turin. He would gaze upon it as he prayed.

I believe that as you grow in fixing your gaze on Jesus, you can learn to turn your inner eyes to him and actually see him. But I'm not proficient at that, so I have a journal I keep in front of me; not a diary, but a journal of key truths I must remind myself of on a daily basis. That he is the God of four hundred billion suns. The Creator of everything I love. That I am his and I have the full rights as his heir.

Fixing your gaze on what is true will help you get into the right frame of mind as you pray.

What are you looking at as you pray? What might help you turn your attention to Jesus?

"SURE, I'LL PRAY FOR YOU!"

The earnest prayer of a righteous person has
great power and produces wonderful results.

JAMES 5:16 NLT

I've come to the place where I've had to stop telling people "I'll pray for you," knowing that despite my good intentions—and these promises are almost always spoken with good intent—I often just don't remember to follow through. Not until much later, and then I feel guilty that I forgot. I don't like promising something I probably won't live up to. You know how these stories go: someone you care about tells you of their pain, need, or struggle, and you respond with, "Oh, I'm so sorry to hear that; I'll pray for you." But then, most of the time, you never do. If all the prayers that were promised were actually prayed, this would be a different world.

So instead of promising future prayer, what I try to do is stop, right there in the moment, and pray. *Right then and there*. It's funny how many Christians this actually throws off guard. "You mean, right now?" "Yes—absolutely. Let's pray." In the restaurant, in the car, wherever. If it's a text or e-mail request, start praying as you type your response, typing out a prayer for them right then and there. Not only does it help to follow through, but it will help them to agree right along with what you are praying, and agreement is *mighty* powerful.

Try it this week—pray in the moment. Maybe silently, maybe out loud, but try jumping straight to prayer instead of putting it off for a "better time" later.

PRAYING FOR GUIDANCE

The LORD . . . guided them during the day
with a pillar of cloud, and he provided
light at night with a pillar of fire.
EXODUS 13:21 NLT

When you are praying for guidance, first you need to reduce any pressure. Pressure nearly always gets in the way of hearing from God. Drama never helps; stress never helps. Give it some breathing room. Take a deep breath yourself.

Second, be open to whatever it may be that God has to say to you. If you are, in truth, only open to hearing one answer from God, then it's not likely you will hear anything at all. More sadly, if you do hear a "yes," you won't trust it. Surrender is the key. Yield your desires and plans to the living God, so that you'll receive his counsel. Consecrate the matter and process of decision making!

Third, don't fill in the blanks! Do not spend half your energy trying to figure it out while you are giving the other half to seeking God. Far better to live with the uncertainty for a while than to be your own counselor.

Finally, give it some time. If you feel you are receiving counsel, guidance, and direction from the Holy Spirit, then ask for confirmation. Confirmation will give you a settled assurance that you are in fact following God's will.

These four points are really helpful when it comes to praying for guidance. Is there a step or two you might be leaving out as you seek God? Can you reduce the pressure? Be open to whatever he says to say? Have you given him some time to "speak"?

WHAT SHOULD I PRAY?

We don't know what God wants us to pray for.
But the Holy Spirit prays for us with groanings
that cannot be expressed in words.
ROMANS 8:26 NLT

The single most significant decision that has changed my prayer life more than any other, the one step that has brought about greater results than all others combined is this (drum roll, please) . . .

Asking Jesus what I should pray.

So simple, and so revolutionizing! Utterly obvious once you consider it, but something so rarely practiced. That is probably one of the side effects of the "prayer is just asking God to do something" view; no doubt it is also more of the negative consequences of the orphan and slave mentality. But if prayer is in fact a partnership, then you'll want to be in alignment with God!

If you pray in line with God's will, you can stand firmly on the promise *it will be done.* Amen will finally become AMEN! "But how do I know what the will of God is?" Now that is the sixty-thousand-dollar question. Let me assure you that you can; God does not torment you by hiding his will from you, though at times it does take a little effort to discern it. We see God's friends in the Old Testament pray with confidence because they clearly heard from God. I believe, dear friend, that confidence is also yours.

Try this—ask Jesus what you should be praying. Give him some time to make it clear. Because then you know you are praying in line with what he is praying!

SHOW ME WHAT TO PRAY

Godliness is profitable for all things, since it holds
promise for the present life and also for the life to come.
1 TIMOTHY 4:8 NASB

When someone asks, "Please pray for_____," I don't necessarily start praying for the specific request. Friend, God doesn't just put Band-Aids on things; and I don't know with any sort of certainty what God is doing in their life at that moment. Whatever the prayer request, I want to live and pray like God's intimate ally, so I turn my gaze toward God and ask, *What do you want me to pray for them? Show me what to pray.*

Those prayers are far more effective because they're aligned with *his will.* They're aligned with what he is doing in the situation at this particular moment. And it is a hard thing to do, because the needs that drive you to prayer so often pull on the heartstrings of your deep love and concern for others.

You're pressing into maturity both in your character and in your partnership with God. It's important to recognize when your sympathies get in the way! Now yes, yes—of course you pray moved by love and concern. But you're talking about the Prayer of Intervention, and the promise you are banking on is that if you're praying in alignment with what God is doing, you'll see results.

Is being in union with God in this way something you typically seek? Who are you praying for today? As you go to pray for them, pause and practice: *God, what do you want me to pray for _____? Show me what to pray.*

JESUS IS INTERCEDING FOR YOU

He always lives to make intercession for them.
HEBREWS 7:25 NASB

That Jesus is interceding for you should be a source of enormous comfort. (Did you know that Jesus prays for you?!) But to be honest, it is also a little sobering to know that you're living in a story where Jesus needs to pray for you! But wouldn't you love to know what Jesus is praying over your life right now? Imagine you could agree in prayer with the Son of God—that ought to add some serious firepower to your prayers!

You might think, *But I need prayer for guidance, or for a job, or a prodigal daughter.* Friend, I understand, but let me assure you—whatever your need, when you have the intimacy and the actual union of being with the Father that Jesus had, you are going to be in a wonderful place, and in a far better position to sort out everything!

And you get to pray and ask for it with perfect confidence and assurance, because you know this is the will of God for you! That is why I love praying the Scriptures. They are, of course, Spirit-breathed and thus so powerful; they also give me assurance that I am praying right in the center of God's will, which fills my prayers with confidence.

Jesus—I agree with everything you are praying for me right now. Jesus, I trust you. I trust your heart for me. I agree with you; I say yes to everything you are praying for me right now!

RESTORING YOUR SOUL

I will bless the LORD who guides me; even
at night my heart instructs me.

PSALM 16:7 NLT

At its very best, all prayer is deep communion, drawing you into intimacy and union with your God. When that intimacy and union reaches the damaged places within you, it's like the spring showers that come to Death Valley—wildflowers burst forth from barren ground; the land looks like Eden again. The inner healing that occurs in you is more beautiful than anything in nature that has taken your breath away. Your heart and soul are worth far more than all the beautiful places in the world. (You may not believe that about your wounded heart, but consider—Jesus didn't die for pine trees. He fully intends to restore this earth he made, but *you* are the prize he ransomed with his life.)

Prayer for inner healing is worth volumes in itself. Your need for it is too great, the fruits far too wonderful to pass it by. You can experience how accessible this form of prayer actually is.

Remember, you are more than a body—you have a heart, and a soul. And Jesus loves to partner with you in that most sacred place; he is most eager to come and make himself known there.

You restore my soul, God; I proclaim it to be true, whatever I may be feeling. You restore my soul. I pray to draw into a deeper communion with you in my prayer life. Holy Spirit—help me do so.

HOW DO YOU INTERPRET UNANSWERED PRAYERS?

How bold and free we then become in his
presence, freely asking according to his will.
1 JOHN 5:14 THE MESSAGE

Be very careful how you interpret "unanswered prayer." Your heart is so vulnerable in those moments. The conclusions come rushing in—*God isn't listening; he doesn't care; I'm not faithful enough; prayer doesn't really work.* Catch yourself! Don't let your heart go there! Ask Jesus to help you interpret what is going on.

The disappointment is real. I appreciate that the Scripture admits deferred hope makes the heart sick, because that sure is true in my experience; it assures me that God knows it does too. He said so. The disappointment of unanswered prayer can be devastating. So, you need to invite the love of God into the disappointment; you need his ministry there. You may need to shed some tears; you may need to grieve; you might need to take a baseball bat to a trash can. However you express your heartsickness, you must invite Jesus there—to comfort, heal, and restore.

Remember, dear friend, God loves you. He is not a betrayer, and he has never betrayed you.

What unanswered prayers have been particularly hard for you? Take those to God. *Jesus—I invite your love into the disappointment of these prayers that have gone unanswered. I ask you to minister to my heart there. Show me what you're up to. I trust you. I love you.*

IDENTITY OF YOUR HEART

Once you had no identity as a people;
now you are God's people.
1 PETER 2:10 NLT

You simply cannot neglect your heart and get away with it. The mind is a beautiful instrument, one you certainly want to develop all your life. God gave you the mind to protect the heart, not usurp it.

So let's think about identity and the heart for a moment. All of us, young or old, have within us a famished craving for *validation*. It will not be denied. You will chase validation wherever you can and you learn pretty quickly what your world rewards, what it shames, what it cares nothing about. The athletes will seek validation by being fast, strong, and winning, while the valedictorians throw themselves into papers, exams, and maintaining their GPAs. The "spiritual leaders" latch on to the praise coming from their giftings, and they give their hearts and souls over to that dance, while the "cool" kids go barefoot and wear dreadlocks. In one form or another, we are all looking for the same thing.

But often it's based on the false self—simply living for what others approve of while famished for validation. But the false self—even when built upon some part of your genuine gifting—will never ever settle the inside issue of needing validation. There is only One who can, and should, give it to you.

Are you aware of your deep desire for validation? Consider where you see yourself looking for it. *Jesus, reveal to me where I'm seeking the validation for the identity of my heart outside of you.*

AN IDENTITY YOU RECEIVED

It's in Christ that we find out who we are.
EPHESIANS 1:11 THE MESSAGE

Identity is *bestowed*, and it's drawn from your impact on others. You long to know that you make a difference in others' lives, to know you matter, and that your presence cannot be replaced by anything. The awful burden of the false self is that it must be constantly maintained.

You believe you have to keep doing something in order to be desirable. Once you find something that brings you attention, you have to keep it going, or risk the loss of attention.

And so you live with the burden of maintaining whatever gets you noticed, but you are never seen for who you really are. You develop a functional self-image, even if it's a negative one. The little boy paints his red wagon with whatever Father left in the can after painting the fence. "Look what I did!" he says, with hope for affirmation. Instead, the angry father shames him: "You've ruined it!" An identity is formed: *My impact is awful; I foul good things up. I am a fouler.* He forms a commitment to never be in a place where he'll foul things up again. Years later, he doesn't accept an attractive promotion because of this—the impact he had on the most important person in his world, and fear of ever being in such a place again.

Friend, Christ has bestowed on you an identity. The best thing you can do is ask him to reveal it to you.

Jesus—I do! I ask you to speak to me about who I am to you, what I mean to you. Speak to me about my identity.

THE FEAR OF MAN

*A considerable number from the ranks of the
leaders did believe. But because of the Pharisees,
they didn't come out in the open with it. They
were afraid of getting kicked out of the meeting
place. When push came to shove they cared more
for human approval than for God's glory.*

JOHN 12:42–43 THE MESSAGE

Motives matter—do you regularly consider yours? Why did Nicodemus visit Jesus *at night*? Fear of what his peers would do if they found out. Dear friend, this fear is a mighty powerful force. The fear of man. Peer pressure. *What will others think?* It can get deadly. And I'm convinced that until we have a healthy appreciation of how deep this actually runs in us, we are kidding ourselves about our motives.

I made a quick list of things "I would never be caught dead doing." It includes: getting a pedicure; having my personal journals read from the podium at the National Religious Broadcasters Convention; yodeling on *Oprah* in a tutu. The fear is way beyond reason; it is gut-level, primal. You have your list, and I have mine. This fear runs deep in the human race. It is ancient, Genesis 3:10 stuff—"I was afraid because I was naked; so I hid." The fear of exposure. It is far more powerful than you like to admit—the origin of every fig leaf and fashion trend. It's what gives power to culture. You long to be praised. You dread exposure. We all do.

Are you aware of your longing to be praised? Your fear of exposure? Are you aware of how they motivate you through your week?

LISTEN TO YOUR HEART

Listen to my cry for help, my King and my
God, for I pray to no one but you.
PSALM 5:2 NLT

Either you have a Father in God or you do not. If you do not, then humanity has no divine intention to it, no ultimate design. And if humanity has no design, you are on your own to create yourself. If you *do* have a Father in God, then you are a son or daughter, and your life has an elegant design to it.

This is the crux of the matter—did God weave divine intent into human nature? Or are we whatever we choose to be?

Jesus believed humanity has a design to it. He said we are made in the image of God—a truth that would do wonders for the cause of justice if the world embraced it. Human worth and dignity would be safeguarded in something far above human opinion. Jesus believed human nature was part of a beautifully, generously created order, filled with divine purpose.

God bless your heart, dear friend, for it refuses to be neglected. It may cry out in the form of anxiety and aimlessness; it will protest in the form of hopelessness, depression, anger, and despair. But it's because it is crying out for more of the life Jesus is offering. Listen to what it is saying.

What is your heart "saying" these days? Are you feeling a cry for comfort, or companionship? A need for meaning, or rest, or a new life? Listen to your heart, friend.

YOU NEED LIFE

You will show me the way of life, granting me the joy of your presence.

PSALM 16:11 NLT

Christianity is often presented as essentially the transfer of a body of knowledge. You learn about where the Philistines were from and how much a drachma would be worth today. The information presented could not seem more irrelevant to your deepest desires.

Then there are the systems aimed at getting your behavior in line. Wherever you go to church, there is nearly always an unspoken list of what you shouldn't do (tailored to your denomination and culture) and a list of what you may do (usually much shorter—mostly religious activity that seems totally unrelated to your deepest desires and leaves you only exhausted). And this, you're told, is *the good news*. Know the right thing; do the right thing. This is life?

You don't need more facts, and you certainly don't need more things to do. You need *Life*, and you've been looking for it ever since you lost Paradise. Jesus appeals to your desires because he came to speak to them. When you abandon desire, you no longer hear or understand what he's saying. But rather you've returned to the message of the synagogue where desire is the enemy. After all, desire is the single major hindrance to the goal—getting you in line. And so you are told to kill desire and call it sanctification.

But Christ came that we may have life—life in all its fullness.

Jesus—I present my life to you today to be filled with your life. You are the Vine; I am a branch. I need your life. I ask for your life.

NAME THE PROBLEM

If you need wisdom, ask our generous
God, and he will give it to you.
JAMES 1:5 NLT

D o you realize that your wounded heart is shaping your experience of Jesus? That's actually good news, dear friend—a fair share of your difficulty with Jesus is simply your brokenness getting in the way. The way to begin to get free of this debris, to remove these limits you've unknowingly placed on Jesus, is first to name what the problem is. Where are you having a hard time with Jesus? Where is your struggle with him?

Do you find it hard to believe he loves you? Do you feel like you are always disappointing him? Is he mad at you?

Invite Christ right into the whole ugly mess. The incarnation is proof enough that Jesus doesn't shy away from getting down in the muck of this world. There isn't *anything* you can show him he hasn't seen before. He's *not* going to be shocked. Or angry. Or disappointed. Jesus *loves* to come; just open the door to him here.

Tell Jesus what you think he thinks of you. Ask him if it's true. Ask him to free your heart from the wounds of your past so that you might know him and love him. This will actually turn out to be a rich part of your learning to love and experience Jesus, this shared journey into and *out of* your brokenness. You'll love him more for it too.

What do you think Jesus thinks about you? Is this how others feel about you? How you feel about yourself? Ask the Spirit of truth to show you how this is connected to your brokenness.

WIELDING HIS
SWORD FOR YOU

Don't fear. Don't hesitate. Don't panic. GOD, your
God, is right there with you, fighting with you.
DEUTERONOMY 20:4 THE MESSAGE

Jesus of Nazareth is frequently misinterpreted as the poster child for tranquility, when in fact his actual teachings are warnings for navigating life, the first one being that evil wants to destroy you. Live like it.

Most folks unfamiliar with Jesus' actual teaching and actions will be surprised by this. I've never heard a Sunday school teaching on Luke 22:36: "If you don't have a sword, sell your cloak and buy one." Jesus knows what you're up against.

Most of us go on to live our actual days with a staggering naïveté that the Son of God himself warned against. You have been dropped into the middle of a terrible battle. Planet-wide. All those Hollywood depictions of the great battle of good and evil pale in comparison to the real thing. You are a warrior in partnership with God. That's why you're here.

There's a sober willingness to accept the reality of the world as it is. But friend, there is a choice to be made about who you want to be, and that person might just change the world.

Where is the battle impacting your life these days? Have you taken up the sword? *Jesus—I take my stand in your victory against my enemies. I bring the truth of God's Word against my foes. You are faithful. You have conquered Satan. He must flee. In Jesus' name.*

MAKE SENSE OF YOUR STORY

By faith we understand that the entire
universe was formed at God's command.
HEBREWS 11:3 NLT

Is there a reality that corresponds to the deepest desires of our heart? Who gets the last word—life or death? You need to know, so you are constantly trying to make sense out of your experiences. You look for coherence, an assurance that things fit together. The problem is that most of us live our lives like a movie we've arrived at twenty minutes late. The action is well under way and we haven't a clue what's happening. *Who are these people? Who are the good guys and who are the bad guys? What's going on?* You sense that something glorious is taking place, and yet it all seems so *random.*

No wonder it's so hard to live from your heart! You find yourself in the middle of a story that is sometimes wonderful, sometimes awful, and you haven't the slightest clue how to make sense of it all. Worse, you try to interpret the meaning of life with isolated incidents, feelings, and images without reference to the story of which these scenes are merely a part. It can't be done, so you look for someone to interpret life for you. Your interpreters were probably the primary people in your life when you were young— your parents, grandparents, or another key figure. They shaped your understanding of the story in which you find yourself, and directed the commitments you made to protect your heart.

This is worth a little reflection. Who were your primary "interpreters"? What was the "story" that they gave you? Is it about survival? Getting a happy little life? Pleasing others?

INVITED TO INTIMACY

*"The sheep hear his voice, and he calls his own
sheep by name and leads them out. When he puts
forth all his own, he goes ahead of them, and the
sheep follow him because they know his voice."*

JOHN 10:3–4 NASB

You're invited into an intimacy with God, who will lead you to the life you are meant to live—he promises to guide you in the details of your life.

What would it be like to yield to Christ in the details of your life? What would it be like to follow his counsel and instruction in all the small decisions that add up to the life you find yourself living? It would be . . . amazing.

You'd find yourself saying, as David did, "You have made known to me the path of life" (Psalm 16:11). This is the privilege and the joy of sheep that belong to a good shepherd. He leads them well. He leads them to life. So, ask Jesus, *What is the life you want me to live?* It is a good question—maybe one of the most important questions we could ever bring to God. He created you, after all. He knows why. He knows what is best for you. If you could learn from him the life he wants you to live—the details, the pace of life, the places you are to invest yourself and the places you are not to—you would be in his will. And there you would find life.

Lord, I don't come to you often enough with my questions. But I long to hear your voice. Open my ears that I might hear you speaking. Holy Spirit, help me hear. What is it you want for my life, God?

UTTERLY HIMSELF

God said to Moses, "I-AM-WHO-I-AM."
EXODUS 3:14 THE MESSAGE

Nobody likes being lied to. Notice your outrage when some trusted leader is exposed as a fake. Think of how strong your reaction is when a close friend lies to you. Some relationships never recover. Now—it is one thing to tell a lie; it is something else entirely to *be* a lie. The man who has two families, carries on two separate lives—he's not just lying about what he does, he's lying about what he *is*.

The most essential gift you have to give is yourself. When you aren't entirely true about that, you aren't true. But we've all grown accustomed to committing dozens of little white lies about ourselves every day.

Except Jesus. You can trust him.

Having given this some thought, perhaps you are better prepared now to understand why God answered Moses the way he did when he spoke from the burning bush. In the midst of the very unnerving encounter, Moses asks him, "Who *are* you?" God simply says, "I Am." In other words, Me. Myself. An answer that is holy and full of integrity, wry and dumbfounding all at the same time. But it is the best possible answer he could have given. God is utterly himself. And he wants you to be utterly yourself, with him.

We often put God in a box. Sometimes we put him in a "justice" box. Or a "Ruler of the universe but not very close to me" box. Often it is the "I have two minutes for you today, God" box. What do you need to do to let God out of the box you've put him in?

YOUR DEEP GLADNESS

*We plan the way we want to live, but
only GOD makes us able to live it.*
PROVERBS 16:9 THE MESSAGE

What is your "deep gladness," the deep passion of your soul? And what are you supposed to do in order to move toward it?

Your dreams will grow and develop over time. More importantly, *you* will grow and develop over time. So let yourself try things. You don't have to nail down the course of your life. You get to do something far more exciting: you get to walk with God. Explore things. Grow as a person.

I'm going to let you in on a little secret: God never gives you the Master Plan for your life. The simple reason is that you'd go run with it. You'd take off with the plan in your hands and leave God behind. So he allows for mystery and setback and obstacles *so that you will seek him.*

He has a place for you. He knows what the next step is toward that place. Give some time to asking him what it is. Not an hour, not a day, but give several weeks or even months. Walk with him. The experience alone will be worth the outcome. So often you'll feel that it is clarity that you need, when in fact your deepest ache is for intimacy with God.

God never gives us the Master Plan—did you know that? Have you been frustrated with that? Tell God how you feel about the way he is working in your life. Be brave—he can handle it.

WHAT IS TRUE ABOUT YOU

Do for GOD what you said you'd do—
he is, after all, your God.
PSALM 76:11 THE MESSAGE

Your fierceness and your warrior heart are just what this world needs right now. I believe you'll continue to see very trying times. The timing of *The Lord of the Rings*, the resurgence of superheroes in film, and all the games and movies like these is curious indeed. Their epic, urgent, heroic battle cry was spoken at *this* moment in history—the moment God called you into. Perhaps it was orchestrated by an unseen hand.

And dear friend, you have the strength and the courage to handle what is before you. You do. But you must not try to play Switzerland in this war; there is no neutral ground. The only safe move is to boldly take sides with the kingdom of God, take your position in the line. Make the decision to be fully in—to become the warrior, live in the Larger Story—and everything else will fall into place. Really.

As I think back on my years as a young man, the words I longed to hear were the very words I still eagerly listen for today: *You're going to be okay. You're going to find your way. You are not alone.*

Friend, this is so encouraging, and it is true about you. These words are your birthright as the son or daughter of the Living One. You are going to be okay. You will find your way. You are not alone.

Just let that be true for one moment: You are going to be okay. Your life is going to work out. You are not on your own. Just let that be true and notice what it does for your soul.

CONVERSATION WITH GOD

Let him tell you what to do; take his words to heart.
Come back to God Almighty and he'll rebuild your life.
JOB 22:22–23 THE MESSAGE

It's a strange feeling to be confronted with undeniable evidence that you're not where you thought you were, and you don't know what to do with your story to make it a good story. So let's stop and get our bearings and talk about what you do from here.

First, let's get rid of the guilt; it only adds to the sinking feeling that you'll never find your way when you feel you've screwed up by losing your way. Let me lift that guilt, if I can, by reiterating one of those truths you won't find in any of those "Find the life you want!" books: *Nobody gets the plan.* I know you think they do, surely somebody does, but it just isn't true. You really have to come to terms with this so you can take hold of what is given: you get a conversation.

Your Father is far, far more committed to that conversation than he is to giving you the plan for your life. And that is the kindest thing in the world.

Do you feel shame because you have made a bad turn with your life, or with a relationship, maybe with work? Invite your loving Father into how you feel about your life these days.

ISSUES OF THE HEART

The God who made the world and everything in it, this Master of sky and land. . . . He makes the creatures; the creatures don't make him.

ACTS 17:24–25 THE MESSAGE

What do you love more than God? What do you look to for security more than you look to God? Where do you draw your sense of identity from, more than you draw it from God? These are the things you must lay on the altar. Here is where your most earnest repentance lies. These things may not in and of themselves be bad, but if you make children more to you than God is, you have made an idol of them, and here you must repent. So if you back into this through the doorway of idolatry, it will free your heart up to love God. Whatever you look to for security or comfort or assurance or validation, whatever you look to to make yourself feel better or to bring you pleasure over and above or quite apart from God, is idolatry.

So, if idolatry is the big issue because loving God is the first commandment, it follows that your repentance ought to be focused mostly on the idols in your life. Idols always take you back to issues of your heart. *That's* where the action is; that's where real transformation takes place.

This is a tough subject—our idols. But we all have them. And God has already forgiven us through Christ. So we can be honest. Ask the Holy Spirit to reveal the idols in your life. As he does, lay them on the altar; give them over to God.

YOUR INHERITANCE

*"A nobleman was called away to a distant empire
to be crowned king and then return. Before
he left, he called together ten of his servants
and divided among them ten pounds of silver,
saying, 'Invest this for me while I am gone.'"*
LUKE 19:12–13 NLT

This allegory is hardly veiled. Clearly, Jesus is the man of noble birth who left to have himself appointed king and will return. Upon his return, he rewards his faithful servants. He repeats the promise but ups the ante in the tale of the sheep and goats: "Come, you who are blessed by my Father, inherit the Kingdom prepared for you from the creation of the world" (Matthew 25:34 NLT). We've gone from silver to houses to cities to kingdoms. We are given *kingdoms.* Which helps make sense of why we are said to reign with him. Can you see the theme here? The victorious king gladly rewards his faithful companions.

It's a mind-set almost entirely lost to our age. Honestly, I have never had one private conversation with any follower of Christ who spoke of their hope of being handsomely rewarded. This isn't virtue, friend. Rather it's a sign of your heart's bankruptcy. But dear friend, your inheritance is one of lavish abundance.

What is evoked in you as you think about reward in heaven? Does it feel almost uncomfortable to consider for too long? Ask God to help you consider "reward" in a new light.

FREE FROM THE FEAR OF MAN

The fear of human opinion disables; trusting
in GOD protects you from that.

PROVERBS 29:25 THE MESSAGE

How much of what we do is motivated by fear of man? Think of it—to be entirely free of false guilt, free from pressure, free from false allegiances. It would be absolutely extraordinary.

This is what gives Jesus the ability to say such startlingly honest things to people. It is what enables him to be so scandalous.

This is the secret of his ability to navigate praise and contempt.

Neither success nor opposition has power over him. One day the crowds love him, the next they are shouting for his crucifixion. Jesus is the same man—the same *personality*—through the whole swirling tempest. Jesus is free from the fear of man. It is something more than integrity, though it certainly encompasses that. He is true to himself, true to his Father, true to what the moment most requires, true to love. In this forest of fig leaves, where you are never sure you are getting the true person, there is nothing false about Jesus.

This man. He is Faithful and he is True.

Jesus—I long to have your trueness fill my being. Fill me with your solid, unshakable life.

SHAPING YOUR CHARACTER

*GOD, you are our Father. We're the clay and you're
our potter: All of us are what you made us.*
ISAIAH 64:8 THE MESSAGE

How does God shape our character? We hate the answer but we know it to be true: affliction.

If you say that God does not intend to use affliction, then what in your mind does he then use? Joy does wonderful things for your soul—it soothes, and strengthens, and heals. But joy does not transform people's characters in the same way affliction does. You do not grow when life is good. Any parent knows this. The child wants ice cream and video games. But the child will grow to be a narcissist if they are allowed nothing but ice cream and video games. The most radiant holiness, the most genuine and glorious love is expressed by those whose lives have known affliction. Jesus best among them.

Our longing for life keeps confusing us about the purpose of life. You ache for life to come together as it was meant to be. And it will, friend; it will. Very soon. But in the meantime, the purpose of life in this hour is not escaping to Hawaii, or whatever your version of happiness may be. Your "education" in this hour, the goal of maturing is holiness, the beauty of Jesus Christ formed in you.

Time for a little more honesty. The purpose of your life is not "happy little life." How does that make you feel? How much of your time and energy are committed to your version of "happiness"?

AUGUST

WAITING

I've kept my feet on the ground, I've cultivated
a quiet heart. Like a baby content in its
mother's arms, my soul is a baby content.
PSALM 131:2 THE MESSAGE

To wait is to learn the spiritual grace of *detachment*, the freedom of desire. Not the absence of desire, but desire at rest. King David describes such a beautiful picture, a young one at peace and safe with its mother. There is no fussing, no insistent tears.

The word *detachment* might evoke wrong impressions. It is not a cold and indifferent attitude; not at all. It doesn't devalue desire, it simply frees your desire to what God promises.

As Thomas à Kempis declared, "Wait a little while, O my soul, wait for the divine promise, and thou shalt have abundance of all good things in heaven." In this posture you discover that, indeed, you are expanded by longing. Something grows in you, a capacity if you will, for life and love and to be Fathered by your God. I think of Romans 8:24–25: "That is why waiting does not diminish us, any more than waiting diminishes a pregnant mother. We are enlarged in the waiting. We, of course, don't see what is enlarging us. But the longer we wait, the larger we become, and the more joyful our expectancy" (THE MESSAGE). There is actually a sweet pain in longing, if we will let it draw our hearts homeward.

Yes, God—I feel the longing. I feel it growing. I choose to let my longing and my disappointments draw my heart toward heaven.

HOLDING THE TRUTH

*They found lush pastures there, and the
land was spacious, quiet, and peaceful.*
1 CHRONICLES 4:40 NLT

The Story is continually being stolen from you by the evil
one—the ultimate deconstructionist. He twists and spins and
pulls apart the truth until the fragments you have left are unrecognizable. Or you lose it yourself in the bombardment of thousands
of messages each day, every one of them marked urgent, leaving
behind the truly important things, the only refuge for your heart.

Friend, you must be intentional about holding on to the truth.
The spiritual pilgrims who aligned themselves with Saint Benedict
took this task seriously with round-the-clock practice of numerous
lessons, verses, prayers, and hymns.

Now, I'm not suggesting that you adopt the Rule of Benedict.
But these men left the distractions of the world to focus entirely on
God. What did they discover? They needed reminders every hour
of the day and night! Do you, who live in the hostile chaos of the
world, think you can do with an occasional visit? You're kidding
yourself if you think you can keep heart without a constant turning to the truth. I suggest you start by reducing constant noise in
your life. If everything is urgent, then nothing is. Unplug from the
clamor, and make room for eternity in your life.

Try this—try a one-minute pause somewhere in your day, every
day this week. No technology, no sound. Just stillness.

WHAT DOES YOUR HEART NEED?

"I will refresh the weary and satisfy the faint."
JEREMIAH 31:25

How would you live differently if you believed your heart was the treasure of the kingdom?

What does your heart need? In some sense it's a personal question, unique to your makeup, and what brings you life. For some it's music, for others it's reading, for others they must garden.

You know what makes your heart refreshed, the things that make you come alive.

Yet there are some things all hearts need in common. We need beauty; that's clear enough from the fact that God has filled the world with it, as he has given us sun and rain, "wine that makes glad the heart of man, oil to make his face shine, and bread which strengthens man's heart" (Psalm 104:15 NKJV).

You need to drink in beauty wherever you can get it—in music, in nature, in art, in a great meal shared. These are all gifts to you from God's generous heart. Friend, those things are not decorations to a life; they are what brings you life. You need silence and solitude. Often.

So let me ask you again: What does *your* heart need? A simple starting place would be to ask God: *What do you have for my heart?* You'll be stunned by what he guides you into.

Try it—ask God, *What do you have for my heart? What beauty or stillness do I need right now? Where can I find it, Lord?*

YOU ARE HIS FRIEND

What is man that You take thought of him?
PSALM 8:4 NASB

In some deep place within, you remember what you were made to be, you carry with you the memory of walking in the Garden. So why do you flee your essence? As hard as it may be to see your sin, it's far harder still to remember your glory.

You are the one that is fought over, rescued, and pursued. There is something desirable within you, something the King of the universe has moved heaven and earth to get.

The Scriptures employ a wide scale of metaphors capturing our relationship with God, and in a breathtaking progression. Down near the bottom of the totem pole you are the clay and he the Potter. Moving up a notch, you are the sheep and he the Shepherd, which is a little better position on the food chain but hardly flattering; sheep don't have a reputation as the most intelligent creatures. Moving upward, you are a servant of the Master, which lets you into his house. Most Christians never get past this point, but you make a swift ascent. God calls you his son or daughter and himself our heavenly Father, which brings you into real intimacy with him. Still, there is something missing in even the best parent-child relationship. Friendship levels the playing field in a way family never can. Friendship opens a level of communion. And "friend" is what he calls you.

Jesus—help me know today who I am, really. Will you tell me what your heart is toward me? Will you surprise me by showing me something that takes my breath away?

LOVE FREELY CHOSEN

*"A man leaves his father and mother and is joined
to his wife, and the two are united into one."
This is a great mystery, but it is an illustration
of the way Christ and the church are one.*

EPHESIANS 5:31–32 NLT

All the breathtaking things in life are a profound mystery. The cross is a great mystery, but we are helped in understanding it by looking back into the Old Testament and finding there the pattern of the sacrificial lamb. Those early believers did not understand the full meaning of what they were doing, but once Christ came, the whole period of ritual sacrifice was seen in a new light, and in turn gave a richer depth to understanding the cross.

We must do the same by looking back and seeing the Bible for what it is—the greatest romance ever written. God creates mankind for intimacy with himself, as his Beloved. You will see it right at the start, when he gives you the highest freedom of all—the freedom to reject him. The reason is obvious: love is possible only when it is freely chosen.

If you're writing a romance, love is the goal; you must allow for the possibility of betrayal. That is precisely what God calls our turning away from him.

But True Love never fails; it always perseveres. God will fight for his Beloved.

Say this to yourself: *I live in a Love Story. I am deeply and profoundly loved.* Linger as you repeat it a couple times. Notice how your heart responds.

YOU CAN HAVE LIFE AND JOY

*"Now is your time of grief, but I will see you again and
you will rejoice, and no one will take away your joy."*
JOHN 16:22

You are familiar with the dilemma of desire—how awful it feels to open your heart to joy, only to have grief come in. They go together, but how do you live in a world with desire so deep in you, and disappointment lurking behind every corner?

Dare you even desire? Do you avoid friendships because they might be taken from you? Refuse to love because you may be hurt? Forsake your dreams because hope has been deferred? To desire is to open your heart to the possibility of pain; to shut down your heart is to die altogether. "Hope deferred makes the heart sick, but a dream fulfilled is a *tree of life*" (Proverbs 13:12 NLT, emphasis added). Your road to life and joy lies through, not around, the heartsickness of hope deferred. A good friend put words to this dilemma: "For decades I've tried to control my life by killing desire, but I can't anymore. However, to allow it is frightening—I have to give up control of my life. Is there another option?"

Oh friend, to kill desire is to kill your heart. And a deadened heart is not what you were created for. God wants to be the Shepherd of your soul, to lead you into the life and joy that you are meant for.

How are you handling your heart's desires these days, dear one?

TRAINING BY ENGAGING

*Prove yourselves doers of the word, and not
merely hearers who delude themselves.*

JAMES 1:22 NASB

You *will* be tested. Like Jesus' desert trial, the enemy comes probing at your weak spots. But this trains you. It's how you develop a resolute heart. You make no agreements with whatever the temptation or accusation is. You repent quickly the moment you do stumble so you don't get hammered. You pray for strength from the Spirit of God in you. You *directly* resist the enemy, out loud, as Jesus did in the desert. You quote Scripture against him and command him to flee.

By the time it's over, you'll wish a few angels would drop in and minister to you as well. I pray they do.

Life will provide a thousand sessions for raising the warrior God calls you to be. Turn your radar on during the day, and intentionally don't take the path of least resistance. Take the road less traveled. If you hate any sort of conflict, then walk into some. When an awkward subject comes up, don't run. Move toward it. Ask hard questions. When the phone rings and it's someone you don't want to talk to, pick it up. Engage. That's the key word— *engage.* Choose to engage and your weary warrior wakes up.

Where in your life do you need to engage right now? In a tough relationship? A moral issue at work? Your children? Tending to your own soul?

YOUR TRUEST SELF

*He climbed a mountain and invited those he
wanted with him [including] . . . John, brother of
James (Jesus nicknamed the Zebedee brothers
Boanerges, meaning "Sons of Thunder").*
MARK 3:13, 17 THE MESSAGE

You're going to need your whole heart in all its glory for this Story you've fallen into. So, who did God mean when he meant you? You at least know that you are not what you were meant to be. Much energy is spent trying to hide that fact, through all the veils you put on and the false selves you create. Far better to spend your energy trying to *recover* the image of God and unveil it for his glory. One means that will help you is any mythic story that awakens the eyes of your heart. It's worth fighting for.

The Bible is filled with characters; the disciples of Jesus were all characters. Take James and John, for instance, "the sons of Zebedee." You might remember them as the ones who cornered Jesus to angle for the choice seats at his right and left hands in the kingdom. Or the time they wanted to call down fire from heaven to destroy a village that wouldn't offer Jesus a place for the night. Their buddies called them idiots; Jesus called them the Sons of Thunder. He saw who they *really* were. It's their mythic name, their true identity. They looked like fishermen out of work; they were actually the Sons of Thunder.

You too have a "true identity." One way to find it is to think of the movies you love, the characters you wish you could be. Who are they? Why do you love those characters?

THE GLORY YOU WERE MEANT FOR

Those he justified, he also glorified.
ROMANS 8:30

When you find yourself taking a second glance in the mirror, when you pause to look again at a photograph, your heart is looking for the glory you were meant to have, if only because you know you long to have it. You remember faintly that you were once more than what you have become.

Your story didn't start with sin, and thank God, it does not end with sin. It ends with glory restored. And in the meantime, you have *been* transformed, and you are *being* transformed. You've been given a new heart. Now God is restoring your glory. He is bringing you fully alive. Because the glory of God is you fully alive.

"Well, if this is all true, why don't I see it?" Precisely. The fact that you do not see your good heart and your glory is only proof of how effective the assault has been on you. You don't see yourself clearly. You're under a spell, alert and oriented times zero, with no idea who you really are. Whatever glory was bestowed, whatever glory is being restored, you thought this whole Christian thing was about trying not to sin, going to church, being nice. Jesus says it is about healing your heart, setting it free, and restoring your glory.

Spend a few minutes in front of a mirror. What arises in your heart? What do you say to yourself? Most of the time, it isn't very kind. It might be good to renounce those things, so your heart can come out from under your own self-contempt. Try it.

YOU HAVE A NEW HEART

"I will give you a new heart, and I will put a new
spirit in you. I will take out your stony, stubborn
heart and give you a tender, responsive heart. And
I will put my Spirit in you so that you will follow my
decrees and be careful to obey my regulations."

EZEKIEL 36:26–27 NLT

No one but God sees who you truly are. This is usually received with *Yes, God sees me, and what he sees is my sin.* Dear friend, this is wrong. Do you believe your sin has been dealt with? It's true. Your Father has removed it from you "as far as the east is from the west" (Psalm 103:12). Your sins have been washed away (1 Corinthians 6:11). When God looks at you he does *not* see your sin. But there's more. You have a new heart, the promise of the new covenant—and what good news!

Too many of us are living in the old covenant, having it drilled into us that our *hearts are deceitfully wicked.* Not anymore. God announces your hope: "I will put my instructions deep within them, and I will write them on their hearts. I will be their God, and they will be my people" (Jeremiah 31:33 NLT).

Friend, sin is not the deepest thing about you. You have a new heart. *Your heart is good.* What God sees when he sees you is the *real* you, the true you, the one he had in mind when he made you.

Do you believe that your heart is good? That it has been made good by the new covenant, and the work of Christ for you?

GOD AS MASTERMIND

In the beginning God created the heavens and the earth.
GENESIS 1:1 NLT

Does God have a good heart? When we think of God as Author, the Mind Behind It All, we tend to doubt his heart. When you're reading a novel or watching a film, caught up in the action, do you even think about the author? You identify with the characters because they are *in* the story. Their struggles win your sympathy because they're your struggles also. You love the hero because he is one of us, somehow rising above the fray to be better and wiser and more loving as you hope one day you might prove to be.

The Author, however, lies beyond. His omniscience and omnipotence may be what creates the drama, but they are also what separates us from him. Power and knowledge don't qualify for heart. Indeed, the worst sort of villain is one who executes plans with cold and calculated precision. He is detached; he has no heart. If we picture God as the Mastermind behind the Story—calling the shots while we, like Job, endure the calamities—we can't help but feel at times God's an experimenter, even though he may have our good in mind.

But what if we saw God not as Author, the cosmic Mastermind behind all human experience, but as the central character *in* the Larger Story? What then could we learn about his heart?

What do you really believe about the heart of God?

A DEEPER WELL

*I saw heaven opened, and a white horse was standing
there. Its rider was named Faithful and True.*
REVELATION 19:11 NLT

Every era has its problems when it comes to knowing Jesus. One of ours is this: having lost all confidence in the noble, the heroic, even the consistently good, we have come to celebrate the neurotic. Really. The heroes of our novels and movies are anti-heroes, broken characters riddled with addiction and self-doubt. People of strong conviction and bold claims are suspect. We fear them. They might be a terrorist, or a Christian. Skepticism has become a virtue.

This has quietly shaped a popular version of Jesus as a man not so much heroic as humanitarian, not a warrior operating behind enemy lines but just a humble man trying to do good in a hurting world. Now yes, yes—Jesus had his dark night of the soul. He didn't stay there. It was an abyss through which he passed. Through which he was *able* to pass, because of something much deeper within him.

When Jesus returns mounted on a white horse, army by his side, to end this horrific age and usher in the next, he is called by a name we haven't heard in the Gospels. That name is *Faithful and True.* By that point in the story, it's what he deserves to be called, and it's what the world needs to be assured of too.

Are your heroes heroic, or are they more broken characters struggling to find their way? Has that shaped your personal view of Jesus?

RE-CREATED YOU

I heard a company of Angels around the Throne,
the Animals, and the Elders . . . in full song.
REVELATION 5:11–12 THE MESSAGE

The promised kingdom will be a glorious place whose presence allows us to think about the renewal of the arts and sciences, education, and the trades. The promise is that God will make not "some things new" but *all things new.*

Let's start with the obvious. You know there's music in the kingdom. Imagine what the music will be! We get to hear the work of the great composers, played by their own hands. You'll hear the angels sing in their own tongues. But who else makes that music? The instruments?

You do, my friend. At least those who want to will. I'd love to learn to play the cello. I wonder what instrument Jesus plays. I wonder what our Father's voice sounds like, how far it carries. (You will hear your Father sing!) Oh my, what joy!

And what of the trades? I've always wanted to work with my hands. I would love to have the time and skill and mentors to build boats with hand tools and sail them, learning to navigate by the stars. What have you always wanted to be good at? I am not being fanciful; you will be restored with all the faculties of personhood given to you by God, and your talents will be even more glorious in the re-created you. Dream, my friend.

Think about what you have always dreamed of doing. What gifts have you yearned to express? Ask God to show you what's possible.

YOU MUST BE BEAUTIFUL

*Jesus said to them, "Why are you bothering this
woman? She has done a beautiful thing to me."*
MATTHEW 26:10

"Beautiful" is not an expression often used by men, but it ought to be. Older philosophers and saints evaluated the universe using three categories: the good, the true, and the beautiful. Recall the story of Jesus being lavished with expensive perfume. The disciples were appalled at the waste. But Jesus describes the act as "beautiful." Though the Master named it as one of the best things ever done to him—thus exalting the beautiful forever—it seems Christians have lost the longing for the quality Christ saw here.

As truth all but vanishes from cultural value, some corners fight for what is true; others want to be more relevant and commit themselves to "doing good." Both are important, but both can fall short of a better way.

I know many whose lives are far from perfect. In no way could they be called efficient or "maximizers." Yet there's something in the way they love, in what they love. Something in the manner in which they tell a story. They love the true, and the good, but they love the beautiful even more, and in doing so, their lives have become beautiful. Friend, you must not only be true, you must be beautiful.

I don't mean physical beauty, though that is a gift from God. I mean the beauty of goodness, trueness, loving-kindness. Have you thought about your life as beautiful?

WHAT DO YOU THINK OF ME, GOD?

It has come at last—salvation and power and the Kingdom of our God. . . . For the accuser of our brothers and sisters has been thrown down to earth.

REVELATION 12:10 NLT

You must ask God what he thinks of you, and you must stay with the question until you have an answer. The battle will get fierce. And what God thinks of you is the *last* thing the evil one wants you to know. He will play the ventriloquist, whispering to you as if he were the voice of God.

Once, coming home from a brutal trip, I was under intense spiritual attack. Tired to the bone, I needed to hear words from my Father. So I began to pour my heart out to him in my journal.

What of me, dear Lord? Are you pleased? I wish I knew without asking. Fear, I suppose, makes me doubt. Still, I yearn to hear from you—a word, a name. . . .

This is what I heard: *You are the man in the arena, face covered with blood and dust, who strove valiantly . . . a great warrior.* And then: *You are my friend.* God knew I needed those specific words. I'm a little embarrassed telling you, it feels arrogant. But I share this in hopes that they will help you find your own. They are words of life, words that heal my wound and shatter the enemy's accusations. May it do the same for you.

What would you really love for God to say to you? Will you take a risk and ask him? It may feel foolish, but ask. And believe it.

HE KNOWS YOUR NAME

*There is now no condemnation for
those who are in Christ Jesus.*
ROMANS 8:1

Oh, what wonderful and redemptive stories I could share of how God has spoken when asked: *What do you think of me?* Friend, it is available to you too. He wants to tell you what is true about you. He wants you to know.

It's a battle to get to this place, but stick with it. And be on guard, because once you hear words from God, the enemy rushes in to steal them. Remember how he assaulted Christ in the wilderness, right on the heels of hearing words from his Father. A friend and I were talking about these stories and many more like them. He sort of sighed and said, "I remember a time in church when I heard God say to me, 'I am proud of you, right where you are.' But I could not believe it. It just doesn't seem true."

That's why we always rest on propositional truth. Dear friend, stand on what Scripture says about you. You are forgiven. Your heart is good. The Father's voice is *never* condemning. (If you hear words of contempt, that is the voice of your enemy, not God.) From that place, ask God to speak *personally* to you, to break the power of the lie that was delivered with our wound. Trust that he will.

He knows your name.

Take time today to journal with these questions: What do you believe God intended for you when he created you? What does he name you? How do you think he's begun to restore your true identity there?

GETTING TO KNOW HIM

*We take our lead from Christ, who is the source
of everything we do. He keeps us in step with each
other. His very breath and blood flow through us.*

EPHESIANS 4:15–16 THE MESSAGE

We have dissected God, and the gospel, and have thousands, if not millions, of facts. It's not that these insights aren't true; it's that they no longer speak to the soul. I could tell you a few facts about God, for example. He is omniscient, omnipotent, and immutable. There—don't you feel closer to him? These statements about God forget that he is a person.

How do we get to know a person? Through stories. All the wild and sad and courageous tales that we tell—they are what reveal us to others. We must return to the Scripture for the Story that it is and stop approaching it as if it is an encyclopedia, looking for "tips and techniques."

Reminders of the Story are everywhere, in the natural world around you, and in the stories of your own life. In fact, every story or movie or song or poem that has ever stirred your soul is telling you something you need to know about the Sacred Romance. Even nature is crying out to you of God's great heart. Sunrise and sunset tell the tale every day, remembering Eden's glory, prophesying Eden's return. You must capture them like precious treasure and hold them close to your heart.

Come back again to the movies you love—the reason you love them is that they are telling you something about the True Story, God's Story. Can you see what it is?

ALL THAT EFFORT FOR ONE

*When Jesus woke up, he rebuked the wind and said
to the waves, "Silence! Be still!" Suddenly the wind
stopped, and there was a great calm. Then he asked
them, "Why are you afraid? Do you still have no faith?"*

MARK 4:39–40 NLT

You are probably familiar with the story of Jesus subduing the storm. Then immediately after in Mark 5, Jesus has an encounter with Legion. In all three Synoptic Gospels, these two stories are linked—they tell of a frightening storm, and then a frightening demoniac. In all three accounts, Jesus—who was sleeping in the stern of the sinking boat—rises to confront the tempest like a drill sergeant: "Quiet! Be still!"

Now, why does he need to rebuke the storm? The word—*epitimao*—is the same used when Jesus commands foul spirits to come out of people. Fascinating—the storm needed to be rebuked.

The very next episode in all three synoptics finds Christ stepping on shore to confront Legion. He frees the man, the locals rage against Jesus, and he gets right back in the boat and returns to the other side. Did he go to all that effort for one man? It ended up that way. And Jesus did say something about leaving the ninety-nine to find the one. It certainly is an awe-inspiring doubleheader, and fearsome too. That is, Jesus is fearsome. Everything else trembles before him. And friend, he is fearsome for you.

O Jesus—I long to believe this is true. I long to know in my heart that you are fighting for me right now. Would you reveal this to me?

FATHERLESS

*"I want you all for myself. I'll be a Father to
you; you'll be sons and daughters to me."*
2 CORINTHIANS 6:17–18 THE MESSAGE

Y ou are the sons and daughters of a kind, strong, and engaged
Father, a Father wise enough to guide you along the way,
generous enough to provide for your journey, offering to walk with
you every step. This may perhaps be the hardest thing for you to
believe down deep in your heart, so that it changes you forever.

Your core assumptions about the world boil down to this: you
are on your own to make life work. You are not watched over, not
cared for. When you're hit with a problem, you have to figure it
out yourself, or just take the hit. If anything good is going to come
your way, you're going to have to arrange for it. You may have
called upon God as Father, but frankly, he doesn't seem to have
heard. You're not sure why. Whatever the reason, your experience
of this world has framed your approach to life. You believe you're
fatherless.

Whatever life has taught you, even if it's not those exact words,
you feel that you are alone. You believe deep down inside that
there is no one you can trust to come through for you. And then
you arrange for little pleasures along the way to help ease the pain
of the loneliness, usually through indulging. Dear friend, it's a
fatherless way to live.

Simply notice how your heart responds when trouble hits—bad
news, a disappointment, or worse. Do you feel fathered . . . or
fatherless?

YOUR DEEP LONGING

*"Oh! Ephraim is my dear, dear son, my child in whom
I take pleasure! Every time I mention his name, my
heart bursts with longing for him! Everything in me
cries out for him. Softly and tenderly I wait for him."*

JEREMIAH 31:20 THE MESSAGE

Put your own name in this verse, in the place of "Ephraim" (a name for God's people, and that includes you). Imagine that God's heart bursts with longing for you. Dear friend, this *is* the message of Jesus: there is a good and loving Father who cares so deeply and passionately for you.

He yearns to be your Father now. He will draw near, if you'll let him. No matter how old you are, your true Father wants you to experience being his beloved son or daughter. But it requires opening your heart, which will take you back into some of your deepest wounds, and the cynicism and resignation that shut your heart down a long time ago. God does this so that he might bring his love and healing to the fatherless child within you, the child that still needs to know you are his Beloved.

Your Father God will do many things to try to get you back to this longing in your heart for a father, the longing to be prized, to be the Beloved. Pay attention; he is waiting to father you, if you'll let him.

Did you have a father with whom you felt safe, whom you felt prized by? Did you get to live childhood as it was meant to be? You might want to write out your answers to those questions. It would be healing to tell your story, at least to yourself, and to God.

TURN FOR HOME

Because we are his children, God has
sent the Spirit of his Son into our hearts,
prompting us to call out, "Abba, Father."
GALATIANS 4:6–7 NLT

Most believe that Christianity is an offer of forgiveness. What isn't often grasped is that there's more. Forgiveness was made available to you *so that* you might come home to the Father. Forgiveness is not the goal. Coming home to the Father is the goal.

Remember the story of the prodigal son, one of many stories Jesus told to try to get it into our hearts where we stand with the Father, and how he feels about us. Yes, the prodigal went AWOL, ran off to Vegas with the family fortune, and blew it all. Yes, you have done the same, more or less. But that's not the point of the story. The story isn't primarily about the prodigal. It is about the father's heart. A father filled with compassion and mercy. This is the kind of Father you have. This is how he feels about you. *This* is the purpose for which Christ came.

His first act of provision happened before you were even born, when he rescued you through the life, death, and resurrection of your elder brother, Jesus of Nazareth. Then he called you to come home to him through faith in Christ. Dear friend, when you turn and reconcile to your Father, you'll see many remarkable things.

Most people tend to relate to one member of the Trinity more than the others; they feel safer praying to the Father, or Jesus, or the Holy Spirit. Have you noticed this to be true for you? And if it is not the Father . . . why not?

GOD WANTS YOU TO SEEK HIM

*"I looked forward to your calling me 'Father,'
and I wanted you never to turn from me."*

JEREMIAH 3:19 NLT

You were never made to do life without a father; the desire for a father's love is literally at the center of your universe. It feels like isolation has become your normal and it feels like freedom, but the trade-off just isn't worth it.

What you often seek in life is a plan, an obvious path to begin walking down. Something that makes it clear what is important for you to do, and how to start doing it.

But God doesn't give a master plan, not even a five-year overview—have you ever wondered why? The reason is simple and massively disruptive: God wants you to seek him, draw near to him, learn to walk with him, and frankly you won't do it if you have a plan to follow instead. It's as if there's an allergy to seeking God; it is sad but profoundly true. God laments over this, as we see in Jeremiah.

As you walk through your daily life and seek desperately to find life, your calling—are you asking God to father you along the way? Are you seeking the outside counsel that can help? He will partner with others to father you.

This might be the simplest, most revolutionary step you can take. Will you ask God to father you? Really? Ask him every day: *Father, I need your help today; I ask you to father me.*

CHILDLIKE HEART

You got me when I was an unformed youth,
God, and taught me everything I know. Now
I'm telling the world your wonders.

PSALM 71:17–18 THE MESSAGE

Your heart longs to recover a sense of wonder; it's one of the reasons only the child-heart can receive the kingdom. Remember now—you shall be as a child again.

The adult in you says, *How touching,* and dismisses it the next moment in order to go on with your very grown-up life. But Jesus is being utterly serious, and thank God. For it's the child-heart still in you that loves the fairy-tale worlds that in hope-beyond-hope you long to be lost in yourself. I believe it is right here that you can discern the longing for the kingdom most clearly—the child in you longing for wonder and a "new world."

This resurrection life you received from God is not a timid, grave-tending life. It's adventurously expectant, greeting God with a childlike "What's next, Papa?" God's Spirit touches your spirit and confirms who you really are. You know who he is, and you know who we are: Father and children. And you know you're going to get what's coming to you—an unbelievable inheritance! You go through exactly what Christ goes through. If you go through the hard times with him, then you're certainly going to go through the good times with him!

"What's next, Papa?" indeed.

Have you lost your sense of wonder in life? In the world God made? Ask Jesus to restore, or simply increase, your sense of wonder.

A HOLY WAY TO HANDLE POWER

Jesus now called the Twelve and gave
them authority and power to deal with
all the demons and cure diseases.

LUKE 9:1 THE MESSAGE

There is no false humility in Jesus. Most of us soften to flattery, but not Jesus. This is *so* rare; most leaders surround themselves with those who flatter them.

When you read how Jesus leads his disciples, you see he has no need to be the center of the action. He sends his friends out to do the very things he does; he gives them a major role in his campaign. "You go do it. Do everything you see me doing." This is humble and this is extraordinarily generous; Jesus is openhanded with his kingdom. There is no need for the whole thing to be always about him. He is delighted to share his kingdom with you.

Most men get power and then crave more; as their stars rise they can't bear to have others in the spotlight; they typically abuse the power they have; and in the end, it winds up crushing them and everyone around them. You recall the expression "Power corrupts, and absolute power corrupts absolutely." It was a lesson learned through the long, soiled history of abused power. But then you have Jesus, who walks right through the snares as if they weren't even there, handling immense power with casual grace.

Did you know that Jesus wants to share his kingdom with you? That he has a role for you now, and an inheritance later?

FIRST THINGS FIRST

For in Christ, neither our most conscientious
religion nor disregard of religion amounts
to anything. What matters is something far
more interior: faith expressed in love.
GALATIANS 5:6 THE MESSAGE

Doing things *for* God is not the same thing as loving God. Jesus loves the poor—so movements have arisen that make service to the poor the main thing. The latest craze is justice—so we rush off to the corners of the globe to fight for justice and leave Jesus behind. We actually come to think that service for Jesus is friendship with him. That's like a friend who washes your car and cleans your house but never goes anywhere with you—never comes to dinner, never wants to take a walk. But he or she is a "faithful" friend. Though you never talk.

How many children have said, "My dad worked hard to provide for us—but all I ever really wanted was his love"?

This is one more cunning ploy of the religious to keep you from the intimacy with Jesus that will heal your life. And change the world. You're not meant to merely love his teaching, his morals, his kindness, or his social reforms. You're meant to love the man himself, know him intimately; keep this as the first and foremost practice of your life. It's fact that people most devoted to the work of the Lord actually spend the least amount of time with him. First things first. Love Jesus.

Jesus, I need you. I need your life and your love. I give my life to you.
I love you.

A TESTIMONY OF GOD'S FRIENDS

"I will give you shepherds after my own heart, who will guide you with knowledge and understanding."

JEREMIAH 3:15 NLT

My hope for you is that you will find a few folks who walk with God to also walk with you through the seasons of your life. But honesty—and Scripture—forces me to admit there are few who find them. All the more reason for you, dear friend, to make the number less scarce, by becoming someone who walks with God and teaches others how.

You can look to those who have walked with God down through the ages. Certainly that is why the Bible is given to us. If God had intended it to be a textbook of doctrine, well then, he would have written it like one. But it's not; it's overwhelmingly a book of stories—tales of men and women who walked with God. Approach the Scriptures not so much as a manual of Christian principles but as the testimony of God's friends on what it means to walk with him through a thousand different episodes. When you are at war, when you are in love, when you have sinned, when you have been given a great gift—this is how you walk with God. Do you see what a different mind-set this is? It's really quite exciting.

How would you describe your faith? Is it a set of beliefs you hold dear? A moral code you are trying to live by? The hope of salvation? Or is it an exciting, daily, intimate walk with God?

CALL HIM "PAPA"

You received God's Spirit when he adopted you as his own children. Now we call him, "Abba, Father."

ROMANS 8:15 NLT

Even though it seems like the proper thing to do, reverence for God lets in a great deal of the clutter that gets between you and God. "Papa, I come to you this morning" has a *totally* different feel than "Almighty God and Everlasting Father." Addressing God with a coat-and-tie formality you'd never want with your dad will end up starching the relationship. "Papa" is what Jesus gave you.

The point is not the words; the point is the fruit, their effect. Stained-glass language reflects a view of what Jesus is like and shapes your experience of him. Whatever term you use, ask yourself: *Does this sound like his actual personality? Does this capture his playfulness, infuriating the Pharisees; his humanity, generosity, and scandalous freedom?*

These ways of speaking about Jesus perpetuate distorted views of his personality and keep Jesus at a distance, the polar opposite of the intimacy his entire life was committed to. It makes it hard to love him. It actually gets in the way of loving Jesus.

Listen—you can honor him, respect him, insist that others do, and never actually love Jesus. That's not what he wanted. False reverence is a choice veil of the religious fog. It will bring a shroud between your heart and his.

Look at how you pray—is it formal? Or is it the ease of a daughter or son who knows they are loved?

THE ABUNDANCE
OF HIS HOUSE

You feed them from the abundance of your own house.
PSALM 36:8 NLT

Yes, yes—you have heard that you are a child of God; you are his son or daughter. The curse of familiarity with the words has dulled you to the staggering truth it contains. You still act and pray like an orphan, or a slave.

Slaves feel reluctant to pray; they feel they have no right to ask, and so their prayers are modest and respectful. They spend more time asking forgiveness than they do praying for abundance. They view the relationship with reverence, maybe more like fear, but not with the tenderness of love. Of being loved. There is no intimacy in the language or their feelings. Sanctified unworthiness colors their view of prayer. These are often "good servants of the Lord."

Orphans are not reluctant to pray; they feel desperate. But their prayers feel more like begging than anything else. Orphans feel a great chasm between themselves and the One to whom they speak. Abundance is a foreign concept; a poverty mentality permeates their prayer life. They ask for scraps; they expect scraps.

But friend, the Father loves you like he loves Jesus. Is this in your mind and heart as you come to prayer? You are not an orphan. You are not merely a "servant" of God. You are His son or daughter. And with that comes his delightful abundance.

Can you see the "slave" or "orphan" in your life with God—in the things you hope for from him?

ORIENTING YOURSELF IN PRAYER

*Taking the five loaves and the two fish and looking
up to heaven, he gave thanks and broke the loaves.*

MARK 6:41

When Jesus gives thanks and looks up to heaven, he's not looking up like a man trying to recall something he just forgot. He looks up to heaven to fix his attention on his Father's loving face. He is orienting himself to what is most true in the world—not the impossibly inadequate resources for the need of the five thousand, not Mary and Martha's grief over Lazarus, and not even the finality of death sealed with a stone rolled over the tomb. No, Jesus turns his gaze from all that and fixes it upon his Father God and the resources of his kingdom.

We know that faith plays a critical role in effective praying—maybe *the* critical role—and so we feel that somehow we have to generate faith. That never works, nor does it help to try and generate *feelings* of faith. You must look from the debris to God. Peter looks at Christ, and he can walk on the water; he looks at the waves, and he goes down.

Before you pray, you must clarify who you are, and whom you are praying to—or *with*. Effective prayer is not begging God to do something, but rather a partnership with God.

What are you thinking about when you come to prayer? Are you looking at the problem at hand, or at Jesus? What would help you "fix your eyes on Jesus"?

STAY CLOSE

*Thus says the Lord GOD, "Behold, I Myself will
search for My sheep and seek them out."*
E Z E K I E L   3 4 : 1 1   N A S B

An intimate, conversational walk with God is available, and is meant to be normal. I'll push that a step further. I assume that if you *don't* find that kind of relationship with God, your spiritual life will be stunted. And that will handicap the rest of your life. You can't find life without God, and you can't find God if you don't know how to walk intimately with him.

Yet most Christians assume that the way to find the life God has for us is to (A) believe in God, (B) be a good person, and (C) he will deliver the rest. A + B = C. But Jesus says no, there's more to the equation. *I do want life for you. To the full. But you have to realize there is a thief. He's trying to destroy you. There are false shepherds too. Don't listen to them. Don't just wander off looking for pasture. You need to do more than believe in me. You have to stay close to me. Listen to my voice. Let me lead.*

Now there's a thought: by holding on to the same assumptions Jesus does, you can safely find the life he has for you.

Can you see some of that A + B = C approach to life I have described here?

JESUS IS AN ARTIST

*What a wildly wonderful world, GOD! You made
it all, with Wisdom at your side, made earth
overflow with your wonderful creations.*

PSALM 104:24 THE MESSAGE

Sunlight on water, songbirds in a forest, desert sands under moonlight, vineyards just before harvest—these all share something in common—they reflect the heart of a particular Artist. They are his masterpieces, his expression, and his gift to you. Something lies in common between these treasures and Jesus as well—words cannot compare to a personal experience. Sailing the ocean on a bright morning with the wind in your face, wandering under a forest canopy while sunlight filters down, lying on warm dunes beneath a full moon watching shooting stars—these experiences are far closer to what it is actually like to experience Jesus than mere talk of him could ever be.

You need Jesus himself. You can experience Jesus intimately. You were meant to. For despite the vandalizing of Jesus by both religion and the world, he is still alive and very much himself.

For to have Jesus, really have him, is to have the greatest treasure in all worlds. And to *love* Jesus—that is to settle the first question of your existence. Everything else flows from there. Loving Jesus will not be a problem when you know him as he truly is. So open your heart, and ask him to show you.

To know Jesus as you were meant to, it will help to keep close the simplest of prayers today: *Jesus, I ask you for you. For the real you. Reveal yourself again to me today.*

SEPTEMBER

JESUS IS GOD

*Rabbi, we know that You have come from
God as a teacher; for no one can do these
signs that You do unless God is with him.*

JOHN 3:2 NASB

Jesus came to reveal God to you. He is the defining word on God—on what the heart of God is truly like, on what God is up to in the world, and on what God is up to in your life. An intimate encounter with Jesus is the most transforming experience of human existence. To be mistaken about him is the saddest mistake of all.

He didn't go to the lengths of the incarnation to then hide for the next two thousand years. The records of Christ are written so you can experience him, and an intimate connection with the Father and the Son.

So if you don't know Jesus as a person, know his remarkable personality—playful, cunning, fierce, impatient with all that is religious, kind, creative—you have been cheated. If you don't experience Jesus intimately, daily, knowing the comfort of his actual presence, don't hear his voice speaking to you personally—you have been robbed. If you don't know the power of his indwelling life, shaping your personality, healing your brokenness, enabling you to live as he did—friend, you have been plundered.

Do you? Are you experiencing Jesus in these ways? If not, it might be your enemy trying to "jam communications." Ask the Holy Spirit to reveal Jesus to you—that's one of his favorite things to do!

THE PERSONALITY OF JESUS

*The light shines in the darkness, but the
darkness has not understood it.*

JOHN 1:5

Texting has gotten me into a lot of trouble. The reason is simple—my tone of voice cannot interpret the words. It's dangerous.

Likewise, without Jesus' tone of voice, what was in his eyes, a suppressed smile, an unflinching gaze, you can misinterpret a great deal. Reading the Gospels without the personality of Jesus is like watching television with the sound turned off. You get a very dry, two-dimensional person doing strange, undecipherable things.

What comes to mind when you think of Jesus? If you combed through the many books on Jesus for words used most often to describe him, you'd get: *loving and compassionate.*

Beautiful qualities, and certainly true of Jesus. But two-dimensional. Especially when you color these virtues with religious tones. Love turns sickly sweet and compassion soft and limp. Loving and compassionate—it's like trying to love a get-well card.

Young writers are encouraged to "find their voice," because it's *personality* that distinguishes a good novel from a phone book. Both are filled with words. Only one is worth reading. Personality is what makes someone some*one*, and not everyone, or anyone. When you lose Jesus' personality, you lose Jesus.

How would you describe Jesus' personality? Does it sound a little two-dimensional still?

JESUS LAUGHS

We were filled with laughter, and we sang for joy.
PSALM 126:2 NLT

When my boys were teenagers, we badgered them into cleaning the windows one day. When finished, the brothers began—as all brothers do—to give each other grief about the day's work. Sam and Luke had each taken half of a divided window in the dining room; Sam was now bragging about how much cleaner his side was, appealing to the evidence like a trial attorney. We turned our attention toward the window in question—at that exact moment a robin smacked into Luke's pane, fell to the ground stunned, shook itself, and flew away. We looked at one another, mouths open, eyebrows raised, and burst into laughter.

Nature had voted. *God* had voted. His timing could not have been richer. "Whose window is clean? Who slacked on the job?" *Thwack.* Brilliant. You couldn't have asked for a more choice reply. The whole episode was hysterical. Now, if you have any belief in the sovereignty of God, you discover that these moments are *orchestrated.* Not a sparrow hits a window without your Father knowing it.

Haven't you seen something in nature that made you laugh? Perhaps you did not make the connection—that you were *meant* to laugh. That it was God who made you laugh. That he laughed with you. Now you know something very important about Jesus.

Oh friend—do you live with a deep awareness that God has a sense of humor? That Jesus does? Ask him to be playful with you this week!

A HEART FOR PEOPLE

Jesus intervened: "Let the children alone,
don't prevent them from coming to me. God's
kingdom is made up of people like these."

MATTHEW 19:14 THE MESSAGE

A simple story, very Sunday school. But we've made a precious moment out of it and thus missed both the reality and the beauty. Our church held a meeting, and apparently child care wasn't available because the little ones were dashing about. Most people tried to put a good face on it, but after several interruptions, you could feel the irritation. This is at the core of human nature, this thing in us that growls, *Do not mess with my agenda.* If you aren't aware how deep this runs in you, how do you feel when people cut you off on the highway or make it difficult for you to get your job done? What angers us is almost always some version of *You are making my life even harder than it already is. Get out of the way.*

Friend, I hope you understand this: far and above the most revealing aspect of anyone's character is how one handles people. How is Jesus with people? He welcomes intrusion. He stops what he's doing and gives undivided attention. He's such an immensely gracious person. I love him for that. I yearn to be like that.

Most people I know feel like they are sort of interrupting God with their prayers; that surely he is about more important things. But now you know that Jesus likes being interrupted. So go ahead—interrupt!

JESUS IS FULLY HUMAN

He became deeply troubled and distressed.
He told [his disciples], "My soul is crushed
with grief to the point of death."

MARK 14:33–34 NLT

The Gospels are filled with beautiful and haunting descriptions of the humanity of Jesus. But when you read what you'd call the more human moments, it feels like Jesus was sort of . . . cheating. After all, we're talking about Jesus here. The guy walked on water, raised Lazarus from the dead. He never broke a sweat, right?

Dear friend, I cannot say this more emphatically—life affected Jesus.

Jesus never did anything halfheartedly. When he embraced our humanity, he didn't pull a fast one by making a show of it. He embraced it so fully and totally that he was able to die. God can't die. But Jesus did.

It will do your heart good to discover that Jesus shares in your humanity. He was, as the creeds insist, fully human. (Yes, yes—more than that to be sure. But never, ever less than that.) I'm sure the chipmunks made him laugh. The Pharisees sure made him furious. He felt joy, weakness, sorrow. The more you can grasp his humanity, the more you will find him someone you can approach, know, love, trust, and adore.

These questions about Jesus are truly important to your relationship with him. So—do you believe in Jesus' humanity? That he really was tired, thirsty, hungry; that he really did feel emotions like you do too?

JESUS IS GENUINELY GOOD

We believe, and we know you are the Holy One of God.

JOHN 6:69 NLT

Most Christians desire very deeply to be known as gracious, kind, patient, and forgiving. You feel that you "owe" it to Jesus to be seen on your best behavior. This is even truer for those of us in "the ministry," whose lives are publicly attached to Jesus. Some of the motivation behind this is beautiful. Religion has horribly distorted the world's view of God, so you go to great lengths to reassure the wary that those aligned with Jesus are really great people. In fact, nowadays most Christian leaders bend over backward to come across as very cool and hip and in no way whatsoever judgmental or condemning.

The problem is, in an effort to be a good poster child for Christianity, you've sort of hidden or left off this other side of Jesus' personality. The man is dead serious about holiness. You can't ignore the deeper issues of the soul.

As far as Jesus is concerned, holiness is a matter of the heart. The model of personal transformation that Christianity offers is internal to external. It's a transformation of the heart, the mind, the will, the soul—which then begins to express itself externally in our actions. This is absolutely critical in order to understand Jesus and his genuine goodness.

I've used the word *holiness* many times thus far in this devotional. Do you like the word? What connotations does it have for you?

JESUS IS BEAUTY

*. . . That I may dwell in the house of the LORD all the
days of my life, to gaze on the beauty of the LORD.*

PSALM 27:4

Beauty is essential to God. No—that's not putting it strongly enough. Beauty is the essence of God.

The first way you know this is through nature, the world God has given you. In what way? Primarily through its beauty. When spring arrives here in Colorado, the wildflowers come up everywhere—lupine and wild iris and Shasta daisies. The aspens have their heart-shaped leaves, trembling in the slightest breeze. Massive thunderclouds roll in, bringing with them the glorious sunsets they magnify. The earth in summer brims with beauty, beauty of such magnificence and abundance it is almost scandalous.

Nature is not primarily functional. It is primarily beautiful. Stop for a moment and let that sink in. We're so used to evaluating everything (and everyone) by its usefulness that this thought may take a minute to dawn on you. Nature is not primarily functional. It's primarily beautiful. Which is to say, beauty is in and of itself a great and glorious good, something you need in large and daily doses (for your God has seen fit to arrange for this). Nature at the height of its glory shouts, *Beauty is essential!* revealing that Beauty is the essence of God. The whole world is full of his glory.

So, if beauty is in and of itself a great and glorious good, something you need in large and daily doses—are you getting it daily? Your soul needs beauty!

GO AHEAD, ASK HIM

You do not have because you do not ask God.

JAMES 4:2

God loves it when you ask; he yearns for you to turn to him and seek him with all your heart.

And yes—God sometimes seems to "wait" to move until you ask. Any good parent knows this. I have resources to help my children. But for several reasons I will wait until they ask. Often they're not ready to receive my help until they've exhausted their own resources. Often there are vital lessons for them to learn, and if I stepped in prematurely, they would be robbed of those precious lessons. Do you see the parallels in your life with God? There is the beauty of humility that he's cultivating in your heart; it takes humility to ask. It's a beautiful form and expression of prayer to ask God to move on your behalf.

Many are of the mind-set that God is waiting for them to ask enough times, or with enough faith, or whatever, until he moves. Oh friend, God is not a reluctant participant in your life, bothered by your requests, unwilling to act until he gets tired of hearing the sound of your voice.

You know who he is and who you are. You understand the invasion, and that you are partners with God invoking the kingdom. Your prayer is not begging God. Kill this religious deception. Ask your Father God for the treasures of your heart. He is eagerly waiting.

What have you been asking for lately?

JESUS IS FULLY ALIVE

*"Why are your hearts filled with doubt? Look at my
hands. Look at my feet. You can see that it's really me."*
LUKE 24:38–39 NLT

Jesus is human, even now. It's true, dear friend. He's at the right hand of the Father in glory.

He is alive. Recall the very funny moment after his resurrection when the two fellows from the Emmaus road see Jesus alive. The pair are in the middle of telling their incredible story when Jesus just appears in the room, as if to illustrate everything they've said. *Yep, that was me. Yep, I did it just like that.* Suddenly he's just standing there and all he says is, "Peace be with you." Here the most fantastic thing in the world is happening before their eyes, and all Jesus says is "Hi"?! His understatement is very, very funny.

The disciples are stupefied, dumbfounded; they don't believe that he is real. Jesus says, "Look at my hands and feet." He's clearly showing them the holes the nails pierced. They *still* think he's a ghost. Finally he asks, "Is there anything here to eat?" like a neighbor dropping by for some chips. He chews it carefully in front of them, swallows it, and waits a few seconds for everyone to digest the lesson. You have got to love this moment. And the point he's making. Jesus raised is still Jesus, a man—flesh and bones and all.

Jesus' was the most human face of all. This will open up wonders for you.

O Jesus—I keep losing track of who you really are. Bring me back to your true heart, your true personality, your reality even now.

JESUS IS RELATIONAL

*"You will seek Me and find Me when you
search for Me with all your heart."*
JEREMIAH 29:13 NASB

What a comfort to know that this universe you live in is relational at its core, that your God is a tenderhearted God who yearns for relationship with you. Not only does God long for you, but he longs to be loved by you. Oh, how we've missed this. Do you see God as longing to be loved by you? You see him as strong and powerful, but not necessarily as needing you.

Do you have any doubt that God wants to be sought after? He *wants* you to love him. God longs to be *desired*. Just as you long to be desired. This is not some weakness or insecurity. Remember the story of Martha and Mary? Jesus said, "Mary has chosen what is better" (Luke 10:42). *She chose me.*

God yearns to share a life of intimacy and adventure with you. The whole world was made for it—the rivers and the glens, the meadows and the beaches. Flowers, music, a kiss. We have a way of forgetting all that, losing ourselves in work and worry. But God will never cease inviting you. Through his creation, God makes romance a priority of the universe. Your God has a passionate heart.

Do you believe God wants a *romance* with you? (This is especially hard for men.) Try thinking about it this way: God knows your heart. He knows what moves your heart. Can you see ways that he has been "moving" your heart lately, with little gifts and reminders? A song on the radio? A sunset? The laughter of your child?

JESUS IS CUNNING

*"I want you to be smart in the same way . . . not
complacently just get by on good behavior."*
LUKE 16:9 THE MESSAGE

Idon't recall a worship song with the word *cunning* in it. "Thou
Art Cunning," or "Cunning, Cunning, Cunning." Do you
interpret God's actions in your life as perhaps part of some cunning plan? That delayed answer to prayer—is there something
brilliant about the timing? Would it help you to rest if you thought
so? When he answers your prayers with "No," do you see him spar-
ing you some unseen danger? And when it comes to your own
"imitation of Christ," do you approach your days wondering, *How
would Jesus have me be snakelike today?* Doesn't it sound a little
unchristian?

You don't appreciate Jesus' cunning because you insist on
clinging to a naive view of the world. You just want life to be easy;
you just want life to be good. You don't want to deal with evil,
so you pretend you don't have to. You don't want to navigate sin
either. You prefer your coffeehouse chitchat, your Twitter-level
engagement. It's as though you think your mission and your context are something other than what they were for Jesus. But no, he
says: *Just as the Father sent me, I send you* (John 20:21).

*Jesus—I have totally missed this part of your personality. Show me
how you are being cunning in the world right now . . . and in my life.*

JESUS IS HUMBLE

Being found in appearance as a man, He humbled
Himself by becoming obedient to the point of death.
PHILIPPIANS 2:8 NASB

The coronation of Jesus is perhaps the most joyful, triumphant moment in history, second only to the resurrection. His crowning ensures the triumph of a kingdom of laughter and beauty and life, forever. But it was a long road to that throne. His first step is a staggering descent—the Son of God becomes a son of man by humbling himself. But *humility* hardly begins to describe the incarnation.

It boggles the mind. The eternal Son of God, "Light of Light, Very God of Very God," spent nine months developing in Mary's uterus. He had to learn to walk. The Word of God had to learn to talk. He who calls the stars by name had to learn the names of everything, just as you did. "This is a cup. Can you say cup? Cuuup." Or did you think baby Jesus came into the world with the vocabulary of Dictionary.com?

For ages upon ages, his generous hand fed every creature on earth; now it is he that has to be spoon-fed, drooling most of it down his chin like any toddler. The Son of God doesn't even know how to tie his shoes. Someone had to teach him how to tie those sandals John the Baptist said none of us were worthy to untie.

I take my shoes off. The humility of this is beyond words.

Let this sink in for a moment—Jesus had to be spoon-fed. He had to learn words like any toddler. He had to learn how to tie his shoes. What does this do for you as it sinks in?

JESUS IS TEACHER

*He began to wash the disciples' feet, drying
them with the towel he had around him.*

JOHN 13:5 NLT

O nce Jesus chooses his band of brothers, he needs to disciple these fishermen, tax collectors, and political revolutionaries who dropped their careers to follow him. I'm not sure you've understood the ramifications of his decision. You just think, *Oh, yeah, the disciples*, and forget what was actually required for them to become apostles. This is going to take a lot of work. There's no fairy godmother waving her wand here; these pumpkins don't just turn into coaches.

But the way Jesus discipled each man proves his humility. To be a crowd-drawing teacher can be a rather heady experience, all eyes looking to you for the next bit of wisdom to drop from your lips. It's easy to be gracious when you're adored. But when your class keeps missing the point, challenging you, running down rabbit trails, changing the subject, misunderstanding, breaking out into a brawl—that's when your character is exposed. I never really saw Jesus' endurance with his disciples. The shining brilliance of *what* Jesus is teaching has obscured the *process* involved, all that it required of him. You've become so used to Jesus being gracious, kind, and patient, you miss the humility of it.

There's no fairy godmother waving her wand here; these pumpkins don't just turn into coaches. How does this help you understand God's work discipling your life? Can you see the *process* better now?

JESUS IS YOUR EXAMPLE

Jesus cried out in pain and wept in sorrow as
he offered up priestly prayers to God. Because
he honored God, God answered him. Though he
was God's Son, he learned trusting-obedience
by what he suffered, just as we do.

HEBREWS 5:7–8 THE MESSAGE

The divine nature of Christ is a mystery we cannot fully explain nor explain away—the choice Jesus made to "empty" himself of his divine powers and prerogatives in order to take on the limitations of humanity. There is debate on exactly how much Jesus emptied himself, but if Jesus was pretending to be a man, then his life is so far beyond ours it can't really be a model for us to follow. To err is human, to forgive is divine and all that. But if Jesus chose a genuine humanity and drew his power from the Father as we must do, then we *can* live as he did.

The Son of God laid down his glory to become a human being. It is the humility of utter dependence. Jesus wept, he prayed, he *learned obedience*—so that we might learn to do the same. What we are witnessing when Jesus "disciples" his followers is something like the emperor stepping down in the arena to face the lions with us, to show us how it's done, using only the tools available to us. Staggering. And so hopeful.

Jesus, thank you for inviting me to live in union with you. In your humility, you show me what it is to be your son/daughter. Help me learn to do the same.

JESUS IS SIMPLY HIMSELF

*Every desirable and beneficial gift comes
out of heaven. The gifts are rivers of light
cascading down from the Father of Light.*
JAMES 1:17 THE MESSAGE

Jesus is simply himself. Playful, cunning, generous, fierce—not one moment of it is contrived. Jesus never plays to the audience, never kowtows to the opposition, never takes his cues from the circus around him. He is simply himself.

I think this will help you with one of the confounding experiences you have reading the Gospels.

The diversity of Jesus' actions, timing, manner, words, dare we say moods; his sudden changes of direction, then his stillness—it's hard to keep up with. It certainly is colorful, but almost dizzying, alive and shifting like the northern lights. Dazzling, but nearly to the point of leaving you confused. As soon as you've grabbed on to one dimension of Jesus—his generosity, his compassion, his honesty—he seems to turn it on its head, or you on yours.

Perhaps the gospel stories seem dizzying only because you've never seen anyone act like Jesus acts before. Maybe what you are witnessing is actually one single quality, not many. Maybe Jesus is simply being true. Knowing this will help you to love him more than anything else.

Loving Jesus is what it's all about, friend. Take some time right now just to tell him you love him.

JESUS IS LOVE IN ACTION

*"I've told you these things for a purpose: that
my joy might be your joy, and your joy wholly
mature. This is my command: Love one another
the way I loved you. This is the very best way to
love. Put your life on the line for your friends."*

JOHN 15:11–13 THE MESSAGE

Jesus has the ability to live in such a way that there's always something of an element of surprise to him, and yet however he acts turns out to be exactly what was needed in the moment. His brilliance shines through, but never blinding, never overbearing. He is the playfulness of creation, scandal and utter goodness, the generosity of the ocean and the ferocity of a thunderstorm; he is cunning as a snake and gentle as a whisper; the gladness of sunshine and the humility of a thirty-mile walk by foot on a dirt road. Reclining at a meal, laughing with friends, and then going to the cross. Jesus is beautiful.

But most of all, it is the way he loves. In all these stories, every encounter, you watch love in action. Love as strong as death; a blood, sweat, and tears love, not a get-well card. You learn a great deal about the true nature of a person in the way he or she loves. And it takes a beautiful heart to recognize the beauty in a scandalous act, and to still love as Jesus does.

Pause and give this a moment—Jesus has such a beautiful heart. It will help you love him and trust him.

JESUS IS APPROACHABLE

*When Simon Peter heard that it was the Lord,
he put his outer garment on (for he was stripped
for work), and threw himself into the sea.*

JOHN 21:7 NASB

After his resurrection, Jesus appears on the shore where the disciples are fishing. He acts like a guy out for a stroll, asks if they had any luck, suggests they try another spot, and reproduces the catch that caught them all in the beginning.

Peter is a hundred yards offshore. That's about three city blocks—a long way to swim, especially in a full-length robe. Peter doesn't care. He doesn't wait for the boat, forgets about the fish, and as quick as you can say, "Jack be nimble" he hits the water, swimming, thrashing, gasping for air, then stumbling ashore fast as he can to get to Jesus. Do you think he then drew another line in the sand? "Hello, sir. Mr. Christ, may I approach?" Peter is a passionate, impulsive guy. He just swam a hundred yards in his bathrobe. I'll bet dollars to donuts he ran right up to Jesus, sopping wet as laundry from the washer, and hugged him, soaking the risen Lord.

If Peter didn't do it, you know Jesus did, adding his tears of joy to the wet embrace. Beautiful. That's the way to do it, friend. Just begin to make a practice of loving Jesus. Relate to him as you see his friends did in the Gospels.

Make a practice of loving Jesus; make it one of your daily disciplines. Try relating to him as you see his friends did in the Gospels.

JESUS IS LIFE

In Him was life, and the life was the Light of men.
JOHN 1:4 NASB

The word I choose to describe Jesus is *life*. Pure, lush, exuberant life. Life that proves to be unquenchable, unstoppable.

Let's turn again to nature. It's such a liberating force from the religious fog, because it's God's and it speaks volumes about his true—pardon the pun—nature. What does creation say about his life? A single tree is enough to make me worship—the beauty, the elegance, the perseverance, the life coursing through it.

Have you ever wondered how many fish are swimming our oceans and seas? And take a microscopic view of your world— the thousands of organisms in a single drop of pond water. How many drops fill a bucket, how many buckets a pond? The earth is teeming with life in such staggering diversity and abundance that science still hasn't come close to cataloging it all.

Now, what would happen if this sort of life expressed itself in a man? Exactly. It did.

When Jesus fed the five thousand, he did so from five loaves and two (small) fish. With leftovers. With a shout he raises Lazarus from the dead. One word best describes what is going on here: life. Jesus really is the Lord of life.

Now for a wonder of wonders—not only do you get Jesus, you get to live his life. Really. This life is yours for the asking.

O Jesus, I need your life in me more than I even know. So I give my life again to you today, to be filled with your life. Fill me with your glorious life, Lord. Unite my life with yours.

JESUS IS FIERCELY INTENTIONAL

Zeal for your house consumes me.
JOHN 2:17 THE MESSAGE

Jesus is a fierce, intentional man to be sure. But his passions are neither reckless nor momentary.

Could a small, unintimidating figure accomplish such a sustained riot? To pull off driving money changers from the temple would require more than a few seconds and repeated blows. This is a sustained assault. If a frail man with a meek voice tried this, he'd be log-jammed by the sheer number and inertia of the traffic. Jesus is a locomotive, a juggernaut. For all practical purposes in John 2, he *is* the bull in the china shop.

This is your Jesus. But is this the Jesus of your worship songs? The religious fog sneaks in to obscure Jesus with lines comparing him to "a rose trampled on the ground." Helpless, lovely Jesus. Vegetarian, pacifist, tranquil. Oh, wait—that was Gandhi. Not Jesus.

This is a breathtaking quality—*especially* when compared to our present age where doubt masquerades as humility, passivity cloaks as rest, and emasculated indecision poses as laid-back enlightenment.

Oh, Jesus could be soft, and he certainly was humble, but his fierce intentionality is riveting to watch.

Fierce—have you believed Jesus is fierce? That he is still fierce today? How would things change if you *really* believed it?

A LOVE AFFAIR

Devote your heart and soul to
seeking the LORD your God.
1 CHRONICLES 22:19

Francis of Assisi was called "the second Christ" because his life was so totally given over to expressing the life of Jesus. What can be learned from this man devoted like no other? "As Saint Francis did not love humanity but men, so he did not love Christianity but Christ," wrote G. K. Chesterton. Wow. Just let that sink in. Francis didn't fall in love with church; he fell in love with Jesus. "His religion was not a thing like a theory but a thing like a love-affair."[8]

Who even remembers him for that? If people know him now, it's only as the statue in the garden of the friar with the birds and bunnies. He's been made a cartoon by the religious fog, just as it happened to Jesus. Which brings us back to something essential for loving Jesus, for making your faith more like a love affair—you are going to have to break with the religious. If you want Jesus, if you want his healing, his life, you're going to have to end the relationship with the religious glaze.

"Religion" has done a lot to veil and distort people's view of Jesus. How about for you—can you see ways you still hold to a very "stained glass" view of Jesus?

DIGNITY OF CAUSATION

When tempted, no one should say, "God is tempting me." For God cannot be tempted by evil, nor does he tempt anyone.

JAMES 1:13

One of the most crippling convictions held by believers today is the idea that everything that happens is the will of God. It is a poisonous belief that will destroy your confidence in God; you will end up believing terrible things about him. The news report about a pack of teenage boys who repeatedly raped a little girl with Down's syndrome: *That was the will of God?*

The Bible makes it perfectly clear that God never causes anyone to sin. God does not tempt, nor does he cause you to sin. But people sin every day, and their sins have devastating consequences. So there are all kinds of events happening every day that are not *caused* by God.

Remember—we live in a world where God has granted to human beings and to angels the dignity of causation, the dignity of making things happen. You get to make things happen, just as God does. God did not cause Adam and Eve to sin, nor did he prevent them from doing so. And their sin had staggering consequences.

You get to make things happen—it opens up endless opportunities for prayer.

Notice in the Lord's Prayer that we are told to pray that his will be done on earth as it is in heaven. Now, if God's will is always done on earth as it is in heaven, why would Jesus have his church pray for that down through the centuries?

DEEP COMMUNION WITH GOD

*Your GOD is present among you, a strong
Warrior there to save you. Happy to have
you back, he'll calm you with his love.*

ZEPHANIAH 3:17 THE MESSAGE

There are no formulas with God. The way in which God heals your wound is a deeply personal process. Jesus is a person and he insists on working personally. For some, it comes in a moment of divine touch. For others, it takes place over time and through the help of another, maybe several others.

But there have been other significant ways in which God will work—times of healing prayer, times of grieving your wound and forgiveness. Most of all, times of deep communion with God. The point is this: healing never happens outside of intimacy with Christ. The healing of your wound flows out of your union with him.

Oh friend, let God love you; let him get really close to you. I know it seems painfully obvious, but I'm telling you few are ever so vulnerable as to simply let themselves be loved by God. Abiding in the love of God is your only hope, the only true home for your heart. It's not that you mentally acknowledge that God loves you. It's that you let your heart come home to him, and stay in his love.

Are you comfortable letting God get really close, and love you? All of you?

YOUR AUTHORITY

He embraced us. He took our sin-dead lives and made
us alive in Christ. He did all this on his own, with no
help from us! Then he picked us up and set us down in
highest heaven in company with Jesus, our Messiah.

EPHESIANS 2:5–6 THE MESSAGE

Adam and Eve were given the earth to rule, but when the test came—they folded. Adam didn't act on Eve's behalf. Satan was there, threatening the whole kingdom, and Adam didn't do squat. Passivity was how Satan became "the prince of this earth," as Jesus called him. Might I point out that many of us fail through some sort of passivity? We refuse to make the tough decisions. We look for a comfortable life.

The earth was given to us, but Satan usurped the throne, as Scar does in *The Lion King*. Jesus came to win it back—to break the claims of his rule. Through his absolute obedience to God and through his sacrificial death, he did indeed break every claim Satan might make to the kingdoms of this earth. Now "all authority in heaven and on earth has been given" to Jesus (Matthew 28:18).

And you, my friend, have been given that same authority. To be seated with Christ in the heavenlies means you share in his authority. And learning to live in this authority, to bring the kingdom of God to your kingdom on earth, is a life-changing turn of events!

Are your prayers primarily characterized by asking God to do things for you, or are you using the authority you have in Jesus Christ to command his kingdom in your domain?

INTERNAL REVOLUTION

*"Unless you do far better than the Pharisees in
the matters of right living, you won't know the
first thing about entering the kingdom."*
MATTHEW 5:20 THE MESSAGE

Jesus gives you a deeper, truer view of holiness. The issues are first and foremost internal, before they are ever external. You can murder someone without ever pulling a trigger. You break the Sabbath if come Sunday night you're exhausted. Especially if you've been exhausted by church. Letter, and spirit. All those external "rules of men" do nothing to promote a genuine holiness. But they do make people Pharisees. By the truckload.

Jesus' freedom is a difficult thing to teach on for many reasons; let me name two. First, there are certain types who will hear this and find it an excuse to live as they please. Many characters in our irreverent age "don't care what others think." Their freedom is abrasive and unholy. The freedom Jesus models is not a crass "giving the finger to the world." Or to the church, for that matter. Others will dismiss the freedom Jesus offers out of fear—either the fear of what people might think (which, ironically, is sin), or the fear of "falling into immorality."

So let me be very clear—the scandalous freedom Jesus models for us is based in an understanding of a holiness much deeper than anything the religious ever concocted. The only possible way that can happen is through an internal revolution, a changed heart. When you have a heart like Jesus'.

Is your life characterized by freedom, or more by rule-keeping?

DEEPER THINGS OF THE HEART

When God, our kind and loving Savior
God, stepped in, he saved us.
TITUS 3:5 THE MESSAGE

God is after something critical: he's after what is going on in your heart. When you find yourself lost or disoriented, feeling discontented, it flushes deeper things in the heart. Stuff begins to surface, like all those feelings of abandonment or fear or self-hatred. But actually, dear friend, that stuff is *gold*. Because it opens you up to deeper healing, deeper freedom; it opens a door for transformation and restoration. It prepares the way for you to become a more wholehearted human being.

Open the door, and Jesus will meet you in your fear, anger, shame. Once he gets access to those places, he can do his healing.

Then you are in a far better place to get back to asking what next thing he has for you. Not The Plan, but the next thing. I know that feels small and inconsequential, but the next thing is going to get you to the next-next thing, which gets you to the next thing after that, and the combination of those steps gets you into the place God has for you. As you practice this approach, you develop the one skill that will determine the outcome of your life more than any other: you learn to walk with God.

Jesus, I don't need to know everything. I just need to know what you want me to do next. What are you saying to me about the next step in my life, Lord?

AN INSATIABLE DESIRE

*"Self-sacrifice is the way, my way, to finding
yourself, your true self. What kind of deal is it
to get everything you want but lose yourself?
What could you ever trade your soul for?"*
MATTHEW 16:25–26 THE MESSAGE

Should the king in exile pretend he's happy there and not seek his own country? His miseries are his ally; they urge him on. Let them grow, if need be. But do not forsake the secret of life or despise those kingly desires. You abandon the most important journey of your life when you abandon desire. You leave your heart by the side of the road and head off in the direction of fitting in, getting by, being productive, what have you. Whatever you might gain—money, position, the approval of others, or just absence of the discontent itself—it's not worth it.

You must return to the "journey of desire." Wherever you are, whatever you're doing, you must pick up the trail and follow the map you have at hand. Desire, both the whispers and the shouts, is the map you have been given to find the only life worth living. You may think you're following the map of desire when all you are doing is serving it slavishly, unthinkingly. It's not the same. You must *listen* to desire, let it guide you through the false routes and dead ends.

Your only fatal error would be to pretend that you have found the life you prize and settle for the same old thing.

Are you listening to your desire these days? What is it saying to you? Can you invite Christ into those desires?

WHO REIGNS?

"If anyone wishes to come after Me, he must deny himself, and take up his cross and follow Me."
MATTHEW 16:24 NASB

The cross sets you free, not only from the penalty of sin but from the very power of it.

Anyone trying to live a whole and holy life knows the grief that comes—regularly—when you cannot seem to live beyond your sin and addictions. You must understand: the unholy trinity Scripture names as the world, our flesh, and the evil one conspire to undermine your character. In that swirling mess, it can feel like you want to (yell at your kids, indulge bitterness or envy . . . just fill in the blank) but what you *must* cling to is that you have died with Christ in the cross; sin no longer has to rule over you. You have a choice!

The cross was not only then, it is now. An essential choice you face daily is whether you'll let the "self" life reign in you, or will Christ reign in you? The first issue is never sin; it's what you do with your internal, natural inclination to play lord of your life. All the hatred and envy you see in social media—that is the "offended self" lashing out. When Jesus invites you to take up your cross daily, he is not saying you have to crucify your every hope and desire. He is saying you must choose not to let "self" reign—neither in your internal nor external world. Christ is Lord of both.

Jesus—I surrender! I'm sorry I keep trying to play "lord" in my life. I surrender my self-determination. Come and be my Lord!

JESUS' TOUCH

A leper appeared and went to his knees before Jesus, praying, "Master, if you want to, you can heal my body." Jesus reached out and touched him, saying, "I want to. Be clean."

MATTHEW 8:2–3 THE MESSAGE

Early on in his public appearances, Jesus gives the famous Sermon on the Mount. It's a "big moment" for Jesus. Then, with the religious leaders watching his every move, we see Jesus touching and healing a leper.

In Israel at that time, to get within a stone's throw of someone so diseased was to jeopardize your own righteousness and reputation. So that is the danger Jesus is faced with. The man comes near Jesus—but not too near. What does Jesus do? He reaches out and touches him. The beauty of this is beyond words. Jesus doesn't need to come in contact with the man in order to heal him. There are many accounts where all he does is say the word and people are healed, even people a county away. Yet he *touches* him. Why?! Because this is the one thing the man needs. No one has touched him for a very long time.

The kindness of Jesus in this one act is enough to make you love him. But so is his scandalous freedom. Jesus doesn't seem to care. Or better, he cares very deeply about the right things.

Do you see Jesus as "scandalously free"? He spoke to women in public—something no rabbi would ever, ever do. He touched the "unclean." Are you being transformed into his likeness in this way too? What is holding you back?

HE WANTS TO HEAL YOU

*It was on the Sabbath that Jesus had
made the mud and healed him.*

JOHN 9:14 NLT

To come to know Jesus intimately, as he is, as he wants to be known, is to release a redemptive landslide in your life. There will be no stopping the goodness. The first purpose of your existence will be resolved, and from there you are set to fulfill all of God's other purposes for you. Now—do you really think that the enemy of your soul, the enemy of Jesus Christ, is simply going to let that happen? Satan is far too subtle to rely on persecution alone. His most masterful works are of deception (ask Adam and Eve about this when you see them). So the Deceiver deceives by means of distortion, and his favorite tool is to present a distorted Christ through the respectable channels of religion.

Consider this one piece of evidence: millions of people have spent years attending church, and yet they don't know God. Their heads are filled with stuffing about Jesus, but they do not experience him, not as the disciples did on the beach. There are millions more who love Jesus Christ but experience him only occasionally, more often stumbling along short of the life he promised, like Lazarus still wrapped in his graveclothes.

He wants to come and heal you. Don't let anything stand in the way.

Jesus, I want to experience you more and more like your friends did, like the disciples on the beach, who got to be with you and hang out. I want to hang out with you, Jesus. Draw near to me.

TIMES OF REST AND RELEASE

"Come away by yourselves to a secluded
place and rest a while."
MARK 6:31 NASB

Unanswered prayer that felt urgent and beyond precious can feel like a knife to the heart. The enemy then rushes in with feelings of betrayal, whispering terrible things about God in your vulnerability. It is never, ever true. But it's good to remind yourself of that.

But like any other form of total-life exertion, you need periods of rest. Even God rested, on the seventh day. It often helps your heart—and your prayers—to give a long prayer vigil a rest now and then. After a rest you will find yourself in a much better place to go at it again, and you may receive new guidance that enables you to adjust your prayers in a more effective direction.

Having said that, I also need to say that there may be a time to let it go.

I do *not* mean you let your faith in the goodness of God go. I do *not* mean you let praying go. But there is a time to let contending go, let go when you have done all you can and more. As you stay close to Jesus he will let you know when that time is, and healing and beauty will come in a way you aren't expecting.

Is there something in your life you have been contending for over a long period of time? Do you perhaps need to rest a bit from all that?

OCTOBER

WHOLE AND HOLY

Long before he laid down earth's foundations, he
had us in mind, had settled on us as the focus of
his love, to be made whole and holy by his love.

EPHESIANS 1:4 THE MESSAGE

God has plans for us. Those plans give God great joy. The heart of those plans is this: to make *you* whole and holy, by his love. Whole, and holy—this is what you ache for. At least, you ache for the wholeness part. The holy part seems optional. But you will soon see why it is not. Whole and holy—this is your destiny. Once the truth of it seizes you, you'll run around the house whooping at the sheer promise.

Now, we probably have some idea what wholeness might look like, even feel like. But what about the holy part? It almost seems a disconnect—summer vacation and clean your room; gelato and Brussels sprouts. What does this have to do with that? For years I thought of holiness as something austere, spiritually elite, and frankly rather severe: giving up worldly pleasures, innocent things such as sugar or music or fishing; living an entirely spiritual life; praying a lot; being a very good person. Something that only very old saints attain.

But you cannot become whole without becoming holy; nor can you become holy without becoming whole. The two go hand in hand.

What comes to mind when you read or hear the word *holiness*? Write down what assumptions you have about holiness. Then ask God, *Is this really what it means to be whole with you?*

ONENESS WITH GOD

"I will make My dwelling among you."
LEVITICUS 26:11 NASB

As you experience the many beautiful and intimate ways Jesus comes to heal your inner being, keep in mind that the essence of healing prayer is always to facilitate the presence of Jesus into the specific places of brokenness. Whatever else might be involved, always begin with, "Jesus, come into this and heal."

Oswald Chambers, a man who wrote on prayer, said, "The idea of prayer is not in order to get answers from God." Good heavens—it's not? What then is the purpose? "Prayer is perfect and complete oneness with God."[9] A mighty truth is being uncovered here.

Oneness with God is the goal of your existence. It's not merely to believe in God, although that is better than not believing in him. It's not merely to trust in God, though that is far better than simply believing in God. It's not even to worship God, which is higher still.

The destiny of the human soul is union with God. The same oneness that Jesus talked about with his Father is your destiny as well. That's what you were made for. Prayer is one of his primary means of drawing you to himself, getting you to pour out your heart before him so that you can receive his heart toward you. You have a soul. God has a soul too.

Is union with God something you seek on a regular basis? Pray: *Father God, Spirit, Jesus, I invite your heart and soul into union with my heart and soul. Show me where I need more—more healing, more of you. I pray for union with you, God!*

HOPE OF FREEDOM

*Sin can't tell you how to live. . . . You're
living in the freedom of God.*
ROMANS 6:14 THE MESSAGE

You *do* need to find healing for the wounds, but you also need to deal with the sin. In most cases, this comes first. You start with repentance, you start with what you know.

You will discover that freedom comes only as you bring unsanctified and unholy places under the rule of Jesus Christ, so that he can possess these very places deeply and truly. Therefore, part of this first step involves sanctifying the place of bondage to Christ. If it's emotional (as with rage) you sanctify your emotions; if it involves addiction you sanctify your obsession, and your body. At the retreats we do, we walk through this process in prayer, and many people are shocked to realize that they have never taken the first, simple step of sanctifying their issues to Jesus Christ. But if you want to be free in this place, it must come under the total, intimate, ongoing rule of God.

There is hope of freedom because of what Christ has done. Now you have an option. But you do have to stop presenting yourself over to sin as best you can. Your choices matter. You need to renounce the ways you have presented yourself to sin, and represent yourself to Christ.

Lord Jesus, I confess I have been offering myself over to sin, and now I am its slave. I renounce [specifically name your sin here]. *Jesus Christ, may your atoning blood cover my sins and cleanse me. In your name.*

WELCOME JESUS TO YOUR WOUNDS

Christ has set us free to live a free life.
GALATIANS 5:1 THE MESSAGE

God promises to heal the brokenhearted. So invite Jesus into your past. Linger with Jesus in prayer there. Pay attention. Often Jesus will bring up something necessary to your healing through a memory he awakens. As you are inviting Jesus into your wounds, what is so very beautiful is the fact that—not every time, but more than you'll expect—Jesus will show you what he's doing; you'll see him come. Call it seeing with your mind's eye or Christ using your imagination or seeing with the eyes of your heart or your spirit—however you want to describe it. Often you'll see Christ come back into your past. You might see him step between you and the one who wounded you, or he might simply tell you, *You are forgiven, you are safe, I love you.*

Healing doesn't necessarily have to be dramatic. Oftentimes it is very quiet. Jesus simply comes as you invite him to, and though you may not "see" him or "hear" him, he comes, and you'll sense a new peace or quietness in your soul. Your heart *feels* better somehow. The important thing is for you to give him permission to enter these wounded places, invite his healing love, and wait in prayer for him to come.

Lord Jesus, I invite you into my wounds and my brokenness. Come and find me here, in these very places. Gather my heart into your love and make me whole.

A CREATIVE HEALER

"He'll steadily and firmly set things right."
ISAIAH 42:4 THE MESSAGE

The human soul is a place of profound mysteries, and God is infinitely creative when it comes to healing your soul. Sometimes he goes straight for the wound or the brokenness. And friend, having had that healed, it's far easier to resist the enemy and renounce your sins. Sometimes it requires binding the enemy first, simply so you can think clearly enough to find the healing you need. Jesus will guide you. Ask him to guide you.

Do not be discouraged if you find that it takes more than one round of prayer. It didn't take you a day to get into this mess. Sometimes you'll have to pray again in a month, and then again in six months. This doesn't mean that "it didn't work." Quite often Christ comes back in your life for a *deeper* work of healing.

No matter your age, the sun has gone down a lot of times in your life; there's a lot of past there. There's a whole lot to your story. And Jesus was with you through all of it. So be gracious, be patient; it doesn't mean you're blowing it if Christ brings it up again. It simply means it's time for another round, and so you continue to invite Jesus into your brokenness, and he will continue to guide you toward deliverance and healing.

Linger with Jesus and ask for his healing grace by simply allowing him to love you: *Jesus, you have come to heal my broken heart. Lord, comfort me where I am hurting; release over me your love and wholeness.*

CHOOSE HOLINESS

*All who are being led by the Spirit of
God, these are sons of God.*
ROMANS 8:14 NASB

As you become more whole, you can become holier. And as you become holier, you can become more whole. Trying to choose one without the other can bring people a great deal of distress, and to the conviction that no real change takes place in this life. It's not true. It's just that discipline is not enough.

Dear friend, you can't repent your way out of brokenness. It simply doesn't work. You repent of your sins; the brokenness must be healed. Furthermore, this isn't simply about the sweet love of Jesus. You have an enemy, strongholds are real, and you must break those agreements and banish the enemy.

After a broken leg has been set, and had time to heal, it needs to be strengthened. The same is true of your soul. God urges you to make "level paths" for yourself, so that you can be restored.

In those hundreds of little decisions each day, choose holiness. The more you do, the more you will find yourself able to. The more you make choices that compromise your integrity, the weaker you feel and the more the enemy pours it on. However, the more you side with the Spirit in you, the stronger you feel. Over time it becomes easier to choose; your will gets stronger; you discover that in fact, you really do want goodness and nothing else.

You can't repent your way out of brokenness. It doesn't work. You repent of your sins; the brokenness must be healed. Does this help you understand how you are handling your struggles?

CLING TO JESUS

For the joy set before him he endured the cross,
scorning its shame, and sat down at the right
hand of the throne of God. Consider him who
endured such opposition from sinners, so that
you will not grow weary and lose heart.

HEBREWS 12:2–3

Your suffering is neither pointless nor isolated. Somehow Jesus' sufferings overflow into our lives; somehow ours are linked to his. This is a great honor. It grants our sorrows an incredible dignity; it invites us to know an intimacy and connection with Jesus in them, *because* of them. The sufferings of Jesus are the noblest part of his life story: the cross, the crown of thorns. What an unspeakable honor that he would share even this with us. This fellowship is a treasure we have not tapped into but one we will need.

When his suffering overflows into our lives, God's promise is that his comfort will overflow to us as well. We can cry out for the comfort of God. Whatever your circumstances may be, he *will* heal your wounded heart; he *will* comfort. This is what Hebrews is trying to say: Do not lose heart because of your suffering. Cling to Jesus; cling to Jesus. He is with you now.

Jesus in me, come for me today into the places where the suffering is deep. Jesus, I believe that your life is the ruler of my life. Fill me today with your life.

STAY TRUE TO GOD

*Through their faith, the people in days
of old earned a good reputation.*
HEBREWS 11:2 NLT

All are commended for faith—those who shut the mouths of lions, or who died by the sword. Yes, Peter was freed. But James—who died by the sword—ultimately won. Death never defeats the Christian. Also, none of them received what was promised—because Eden will not be restored on the earth until Jesus returns.

The mighty victory is staying true to God. It is maintaining a mature perspective—where God means everything to you—through glorious breakthrough and in the midst of terrible affliction. If you do not hold fast to this, you will be shaken when your prayers do not seem to prevail; you will fall prey to feelings of failure or despair. Or you will be grasping at promises of unending victory, looking down on those who do not see things as you do. You will be forced to ignore the sufferings of Christ, and your honor in sharing in them.

And you will miss the goal of this life, which is not unending breakthrough, but something far more beautiful and everlasting—the beauty of Jesus Christ, which your Father is committed to forming in you.

Oh friend—how we handle our suffering and disappointment is so critical. Have you been losing heart? Ask Jesus to strengthen you where you are weary.

HIS BEAUTY HEALS

Splendor and majesty are before Him,
strength and joy are in His place.
1 CHRONICLES 16:27 NASB

There is something profoundly healing about beauty. After I lost my dearest friend, there were months when only beauty helped. I couldn't hear words of counsel, read, or even pray. Only beauty helped comfort. It soothes the soul.

Beauty inspires. Imagine being in the presence of a woman like Mother Teresa. Her life was so beautiful, and it called us to something higher. A teacher in the inner city insisted on putting a fountain and flowers in the courtyard of the school, "because these children need to be inspired. They need to know that life can be better." Beauty inspires.

Beauty is your most immediate experience of the eternal. Think of what it's like to behold a gorgeous sunset or the ocean at dawn. You yearn to linger. Sometimes the beauty is so deep it pierces you with longing for life as it was meant to be. Beauty reminds you of an Eden you have never known, but you somehow know your heart was created for it. Beauty says, *There is a glory calling to you.* And if there is a glory, there is a source of glory. What great goodness could have possibly created this? Beauty draws you to God.

Beauty is, without question, the most essential and the most misunderstood of all God's qualities.

Beauty ministers to us in our suffering and disappointments. Where can you find some beauty this week?

THE PARTIAL

*They placed their hope in a better
life after the resurrection.*

HEBREWS 11:35 NLT

The longing for life is the driving force of humanity. It's your longing for life that compels you to pray. When you see what's possible as God comes, hope surges within you and that's good.

What's not good is the subtle shift that sometimes follows. When life comes together in a way you've longed for, something whispers, *Maybe it can always be like this*—your longing for Eden rises within you, and it's beautiful. Only it's premature.

Paul saw some pretty staggering answers to prayer, but he also knew exposure, hunger, and cold. And remember—all of heaven was committed to this man being successful. His life was powerful. But Paul knew there is only one paradise—and we are not there yet.

Most people just hope things work out, tossing up prayers, hoping to score on a Jesus lottery ticket. They have little to show for it. Others discover the possibility of breakthrough; they begin to experience breathtaking results. Then their Eden-hearts get confused about what it means to be victorious.

You can always be victorious—it just depends on what you mean by *victorious*. Or better, it depends on what God means by victorious.

O Jesus, my heart longs for Eden. But here and now, I need your grace to be grateful for partial healing and freedom. Help me here, Lord.

AN EPIPHANY

Christ lives in me. The life you see me living is not
"mine," but it is lived by faith in the Son of God.
GALATIANS 2:20 THE MESSAGE

The point of encountering those things in your life you cannot handle is that you are forced to turn to Christ. Did you really think you could be kind for the rest of your life without the inner help of Jesus? One day of kindness is a miracle. What about being forgiving? Generous? Honest? Did you really think you could overcome your lifelong strongholds without the life of Jesus in you?

This realization was an epiphany for me. I have spent most of my adult years trying to find those keys that would enable people to become whole. Like an archaeologist raking for buried treasure, I've combed through the provinces of counseling, spiritual discipline, inner healing, deliverance, addiction recovery—anything that would help me help others get better. The epiphany I had come to is this: Jesus has no intention of letting you become whole apart from his moment-to-moment presence and life within you.

Your brokenness and your sin are not something you overcome *so* that you can walk with God. They are the occasions for you to cry out for the life of God in you to rescue you. Not God outside you, up in the sky somewhere. Christ *in* you, your only hope of glory.

This is big, friend. Do you approach your spiritual life with the aim that it is Jesus-in-you that enables you to live? Or are you trying it in your own strength?

GRATITUDE AND AWE

"I'll lead them up and present them by
name to my Father and his Angels."
REVELATION 3:5 THE MESSAGE

A time will come to look back with your Lord over the story of your life. The whole idea of judgment has been terribly twisted by our enemy. How will this not be an utter horror? One evangelistic tract conveys that at some point shortly after your arrival in heaven the lights will dim and God will play the videotape of your entire life before the watching universe: every shameful act, every wicked thought. However, if there is "now no condemnation for those who are in Christ Jesus" (Romans 8:1), how is it possible there will be shame later? Would he truly strip his Beloved for the universe to gawk at you? Never.

God may choose to evaluate your life, but whatever memory of your past you have in heaven, know this: it'll only contribute to your joy. You'll read your story by the light of redemption and see how God has used both the good and the bad, the sorrow and the gladness for your welfare and his glory. With the assurance of total forgiveness you will be free to know yourself fully, walking again through the seasons of life to linger over the cherished moments and stand in awe at God's grace for the moments you have tried so hard to forget. Your gratitude and awe will swell into worship so strong and kind as to make you fully his own.

It is good to pause and ask ourselves on a regular basis, *What am I looking forward to in the coming kingdom?* What part of your story are you looking forward to being redeemed?

REASON AND YOUR HEART

"Walk out into the fields and look at the wildflowers. They never primp or shop, but have you ever seen color and design quite like it?"

MATTHEW 6:28 THE MESSAGE

It's easy to hide behind reason and logic. But friend, you must grow beyond mere reason, or you'll be stunted on your journey, certainly in the way you love. No one wants to be analyzed, and many relationships fail for the insistence of treating others as problems to be solved, rather than as hearts to be known and loved. Jesus could hold his own in any theological debate, but he's also an artist (the Creator of this world of beauty) and a poet, and a storyteller. When he says, "Consider the lilies of the field," he does not mean analyze them, but rather *behold* them, let their beauty speak. He appeals to their beauty to show us the love of God.

You're awakened when you see that beauty is far truer than the propositional and the analytical.

I came to Christ not because I was looking for a religion, but because I was looking for the truth. I yearned for an intellectually defensible case for Christianity, and I found it. My head was satisfied, but my heart yearned for something more. While I found logic in my theology, I was being wooed by beauty in the mountains and deserts, in literature and music. Why did they bring me closer to God than analysis? They speak to the heart.

What are you using these days (besides this devotional) to nourish and strengthen your faith?

REPENT IN THE MOMENT

A righteous man falls seven times, and rises again.
PROVERBS 24:16 NASB

Friend, set perfection aside. You are on your way to being transformed, but the moment you insist on total perfection you set yourself up for bitter disappointment. Sin shall not be your master, because you are under grace. Grace. So what do you do when you blow it?

Repent quickly. The sooner the better. For one thing, you don't want to lose your intimacy with God. For another, you know the enemy is going to jump all over you when you blow it, and you don't want to get hammered by that for days, weeks, months, years. You're after freedom; the longer you wait to repent, the deeper a hold the sin gets in you. Repent quickly: First, run to God. (*Father, forgive me.*) Next, renounce it quickly and summon your soul to the posture that you don't intend to repeat it. (*Father, I renounce [the envy, comment, lust, cowardice]. I renounce giving it a place in my heart and soul.*) Then cleanse and renew—you are blameless before God. (*Father, cleanse me with the blood of Jesus; wash me right here from all of this. I trust you and ask for your holiness here.*)

If you will practice this—instead of giving way to resignation—you are going to love the freedom it brings. Friends, holiness is yours, if you will ask for it, seek it, pursue it.

Jesus, I receive you as my life, and I receive all the work and triumph of your resurrection, through which you have conquered sin, death, and judgment. I have been raised with you to a new life, to live your life—dead to sin and alive to God. Thank you, Jesus.

INTENDED FOR PLEASURE

O Lord, we have waited for You eagerly; Your name,
even Your memory, is the desire of our souls.

ISAIAH 26:8 NASB

Isn't the promise of the return of the life you prize what you've been longing for? Healing for every brokenness, the lost found, and the weary given rest? Life to the limit is your promise.

Christianity takes desire seriously—far more seriously than the stoic or the mere hedonist. Christianity refuses to budge from the fact that man was made for pleasure, that his beginning and his end is a paradise, and that the goal of living is to find life. Jesus knows the dilemma of desire and he speaks to it in nearly everything he says.

When it comes to the moral question, it is neither simply yes or no to desire, but always what we *do* with our desire. Christianity recognizes that we have desire gone mad within us. But it does not seek to kill desire; rather it seeks the healing of desire, just as it seeks the healing of every other part of our human being.

God is realistic. He also knows that happiness is fragile and rests upon a foundation greater than happiness. All the Christian disciplines were formulated at one time or another in an attempt to heal desire's waywardness, and so by means of obedience, bring us home to bliss. Dear friend, the goal of morality is not morality—it is ecstasy. *You* are intended for pleasure!

Just pause and let this sink in: the goal of morality is not morality—it is ecstasy. Your soul is made for pleasure. Where are you taking that need these days?

A LITTLE BIT OF CLARITY

*The unfolding of your words gives light; it
gives understanding to the simple.*

PSALM 119:130

What are you perfectly clear on these days? Your life? Why have things gone the way they have, and where's God in all that? Do you know what you ought to do next, with confidence that it'll work out? Oh, to wake each morning knowing exactly who you are and where God is taking you. It's awesome when you do see. But more often life seems more like driving along with a dirty windshield—you can sort of make out the shapes ahead. . . .

Wouldn't a little bit of clarity go a long way right now?

Let's start with why life is so dang *hard*. You try to lose a little weight, but it never seems to happen. You think of making a shift in your career, maybe even serving God. Perhaps you do make the jump, but it didn't pan out the way you thought. Yes, you have your faith. But even there—maybe *especially* there—it all seems to fall rather short of the promise.

Your heart is a treasure of the kingdom. God wants to shine his light and bring clarity to your soul as he heals and restores what has been stolen from you.

Wouldn't a little bit of clarity go a long way right now? Write some things down that you are seeking God for clarity in. Then ask for his light to shine in these very places.

A HEALED HEART

*He has sent me to comfort the brokenhearted
and to proclaim that captives will be
released and prisoners will be freed.*

ISAIAH 61:1 NLT

I expect that at one time or another you've used the phrase, "Well, part of me wants to, and another part of me doesn't." You're familiar with the feeling of being pulled in different directions. Friend, it's a manifestation from wounds—in this fallen world, none of us are wholehearted.

Certainly we've seen that the mind and will can be broken. This treasure called your heart can also be broken, *has* been broken, and now lies in pieces. When it comes to "habits" you cannot quit, anger that flies out of nowhere, fears you cannot overcome, or weaknesses you hate to admit—much of these come out of the broken places in your heart crying out for relief.

When Isaiah promised that the Messiah will come to heal the brokenhearted, he was not speaking poetically. The Hebrew is *leb shabar*—*leb* for heart, *shabar* for broken. Isaiah uses the word *shabar* to describe a bush whose "twigs are dry" and dead (27:11). God is literally saying, "Your heart is in many pieces. I want to heal it."

This is a new thought for many people. Did you know that your heart can be fragmented? Are you aware of feeling "divided" inside? God can heal our fragmentation, but first we must become aware of it. Are there situations that suddenly make you feel five or nine or sixteen again? Write down a few thoughts about it.

FULLY INTEGRATED

On that day the LORD their God will rescue his
people, just as a shepherd rescues his sheep. They
will sparkle in his land like jewels in a crown.
How wonderful and beautiful they will be!

ZECHARIAH 9:16–17 NLT

A good deal of research is coming forth to confirm that human beings are actually a collection of shattered "pieces." Every person carries within themselves a shattered personality. In other words, we are fragmented beings. You know the internal war this is describing.

Dear friend, it is the unhappiness and isolation of your inner parts that cause so much of the unrest, awkwardness, and sabotage in your life. James describes the poor souls who are "like a wave of the sea, blown and tossed by the wind. . . . Such a person is double-minded and unstable in all they do" (1:6, 8). The Greek here for "double-minded" is *dipsuchos*, which is better translated "two-souled" or "split-souled." Did you just feel that inner tremor? Something in you is responding to this even as you read it. We are all traumatized and fragmented; no one passes through this vale of tears without it.

And your Healer will make you whole again. The little boy or girl in you who has so long hidden in fear, the angry adolescent, the heartbroken man or woman—all of "you" will be brought home to you, a fully integrated human being filled with goodness and glory from head to toe.

UNDIVIDED HEART

*Teach me your way, LORD, that I may rely
on your faithfulness; give me an undivided
heart, that I may fear your name.*

PSALM 86:11

Your healing from brokenness is about fragmentation, or separation from yourself. The "undivided heart" is what you're after. Again, you begin by inviting Jesus in. Asking him to shine his light into the broken places. Sometimes he'll take you back to a memory. Sometimes he'll simply make you aware of a "young" place in your heart that needs his love and comfort. Keep inviting Christ in.

Jesus will often speak words of love or comfort to this specific broken young part of your heart. Sometimes he'll ask a question, like, *Why are you frightened?* Often he'll ask, *Will you let me come to you?* Remember, he waits for your permission to come and heal.

What you're praying toward in these cases of actual brokenness is integration—you want to be made whole again. As you invite Jesus to bind up your broken heart, often you simply feel his love and presence there in ways you've never felt before.

Lord Jesus, you are my Healer. Come into this broken place in me. Love me here, Lord. Comfort me here. I pray you would unite yourself to this fragmented place in me, and that you would make my heart whole here. Jesus will often speak words of love or comfort to this broken part of your heart. Just linger, and let him come.

HIS PRESENCE WITHIN YOU

God's love has been poured out into our hearts.
ROMANS 5:5

It's quite common for the older part of you to feel anger or shame about the younger "stuck" place of your brokenness. And therefore, it's common to express rejection toward this part of you. You need to renounce all self-rejection, for Jesus cannot heal while you're rejecting yourself there.

The enemy will often use places of brokenness as occasions to oppress you. It's common to find spiritual warfare in broken places, because the chasm in the heart and soul provides a place for the enemy to do his work. He is a divider, after all; his main work is to divide—man from God, man from one another, and man from himself. So as you seek integration, ask Jesus to bring his sword against the enemies that are oppressing the young places in you.

You can then ask Jesus to restore you in wholeheartedness, to heal up the brokenness and make you whole again, through his presence within you. We ask him to bring the young place into that wonderful home Jesus had made for himself in your heart (Ephesians 3:17). The young places of you feel safe with Jesus; it is a place filled with love. And in that place Jesus can bring healing about, either in that moment or over time.

We have found it helpful in inner healing prayer to ask, "How does older-you feel about younger-you?" Often older-us doesn't like younger-us; we may feel shame or contempt for our brokenness. It is important for your healing that older-you has compassion for younger-you. Can you offer that to yourself?

YOUR REDEMPTION

"He has sent me to proclaim that captives
will be released, that the blind will see, that
the oppressed will be set free, and that the
time of the LORD's favor has come."
LUKE 4:18–19 NLT

When the Bible tells us that Christ came to redeem mankind, it offers a whole lot more than forgiveness. To simply forgive a broken man is like telling someone running a marathon, "It's okay that you've broken your leg. I won't hold that against you. Now finish the race." That is cruel, to leave him disabled that way. No, there is much more to your redemption.

The Messiah will come, he says, to bind up and heal, to release and set free. Christ comes to restore and release you, your soul, the true you. This is *the* central passage in the entire Bible about Jesus, the one he chooses to quote about himself when he steps into the spotlight and announces his arrival. He is offering it to you. So take him at his word—ask him to release you from all bondage and captivity, as he promised to do.

But you can't do this at a distance; you can't ask Christ to come into your wound while you remain far from it. You have to go there with him. Will you?

Lord Jesus, I give my life to you—everything I am. I surrender myself to you utterly. Come and be my Healer. I give you my wounded heart.

MOMENTS OF SIGNIFICANCE

Today if you hear His voice, do not harden your hearts.

HEBREWS 4:7 NASB

God gives us dozens of encounters every day, opportunities to be honest about what motivates us. What we do with them is up to us.

This is how he honors us. When God created us, he gave us a will, and that beautiful and mysterious inner life called the soul. God steps back a bit to let us make our own decisions. These simple moments of decision are filled with significance. When I choose to avoid whatever it is God has brought up, something feels compromised. It is at least a refusal to mature. But it also feels like a refusal to step toward God. Thankfully, the opposite is true. When I choose to face the uncertain, admit the neglect, or enter into my fears, something in me grows up a little bit. I feel strengthened. The scales tip toward a closer walk with God.

Whatever else we do with these moments, there is no getting to it later or it will just simply go away. So how do we walk with God in the moment? We go with it. Now. As it is unfolding. That is the only way to have any real relationship with Jesus Christ. *Now* is the time, dear friend.

Life with God is in the "now." So—what has been happening this week that has upset you? Confused you? Thrown you? Rather than trying to get past it quickly, invite Christ into the emotion; invite him into the moment.

YOU NEED TO FORGIVE JESUS

*Restore to me the joy of your salvation and
grant me a willing spirit, to sustain me.*

PSALM 51:12

If you're holding something in your heart against Jesus, no amount of ignoring it is going to make it go away—the loss of someone you love, pain from your past, simply the way your life has turned out. In order to move forward, you're going to need to forgive Jesus.

"But Jesus doesn't need my forgiveness!" you protest. I didn't say he did. I said that *you* need to forgive Jesus. To be clear: to forgive a person, you pardon a wrong done to you; "forgiving" Jesus means to release the resentment you hold against him.

This comes *before* understanding. To see the world the way Jesus did—as a vicious battle with evil, against an enemy that has hated you—ushers understanding that will help you not to blame this stuff on God. But in your hurt, part of you believes Jesus could have done something about it *and didn't*. That's why you need to forgive him. You do this so that this part of you can receive his love.

Perhaps as part of the fruit of that restoration Jesus will be able to explain why things happened the way they did. But dear friend, you need Jesus far more than you need understanding. And so you forgive.

This has proven massively effective for many, many people. We feel abandoned by God in some part of our story; we may even feel betrayed. This is why we must forgive God from our hearts, in order to restore the relationship and receive healing here.

A GOD OF PROCESS

*We are His workmanship, created in Christ
Jesus for good works, which God prepared
beforehand so that we would walk in them.*

EPHESIANS 2:10 NASB

We don't know much about stages of development in our *instant* culture. Someone else makes your coffee. You don't have to wait to get in touch with someone—you can text them this moment. Most everything is available at your fingertips.

But God is a God of process. If you want an oak tree, he has you start with an acorn. If you want a healing, you must begin with the young place. God ordained the stages of your development and maturity. They are woven into the fabric of your being, just as the laws of nature are woven into the fabric of the earth. In fact, those who lived closer to the earth respected and embraced the stages for centuries upon centuries. You have known them as the ancient paths. Only recently has culture lost touch with them. In exchange for triple-venti nonfat sugar-free vanilla lattes. The result of having abandoned our ordained initiation is a world of broken-hearted souls.

But it doesn't have to be this way. You needn't wander in a fog. You don't have to live alone, striving, sulking, uncertain, angry. You don't have to figure life out for yourself. Your healing is also a process, and Jesus is with you every step. He always has been.

Process allows us to rest; "instant fix" creates enormous pressure. Have you been fighting the process nature of God's work in your life?

BODY, SOUL, AND SPIRIT

*"A body you can look at and touch. But the person who
takes shape within is formed by something you can't
see and touch—the Spirit—and becomes a living spirit."*

JOHN 3:5–6 THE MESSAGE

Allow me to offer this clarity: you have a body, a soul, and a spirit. Spirit, soul, and body; *pneuma, psuche, soma* in the Greek. Three clearly distinct realms of the human being.

Your spirit is the life breath of God within you, giving life to both body and soul. It is the life force of God within you, animating both body and soul. Your soul is comprised of a number of capacities, including heart, mind, and will. Your spirit is the sunshine; your soul the stained-glass window it shines through.

Your soul is actually a region of vast mystery and beauty, filled with memories and capacities far beyond the reckoning of the average person educated in the scientific era. Both the Old and New Testaments address the heart and soul as distinct entities. They are very real "things" and can be wounded deeply, as anyone who has been heartbroken can tell you. As your own soul will tell you, if you will but listen.

The glorious news is that God restores your soul; he will heal your broken heart: "The LORD is my shepherd. . . . He restores my soul" (Psalm 23:1, 3 NASB).

*Jesus—I need you to come and shepherd my soul. Lead me beside
still waters; make me lie down in green pastures. Restore my soul.
Restore my soul.*

GLORY RESTORED

*"Otherwise they might see with their eyes,
hear with their ears, understand with their
hearts and turn, and I would heal them."*

MATTHEW 13:15

And I would heal them." That's a different offer from: "And I would forgive them." It's a different offer from: "And I will give them a place in heaven." No, Jesus is offering *healing* to you. Look at what he does to people who are broken. How does he handle them? The blind are able to see like a hawk. The deaf are able to hear a pin drop. The lame do hurdles. The corroding skin of the leper is made new. They are, every last one of them, healed.

Now follow this closely: everything Jesus *did* was to illustrate what he was trying to *say. Here—look at this—this is what I'm offering to do for you. Not just for your body, but more important, for your soul. I can heal your heart. I can restore your soul.*

For some reason this has been lost in the recent offerings of the church. Perhaps it's pride, which has kept you from admitting that you are broken. Perhaps it is fear of getting your hopes up. Perhaps it's been the church's almost total focus on sin and the cross. But the Scripture is abundant and clear: Christ came not only to pardon you, but to heal you. He wants the glory restored.

Jesus can, and wants to, heal your heart. What does that rouse in you? Is it hope? Is it cynicism? Is it "I tried that—it doesn't work"? Take whatever your response is to God, tell him honestly. Then take a risk and ask him for the healing you would like to experience in your soul.

BREAK THE STRONGHOLD

Don't sin by letting anger control you.
EPHESIANS 4:26 NLT

Your strongholds are not always based in sin. Paul says, "In your anger do not sin," so note, anger does not equal sin. Anger can be a very appropriate reaction to life's injustices. However, failure to deal with that anger gives your enemy an opportunity to create places of bondage in your life. If you let the sun go down on these unresolved issues in your life—the wounds, the pain, and the sin that goes with them—it'll get messy down the road. A genuine pursuit of holiness requires you deal with them now.

If you struggle with something, there are probably agreements like *I'll never get free of this.* Those agreements serve as permission for the enemy to keep you in bondage. In addition, there are agreements with the sin itself: *I am filled with rage; I am a drunk.* Oh friend, don't make agreements with your sin. You're dead to sin and alive to God. You're forgiven and dearly loved.

You must break these agreements. Some will be obvious to you; others require the presence of the Holy Spirit to reveal them. Ask for revelation.

Pause, and ask God to reveal the agreements you have been making with the lies of your enemy. *Spirit of God, search me, know me, reveal to me the agreements I have been making.* As you become aware of those agreements, take the deliberate step to break them. *I break these agreements in the name of my Lord Jesus Christ. I break agreement with* [fill in the personal agreement here; renounce it in Jesus' name]. *Jesus—set me free in this very place.*

WHOLEHEARTED

*"Be glad and rejoice forever in what I
create; for behold, I create Jerusalem for
rejoicing and her people for gladness."*

ISAIAH 65:18 NASB

No more tears. No more pain. No more death. No longer any reason to mourn. At the renewal of all things, your heart is going to be free from grief. The joy of this will far surpass your physical relief. Think of it—if God would offer today to remove from you just one of your greatest sources of internal pain, what would you ask him to remove? And once it was gone, what would your joy be like?

Oh my goodness—I would be a happy maniac, dancing in my underwear like David before the ark, running about the neighborhood like Scrooge on Christmas morning, leaping housetop to housetop like the fiddler on the roof.

And if all your brokenness were finally and completely healed, and all your sin removed from you as far as the east is from the west—what will you no longer face? What will you finally be? How about your loved ones—what will they no longer wrestle with? What do they finally get to be?

You shall, finally and fully, be *wholehearted*—a wish so deep in my soul I can hardly speak it.

Friend, there is so much healing available now. But our total restoration will take place at the return of Christ. What are you looking forward to at the renewal of all things? Journal a little about that.

CULTIVATING CONNECTION

*He climbed the mountain so he could
be by himself and pray.*
MATTHEW 14:23 THE MESSAGE

The Christian faith is at its center an invitation to intimacy with God. He is an actual person, with a personality and a heart just like you, and just as in any other relationship it is the connection of these two hearts that matters above all else. This is where you separate from religion, and this is what will rescue you from slipping back into it. Friendship with God is the heartbeat of it all; nothing else can substitute (though many things will try).

So the question is, how do you cultivate friendship and intimacy with God? (Isn't that more refreshing than, "How do I get more serious about my religion?") Simply ask yourself, *What would I do to cultivate a deeper intimacy with my spouse or with my friends?* Time together, talking about life, processing both your inner and outer experiences—it seems painfully obvious but it honestly is that simple.

And always, always, always remember *you are at war.* You have an enemy; his attacks are the primary reason you can't "connect" with God. It's not you; it's not God. It's usually some sort of fog, accusation, dullness, or spiritual interference the enemy has brought in. Just as you will need to fight for your relationship with others, you'll need to rise up for your friendship with God.

How do you currently cultivate genuine friendship with God? A good place to start is with what you love to do. Have you connected with God in your love of that?

RELEASING YOUR HEART

Awake, O sleeper, rise up from the dead,
and Christ will give you light.
EPHESIANS 5:14 NLT

God gave you eyes so that you might see; he gave you ears that you might hear; he gave you will that you might choose; and he gave you a heart that you might *live*. The way you handle the heart is everything. A man must *know* he is powerful; he must *know* he has what it takes. A woman must *know* she is beautiful; she must *know* she is worth fighting for. "I don't know when I died," said a man. "But I feel like I'm just using up oxygen." I understand. Your heart may feel dead and gone, but it's there, just waiting to be released.

This isn't about the seven things you ought to do to be nicer. This is about the recovery and release of your heart, your passions, your true nature, which you have been given by God. It's an invitation to rush the fields and to leap from the falls. For to know who you truly are, to find a life worth living, to love deeply, you simply must get your heart back. You are already aware of what makes your heart come alive. Keep listening. Stay close to God, he will show you how to keep pursuing life. He wants it for you more than anything.

As you have discovered in this devotional, there are so many facets to our journey toward wholeheartedness. A man must *know* he is powerful; he must *know* he has what it takes. A woman must *know* she is beautiful; she must *know* she is worth fighting for. Do you? Where do you still need your Father to speak validation to you?

EXPERIENCING JESUS

Your flesh will be restored and you will be cleansed.
2 KINGS 5:10

As a wise sage was praying with me through some memories, I was reminded of the time in middle school when my first girlfriend broke my heart. These wounds can linger for a lifetime if you let them. I invited Jesus into the memory. I saw the girl and me, that fateful summer day in the living room. Then Jesus entered the room. He was quite stern with her, and it surprised me. *That mattered to you?* I wondered. *Very much,* he said. Then Jesus turned to me. I felt his love. I was able to let the heartbreak go. It was so healing.

Friend, to understand that Jesus is angry about what happened to you is very, very important in understanding his personality and for your healing. What I love about these encounters is that every time Jesus is so true to his real personality. Sometimes fierce, sometimes gentle, always generous, and often very playful.

Experiencing Jesus doesn't have to be dramatic. The "big-time" miracles actually account for a small portion of the three years he spent with the disciples. There was just a lot of ordinary living. Jesus comes here too. In a tulip, a smile, a cup of coffee, the night sky.

If you get rid of the limits and the religious constraints, you'll see him everywhere.

Jesus—I need to experience you in some fresh ways. Open my eyes to see how you are coming to me today, and this week.

NOVEMBER

YOU ARE PART OF AN EPIC

His heart was devoted to the ways of the LORD.

2 CHRONICLES 17:6

As God leads you through the healing of your broken heart, it's important to remember the Story written deep in your heart. Christianity, in its true form, tells that there is an Author to your story and that he is good, the essence of all that is good and beautiful and true, for he is the source of all these things. It tells that he has set your heart's longings within you, for he has made you to be this way. It warns that the truth is always in danger of being twisted and corrupted and stolen from you because there is a villain in your story who hates your heart and wants to destroy you. It calls you up into a Story that is truer and deeper than any other, and assures you that there you will find the meaning of your life.

You won't begin to understand your life, or what this so-called gospel is that Christianity speaks of, until you understand the Story in which you have found yourself. For when you were born, you were born into an Epic that has already been under way for quite some time. It is a Story of beauty and intimacy and adventure, a Story of danger and loss and heroism and betrayal.

Story is the language of the heart. Story is the shape of the reality in which you live. How have you been thinking about the Story this week? (Have you been thinking about it at all?) Go back to one of your favorite movies—watch it, and let it speak to you about the Story.

GOD'S POWER AND GOODNESS

*God made the two great lights, the greater
light to govern the day, and the lesser light to
govern the night; He made the stars also.*

GENESIS 1:16 NASB

God gave us *the sun*—this ought to answer any doubts about his power and goodness. All life on this planet derives its life from the sun. This is helping me realize God is powerful enough for whatever need I am praying over.

Now get this—there are roughly one hundred billion stars of all sizes in a galaxy, and one hundred billion galaxies in the universe. Which means there are approximately four hundred billion billion suns like ours that God has made. Meanwhile, God is providing the energy of those suns every moment. J. B. Phillips nailed the predicament of too many Christians: "Your God is too small."[10]

Words seem ridiculous at this point, but let us say clearly: power is not an issue with God. His resources are unlimited. Is this the Person you have in mind as you pray? You must turn your gaze in the direction of God, or something that reminds you just who he is.

Like four hundred billion billion suns, this was the very lesson Jesus was trying to get across to his disciples when he fed the five thousand with a few loaves and fishes (John 6:1–14). *His resources are unlimited.*

O Father, it's true—my view of you is too small. I pray for a revelation of your glory this week; I pray to see the vast resources of your power and goodness. Enlarge my view of you, God.

ORIENTATION

"Call on me in the day of trouble; I will deliver you."
PSALM 50:15

The deep, unshakable conviction that you were born into a great war is such a critical belief that you *must* lay hold of it. Otherwise, you'll have a very hard time maintaining a belief in the goodness of God. For the very simple reason that the horrors of the world and the assault on your own hopes and dreams will erode your faith. *Why isn't God answering? How could a kind and loving God allow . . .* fill in your story.

Now, I'd rather believe that life is about simple happiness under the tender care of Jesus. I'd much prefer to be lifted out of all trouble simply by praising God. But it simply isn't true, and the sooner you accept this life is far more like a D-Day landing than a church service, the sooner you'll be able to orient yourself, interpret your story, and learn how to navigate your way forward.

One of the great lies people cling to is that victory can come without a fight. "I have to fight for this?" Dear friend, this is not discouraging; it's *orienting*. Your Jesus has *already won*. He certainly followed through with everything he could give. Such honor. Bravery. Selflessness. What, after all, do you really believe this life is about?

Again, we come back to one of the critical truths about the Story we find ourselves in—we are at war with evil powers. So much of the life we seek—the joy, freedom, and restoration—are opposed not because God isn't coming through but because we live in a *war*. How has that factored into your thinking and prayers these days?

LIFE WILL WIN

If we are thrown into the blazing furnace, the God we serve is able to deliver us from it, and he will deliver us.

DANIEL 3:17

J esus' life was the life of perfected humanity. He was the best man who ever lived. His life was filled with joy. And it was also a life familiar with suffering. More than that—he learned obedience through what he suffered, was perfected through his suffering.

This is not a discouragement to pray. It is the higher context within which you pray. It is a higher end than trying to eliminate all suffering. Oh yes—sometimes that overcoming looks like a healing, and sometimes it looks like sorrow.

But dear friend—*life wins.* Sometimes now, especially if you will pray. But life wins fully, and very soon.

Just as you must fix your eyes on Jesus when you pray, you must also fix your heart on this one undeniable truth: life will win. When you know that unending joy is about to be yours, you live with such an unshakable confidence it will almost be a swagger. You can pray boldly, without fear, knowing that if this doesn't work now, it will work totally and completely very soon. You can have that kingdom attitude of Daniel's friends, who said, "God is able to deliver, and he will deliver. But if not . . ." You will not lose heart.

Write down a few key truths you need to remember each day, and tape them somewhere you will see them often. Like the bathroom mirror, or your computer. Perhaps it is "Life will win." Perhaps it is "God is so generous and good." Whatever you need, write it down!

I ACCEPT YOUR INVITATION, GOD

*Endure hardship as discipline; God is
treating you as his children.*
HEBREWS 12:7

Victorious moments where you are able to break free of shame and the false self are breakthrough moments that will give you courage to step forward and live from that place.

I think of stories where the hero needs to come to terms with his true identity. Peter didn't exactly have a high view of himself, but Jesus called him a rock. Their peers thought James and John were knuckleheads; Jesus called them Sons of Thunder. Dear friend, you must hear who you really are, receive genuine validation, so that you can tear up the other scripts you've been handed.

You reframe everything by one simple choice: *I am accepting God's invitation to become my truest self.* From there, you interpret jobs, money, relationships, flat tires, even your play time as the context of who you are becoming. You take an active role, asking your Father to speak to you, speak to your identity, and to validate you. You step into your fears and accept "hardship as discipline." As you do, an inner strength grows. Which will change everything when it comes to how you love God, yourself, and others.

Time to reevaluate this too—how are you viewing yourself these days? What identity are you currently living under? Write it down; name it, expose it, put it into words. Then ask your Father to come and speak what is true!

THE BEAUTY OF
WHAT YOU KNOW

The fear of the LORD is his treasure.
ISAIAH 33:6 NASB

For years, whenever I'd hear one of those dramatic stories reported by missionaries—the ones where Jesus appears in the midst of a kidnapping or attempted execution, blinds the group of rebels, and the would-be martyr walks out unharmed, then leads the village to Christ and becomes best friends with the witch-doctor—I would think to myself, *Geez. I'm such a loser when it comes to Jesus. I don't have anything like that to share. That's the real stuff. I'm playing with blocks on the kindergarten floor.* Something I haven't experienced eclipses *all* that I have known of God. Jesus is trying to prevent that plunge into diminishment by saying that your "old" treasures are treasures.

Don't let someone else's remarkable encounter with Jesus diminish the beauty of what you know of him. Hold fast to the treasures you have.

And, at the same time, be encouraged that you haven't experienced all there is with God. There is more. Much more. Those new possibilities are often opened to us through hearing the ways Jesus is working in other people's lives. Dear friend, let's discover more of Jesus, together.

No doubt you have at some time heard someone describing God in ways you haven't experienced him, but would love to. What new way would you love to know God? Experience him? Ask for it!

A QUESTION

Create in me a clean heart, O God.
P S A L M 5 1 : 1 0 N A S B

Right now, this week, what is it that you are repenting of? If you don't have a ready answer, how can you be taking holiness seriously? If your answer focuses on something external, what about the matters of the heart behind it? It's worth a pause.

I remember sitting in a church service several years ago while the congregation sang a worship song about holiness. It's a beautiful song that sings about having only holiness as our heart's desire. I found myself squirming; I just couldn't sing the song with integrity. My heart's *one* desire? I don't think it's even on the top-ten list. I want life; I want love; I want beauty, joy, laughter, friendship, adventure. Few understand the link between holiness and the life longed for.

I can't say it enough, dear friend: you were created for life, love, beauty, joy, laughter, friendship, adventure. These are the very things God wants for you. But you cannot find that life, let alone sustain it, until you're restored. The more you get to know Jesus, the more he changes your understanding of what holiness is all about. And the more you see him operate, the more you'll be captured by the beauty of his life.

So . . . what *are* you repenting of these days? If you don't have a ready answer, how can you be taking holiness seriously? If your answer focuses on something external, what about the matters of the heart behind it? It's worth a pause.

FORGIVENESS AND HEALING

The Spirit of the Sovereign LORD is on me, because
the LORD has anointed me to proclaim good news.

ISAIAH 61:1

J esus is not finished with you just because you're "forgiven." Not at all. Would a good father feel satisfied when his child is rescued from an accident, but left in the ICU? No, he wants healing as well. God has much more for you.

Of all the Scriptures Jesus could have chosen, he picked Isaiah 61 when he began his ministry here on earth and first publicly announced his mission. It must be important to him. What does it mean? It's supposed to be really good news, that's clear. It has something to do with healing hearts, setting someone free. Let me try and state it in more familiar words:

God has sent me on a mission. I have some great news for you. God has sent me to restore and release something. And that something is you. I am here to give you back your heart and set you free. I am furious at the enemy who did this to you, and I will fight against him. Let me comfort you. Dear one, I will bestow beauty upon you where you have known only devastation; joy in the places of your deep sorrow. And I will robe your heart in thankful praise in exchange for your resignation and despair.

Now that is an offer worth considering.

What if this offer is true? I mean, what if Jesus really could do this for your broken heart, your wounded soul? Ask Jesus, *Is this true for me? Would you do this for me?* He can, and he will . . . if you'll let him.

FILLED WITH HIS JOY

"Now I am coming to you. I told them many
things while I was with them in this world
so they would be filled with my joy."

JOHN 17:13 NLT

We don't like to think much about joy, because it can hurt to allow ourselves to feel how much we long for it. But friend, joy is the point. I know it is. God says, "The joy of the LORD is your strength" (Nehemiah 8:10 NASB). I think, *My strength? I don't even think of it as my occasional boost.* But yes, now that I give it some thought, I can see that when I've felt joy I've felt more alive than at any other time in my life. Pull up a memory of one of your best moments. The day at the beach. Your eighth birthday. Remember how you felt. Now think what life would be like if you felt like that on a regular basis. Maybe that's what being strengthened by joy feels like. It would be good.

What does Jesus have to say about joy?

"Until now you have not asked for anything in my name. Ask and you will receive, and your joy will be complete" (John 16:24). Your joy complete? The full measure of his joy? That's what Jesus wants for us? I'm almost stunned. Can you believe that it's come down to joy?

Joy is so beautiful, so powerful. Is there joy in your life these days? Thank God for it! Celebrate it! If there is no joy, then by all means ask for it! Father, Jesus, Holy Spirit—increase my joy! Give me your joy, Lord!

A WILL OF YOUR OWN

If you refuse to serve the LORD, then choose
today whom you will serve. . . . But as for me
and my family, we will serve the LORD.
JOSHUA 24:15 NLT

God enables you to love. He gives you the greatest treasure in all creation: a heart.

But just as you have lost your wonder at the world around you, you have forgotten what a treasure your heart is. All of the happiness you have ever known and all of the happiness you hope to find is unreachable without a heart. You could not live or love or laugh or cry had God not given you a heart.

And with that heart comes something that just staggers me. God gives you the freedom to reject him. He gives you a will of your own.

Good grief, *why?* He knows what free-willed creatures can do. He has already suffered one massive betrayal in the rebellion of the angels. He knows how we will use our freedom, what misery and suffering, what hell will be unleashed on earth because of our choices. *Why?* Is he out of his mind?

The answer is as simple and staggering as this: if you want a world where love is real, you must allow each person the freedom to choose.

We do forget what a treasure our hearts are. How are you taking care of your heart this week?

MAKE A DIFFERENCE

We who have run for our very lives to God have every
reason to grab the promised hope with both hands
and never let go. It's an unbreakable spiritual lifeline.
HEBREWS 6:18–19 THE MESSAGE

We need to embody God's love in the world today. The human race is not well; things fall apart. We must care for the planet and all creation; we must fight injustice. But we speak of that work so casually; we do not understand it can be the most demanding, heartbreaking work in the world. Those who serve at the front lines of social justice ministry have a tragically high burnout rate.

Without a glorious hope blazing in your heart, you will be crushed by the pain of the world. "If you read history," wrote C. S. Lewis, "you will find that the Christians who did most for the present world were precisely those who thought most of the next. It is since Christians have largely ceased to think of the other world that they have become so ineffective in this."[11]

If you really want to make a difference in the world, do exactly what the Scriptures command you to do—grab hold of the promised Renewal with both hands and make it your spiritual lifeline.

Most Christians have no solid grip at all on their future; they are fixated completely and entirely on the present moment. But we cannot live without a future. Begin to write down what you are looking for at the restoration of all things, in your life that never ends. You must have concrete hopes or they won't give you hope.

SOUL CARE

Let my soul be at rest again, for the
Lord has been good to me.
PSALM 116:7 NLT

When I'm in a heightened state of sensitivity, I can tell immediately what helps and what hurts my soul. It is very enlightening.

I've found there is a huge difference between relief and restoration; much of what provided me relief in the past (like TV) does not help with restoration. It helps to have perspective on what actually helps my soul grow strong, and what doesn't.

Helpful: Generous amounts of sunshine. Long walks. Swimming. Music. Water. Chocolate. Kindness. Compassion. Yard work. Building something. Beauty. Unhelpful: Television. Traffic. Draining people wanting to talk to me. The news. Social media.

"Soul care" is not a category for most people. They don't plan their week around it. Maybe it feels unnecessary; maybe it feels indulgent. But we are going to want our souls strong and ready for the days ahead, not weary and weak. So we must practice soul care. I for one am trying to make room for it as part of my "routine." It really is helping.

Ask Jesus, *What does soul care look like for me? What will draw my soul to restoration? What do I need to draw my soul nearer to you, God?*

RECOVERING THE ROMANCE

My beloved is mine, and I am his.
SONG OF SOLOMON 2:16 NASB

The sacred romance is a Love Story, but far older and much more reliable than matrimony. Rather it's the Story of how God has pursued you ever since you were a child. Oh friend, God cares about—even yearns for—the life of your heart. That your heart even matters to God is one of the greatest, most hopeful turns of faith that can come into your life.

You are in a process of restoration, at the center of which is a recovery of wholeheartedness.

I believe that sometimes God will invite you back into treasured memories and special places. And if it is by his invitation, you are safe to go there. He takes you back for several reasons—not only for the feast of memories that comes (some of which is needing to be healed), but also to reawaken sleeping places in your heart. Mostly I think he takes you back to show you as an adult all the ways he was wooing you in your childhood, even when you didn't know him at the time.

To be taken back into the memory of an ice cream shop, to a swing in your backyard, the experience can be almost like a waking dream where you revisit the best days of your childhood. When you go there with Jesus, you'll find there is much of the Romance in your story to be reclaimed.

This is a wonderful exercise: Write down a few things from your childhood that were precious memories to you. Ask God to show you how he was "romancing you" at that time.

FOLLOW HIM

*"Whoever serves me must follow me; and
where I am, my servant also will be."*

JOHN 12:26

Only Christianity can teach you to walk with God. But we forfeit that birthright when we take folks through a discipleship program whereby they master any number of Christian precepts, and miss the very thing for which they were created: intimacy with God. Knowing God. After all—aren't we "followers of Christ"? Then by all means, let's actually *follow* him. Not ideas about him. Not just his principles. Him. Now. Today.

You might recall the old proverb: "Give a man a fish and you feed him for a day; teach a man to fish and you feed him for a lifetime." The same holds true here. Teach a man a rule and you help him solve a problem; teach a man to walk with God and you help him solve the rest of his life. Truth be told, you couldn't master enough principles to see you safely through your story. There are too many surprises. Things are hard at work—is it time to make a move? What *has* God called you to do with your life? What does the future hold for you—and how should you respond?

Only by walking with God can you hope to find the path that leads to life. *That* is what it means to be a disciple.

Jesus—how are you leading me this week? How are you shepherding me? Open my eyes to see; open my ears to hear. Help me be a better follower in the daily things of my life.

NOTHING IS LOST

*You will know that your tent is secure . . . you
will visit your abode and fear no loss.*

JOB 5:24 NASB

You may have experienced revelation when the Creator of your mind and soul gives a sweeping understanding, as if by transfusion. As was my experience when my youngest graduated from high school—my heart cried out to God: *How is everything not just loss?* In that moment, Jesus showed me something like this:

When the kingdom comes, my dear, heartbroken friend, nothing that was precious to you in this life will be lost. No memory, no event, none of your story is lost. How could it be lost? It is all held safe in the heart of the infinite God, who encompasses all things. Held safe outside of time in the treasuries of the kingdom, which transcends yet honors all time. This will all be given back to you at the Restoration, just as surely as your sons will come back to you. Nothing is lost.

Nothing is lost?! The effect of this reality is nearly instantaneous. I went from a desolate parent saying good-bye—not just to our last child but to an entire era—to becoming the beloved child given a sneak preview into the Christmas morning that will come upon all the earth.

Dear friend, *nothing is lost.*

Just pause, and let this be true. Say it over and over to yourself: *Nothing is lost. Nothing will be lost.* What does it do for your soul?

TREASURE CHESTS

*Your heart will throb and swell with joy; the
wealth on the seas will be brought to you.*

ISAIAH 60:5

Oh friend, you have suffered very specific wrongs over the course of your life; God is fully aware of all of them. Jesus your King will make sure it's addressed with very specific reparations; he's furious about what you've endured and *will* make it right.

Imagine—after your enemies are judged and banished, many great treasure chests are set before you. Jesus tells you to open them, saying, *These are the gifts I meant for you in your former life but were stolen. I return them now, with interest.* Imagine what fills those chests. Laughter comes from one, for so much of what has been lost are memories and joy.

Then you turn to others and ask, "And what are these chests, Lord?" *These are the rewards for your choices, your victories, your perseverance, and your service.*

Those treasure chests are yours, friend; their contents will thrill your heart and redeem so much of what you have endured here. Justice shall be yours. Wrongs will be avenged, hurts shall be healed, and all that was stolen from you in this life recompensed far beyond your wildest hopes. You will open those chests, look, and be radiant. Your heart will throb and swell with joy.

What fills your treasure chest? What has been lost to you that you long to be restored? What is the hope in your treasure chest? Journal these thoughts.

SEIZE HIS HOPE

[Cast] all your anxiety on Him,
because He cares for you.

1 PETER 5:7 NASB

You need to make a conscious choice to seize hope of God's promise of renewal. To start, ask yourself, *What have I done with my kingdom heart? Where am I currently taking it?* Do you believe, by now, that God made your heart for joy? So where is your hope for joy set right now? You have a heart for redemption—where are you taking your heart for redemption these days? You ache for restoration, yours and those you love—where is your hope for restoration these days?

You need to begin to make conscious, deliberate decisions to give your heart to the return of Jesus and the renewal of all things. Every time you find yourself getting anxious about an uncertain hope, stop and pray, *Jesus, I give my hope to your true and certain return, and the renewal of all things.* Every time disappointment strikes again, you can pray, *Jesus, I give my heart to your kingdom; I am made for your kingdom and nothing else will do.* When you wake in the morning and all your hopes and fears rush at you; when you come home at night beat up from another long day; when you hear of someone else's great joy and something envious rises in you—make the conscious decision to give your heart to the return of Christ and the restoration of all things.

This is worth an honest moment: Where *is* your hope for joy set right now? Where are you taking your heart for redemption these days? Where is your hope for restoration these days?

FULLY ALIVE

"I am the bread of life."

JOHN 6:48

"The glory of God is man fully alive" (Saint Irenaeus). When I first stumbled across this quote, my initial reaction was . . . *You're kidding me. Really?* Is that what you've been told? That the purpose of God—the very thing he's staked his reputation on—is your coming fully alive? It made me wonder, *What are God's intentions toward me?*

Yes, we've been told any number of times that we matter to God, and there are some pretty glowing promises given in Scripture along those lines. But on the other hand, the days of our lives have a way of casting a rather long shadow over our hearts. I read the quote again, "The glory of God is man fully alive," and something began to stir in me. *Could it be?*

I turned to the New Testament to read what Jesus said he offers. "I have come that [you] might have life, and have it to the full" (John 10:10). Now, that's different than saying, "I have come to forgive you. Period." Forgiveness is awesome, but Jesus says here he came to give us *life*. The more I looked, the more this whole theme of life jumped off the pages. I mean, it's *everywhere*.

Do you believe that the glory of God is people coming truly alive?

CHOOSE THE KINGDOM

"Seek the Kingdom of God above all else, and live righteously, and he will give you everything you need."
MATTHEW 6:33 NLT

Dear friend, you have suffered so many losses already; you hate to admit it, but more will come. But with the hope of the renewal of all things, you can truthfully say to yourself, *Nothing is truly lost.*

Friend, it's as simple as this: if you do not give your heart over to the renewal of all things, you will take your kingdom heart to something in this world. You'll do compulsive things, like collecting way too many shoes. You'll be tempted into far darker things. It's inevitable.

But if you choose the kingdom, if you deliberately give your heart to the renewal of all things, you'll notice the effects immediately. Pressure will be lifted off your current hopes; when things don't go well, you'll find yourself less angry, less dejected. As your heart and soul become anchored in the Renewal, you'll find yourself freer to risk. You can love people, because God will do everything in his power to make sure you will not lose them; the good-byes of his children are only momentary. You can love beautiful places and cultures and things like wilderness because even though it looks like they may be vanishing, they will be restored.

For nothing is lost. He renews all things.

Because you do have the hope of the renewal of all things, for what loss do you need to tell yourself, *This is going to come back to me*?

STONES OF REMEMBRANCE

*Samuel took a stone and set it between Mizpah
and Shen, and named it Ebenezer, saying,
"Thus far the LORD has helped us."*

1 SAMUEL 7:12 NASB

Can you name five beautiful truths that came to you last year? Dear friend, forgetfulness is a spiritual pandemic ravaging humanity. That heart-sickness, where nothing really matters anymore—that's the daily condition for most of the human race. From there, it's an easy slide into resignation, then addiction, the various medications of choice. And that is why God strikes the gong of "remember" so often in Scripture.

Samuel set up standing stones so that every time the Israelites passed them, they would remember what God had done, remember how utterly faithful he is. It does the heart good to remember. Because we all too easily forget.

I have a number of reminders set where I most spend time with God: A bear tooth found on a backpacking trip I don't want to forget. A granite rock from the top of the Grand Teton. A stone from a failed attempt to climb the north buttress of Mount Sneffels. And when I begin a new journal, I copy over critical words I must remember. Because I forget even the most precious things.

Where are your stones of remembrance? Where do you keep all those words that once meant so much to you—the clarity you received on your identity? The counsel you know will save your life if you follow it? The precious truths you know of God? If you don't have a place you record it, start a journal now!

YOU TOO SHALL LIVE

Christ has been raised from the dead. He is the
first of a great harvest of all who have died.

1 CORINTHIANS 15:20 NLT

God knew what he was doing from the very beginning. He decided from the outset to shape the lives of those who love him along the same lines as the life of his Son.

So you too shall live and never die. Creation will be restored, and you will be restored. And we shall share it together. "Today," Jesus said to the thief on the cross, "you will be with me in paradise" (Luke 23:43). Imagine that. Imagine being reunited with the ones you love, and with all the great and noble hearts of this Story, in paradise.

You will walk with God in the Garden in the cool of the day. You will see our Jesus face-to-face. You will hear him laugh. All that has ever stood between us will be swept away, and our hearts will be released to real loving. It begins with a great party, what the Scriptures call the "wedding feast of the Lamb" (Revelation 19:9 NLT).

You'll raise a glass with Adam and Eve, with your grandmother and your grandson. Imagine the stories you'll hear. All the questions that shall finally have answers. And the answers won't be one-word answers, but story after story, a feast of wonder and laughter and gladness.

Just soak that picture in. Just give this a few precious moments of your time. Reread this entry; read it aloud to yourself. Your heart needs this more than you know.

HIS FRIEND OF THE DEEPEST SORT

"The Son of Man came not to be served but to serve others and to give his life as a ransom for many."
MATTHEW 20:28 NLT

God created us in freedom to be his intimate allies, and he will not give up on you. He seeks you still. Not religion. Not good church people. A lover. A friend of the deepest sort.

Yours is the most beautiful of all love stories. However, have you noticed that in the great stories the hero must often die to win the freedom of his Beloved? William Wallace's death breaks the grip of darkness over Scotland. Aslan dies upon the stone table for the traitor Edmund and for all Narnia. Maximus dies in the arena to win the freedom of his friends and all Rome. These are pictures of a greater sacrifice.

Remember, God warned us back in the Garden that the price of mistrust and disobedience would be death. Not just a physical death, but a *spiritual* death—to be separated from God and life and all the beauty, intimacy, and adventure forever. Through an act of your own free will, you became the hostage of the kingdom of darkness and death. The only way out is ransom.

The coming of Jesus of Nazareth was like the opening scenes of *Saving Private Ryan*. A great invasion, a daring raid into enemy territory, to save the free world, but mostly to save you.

O Jesus—thank you for everything you did to ransom me. Thank you for giving your life for me.

PURE GIFT

The heavens proclaim the glory of God.
The skies display his craftsmanship.

PSALM 19:1 NLT

God seems to be rather enamored with beauty, and I want to speak of beauty's healing power, of how it comforts and soothes, and how it moves and inspires. All that sounds ridiculous. You know your own experiences of beauty. Let me call upon them then. Think of your favorite music, or tapestry, or landscape. "We've had a couple of inspiring sunsets this week." A dear friend told me: "It was as if the seams of our atmosphere split for a bit of heaven to plunge into the sea. Simultaneously I wanted to kneel and weep." Yes—that's it. All I want to do is validate those irreplaceable moments, lift any obstacle you may have to filling your life with greater and greater amounts of beauty.

We need not fear indulging here. The experience of beauty is unique to all the other pleasures in this: there is no possessive quality to it. Just because you love the landscape doesn't mean you have to acquire the real estate. Simply to behold the flower is enough; there is nothing in me that wants to consume it. Beauty is the closest thing we have to fullness without possessing on this side of eternity. It heralds the Great Restoration. Perhaps that is why it is so healing—beauty is pure gift. It helps us in our letting go.

The reason I keep returning to beauty in this devotional is for two reasons: 1) we need it far more than we think and 2) very few people seek it out on a regular basis. The best thing you can do this week is get outside; spend twenty minutes outside. Nature heals.

THE SOURCE OF BEAUTY

*You have bedded me down in lush meadows, you find
me quiet pools to drink from. True to your word, you let
me catch my breath and send me in the right direction.*

PSALM 23:2–3 THE MESSAGE

It had been one of those days when everything seems to go sideways from the moment it started. By the time it ended, I was fried. After dinner, I went out on the porch. I knew I needed rescue and nature was my nearest hope.

It was a beautiful evening and I immediately felt the rescue enter my soul and begin its gentle work. I let out a few deep sighs, breathing in the Spirit of God, and found myself letting go of the mess. My heart surfaced, as it often does when I'm in nature, allowing beauty to have its effect on me.

That's when the carnival started. *You oughta go find some cookies,* went the voice, and the carnival of desire started jockeying for my attention. Two kingdoms vying for my soul: The carnival was offering relief. Beauty was offering restoration. They are leagues apart. Relief is momentary sedation. Most turn there when what you really need is *restoration.* Beauty heals, offers restoration. You *need* its healing power. The world you live in fries the soul on a daily basis.

So you must turn to the true Source of beauty, the Maker of all that is beautiful, and ask for his love to come and bring restoration. Much more healing than mere relief.

*Jesus, like David in the Psalms I ask you for your beauty. I pray your
beauty would fill my soul.*

IF ONLY . . .

*You can be sure that God will take care of
everything you need, his generosity exceeding
even yours in the glory that pours from Jesus.*
PHILIPPIANS 4:19–20 THE MESSAGE

As I was praying about my disappointments, something lingered beneath the surface. I was coming to believe that God's love and God's life are not enough—a very subtle and deadly shift that opens the door to despair and a host of other enemies. Isn't that what Adam and Eve were seduced into believing—that God was not enough? He had given them so much, but all they could see was the one thing they *didn't* have. So they reached for it.

What was so compelling that Adam and Eve could turn from the living God to reach for the one missing thing? I think I'm beginning to understand. You start out longing for something, and the more you come to believe it's what you *need* to be happy, the more you obsess about it. The prize swells far beyond its meaning and takes on mythic proportions. You're certain life will come together once you achieve it. You think, *If only I was married. If only I was rich. If only I had* _____ (fill in the blank). Everything else pales in comparison. Even God.

Friend, I'm not minimizing the sorrow of your disappointments. The ache is real. But the ache can swell beyond its nature. The only thing you truly need is God and the life he gives you.

Jesus, I break the agreement that I need _____. *I give that place in my heart back to you. Jesus, come. Fill me with your love and your life.*

GOD RESTORES

See, the former things have taken
place, and new things I declare.
ISAIAH 42:9

When Jesus touched the blind, all the beauty of the world opened before them. When he touched the deaf, they heard laughter. He touched the lame, and they began to dance. And he called the dead back to *life* and gave them to their families.

Wherever humanity was broken, Jesus restored it. These are illustrations of the coming of the kingdom where God *restores* the world he made.

God has been whispering this secret to you through creation itself, every year, at springtime, ever since we left the Garden. After months of winter, I long for the return of summer. Sunshine, warmth, color, and the long days of adventure. Isn't this what we most deeply long for? To leave the winter of the world behind?

If you listen, you'll discover something of tremendous joy and wonder. The restoration of the world played out before you each spring and summer is *precisely* what God is promising us about our lives. Every miracle Jesus ever did was pointing to this Restoration, the day he makes all things new.

Just like the theme of beauty, I am repeating the truths about your glorious future because most people have no grasp—not really—on the future. You need to keep coming back to this. Very soon now God is going to restore the world he made, and you with it. What fun are you looking forward to having?

REDEMPTION, NOT DESTRUCTION

"Behold, I am making all things new."
REVELATION 21:5 NASB

The renewal of everything honestly seems too good to be true. You, the survivor of the wreckage of Eden, have grown so accustomed to living on the faintest traces of happiness and restoration, you must take this proclamation in carefully.

But friend, God promises to make current things new—as opposed to making *all new things*. God is very careful about what he says. It's especially touching that immediately after God adds, "Write this down, because it is true." Perhaps John the Seer was obviously dumbstruck on this point (wouldn't you be?) and needed to be assured by God, *Yes—this is what I mean*.

Many people have the vague but ominous idea that God destroys the current reality and creates a new "heavenly" one. But that's not what Scripture actually says. Paul teaches us that creation—meaning the earth and the animal kingdom—longs for the day of its redemption, when it will be set "into the freedom of the glory of the children of God" (Romans 8:21 NASB). Clearly that does not imply destruction; far from it.

There are glorious times ahead, when all things are made new.

Father God, thank you for the joyful day that is on the horizon, when all of your creation will be released and reunited in the full glory that you created it to have. Holy Spirit, reveal the deep truth of this to my spirit and my soul.

JESUS IS THE FORERUNNER

They knew it was the Lord. Jesus came, took the bread
and gave it to them, and did the same with the fish.
JOHN 21:12–13

Jesus Christ is the forerunner for the Great Renewal, "the beginning and the firstborn from among the dead" (Colossians 1:18). He died, as everyone has and will. But on the third day he was raised to life, leaving his grave clothes folded neatly in the tomb. (A very touching detail, I might add, as if to say, "And that's that," like a man putting away his flannel pajamas now that winter is past.) Jesus walked out of the grave radiantly alive, restored, and everyone recognized him. The "new" Jesus is not someone or something else now; he is the Jesus they loved and knew. He walked with them, had meals with them—just like before. The most striking thing about the post-resurrection activities of Jesus is that they were so remarkably *ordinary.*

Jesus' restored life is surprisingly like his "former" life. As will be the great feast (do you realize you *eat* in the life to come?!). The Great Renewal rescues you from all the vague, ethereal, unimaginable visions you've been given of an eternal life Somewhere Up Above. It is as real as the air you breathe.

We are trying to take hold of hope. How is your hope these days? Why?

RESTORATION OF EVERYTHING

*"Truly I tell you, at the renewal of all things, when
the Son of Man sits on his glorious throne. . . .
Everyone who has left houses or brothers or sisters
or father or mother or wife or children or fields for
my sake will receive a hundred times as much."*

MATTHEW 19:28–29

When Jesus speaks of the Restoration, he does so in very tangible terms, pointing to the recovery of normal things like houses and lands.

There is no bait and switch here. The renewal of all things simply means that the earth you love—all your special places and treasured memories—is restored and renewed and given back to you. Forever. Nobody seems to have heard this or paid much attention to it, because, for one thing, nobody I know is fantasizing about it. When was the last time you eavesdropped on a conversation at Starbucks about the restoration of all things? And for another thing, everybody I talk to still has these anemic, wispy views of heaven, as a place up there somewhere, where we go to attend the eternal-worship-service-in-the-sky.

Meanwhile you fantasize about that boat you'd love to get or the trip to Italy, the chocolate éclair. Of course you do, dear friend—you are made for utter happiness.

What is your heart fantasizing about these days? Be honest. Can you see your longing for Eden-restored in those fantasies?

BEYOND YOUR
WILDEST DREAMS

"My grace is sufficient for you."
2 CORINTHIANS 12:9 NASB

There is only the kingdom, friend. Everything else will slip through your fingers, no matter how strong your grasp. Why do you fight this hope? You nod in appreciation but ask it to stay outside your yard. Pascal understood: "Nothing is so important to man as his own state, nothing is so formidable to him as eternity; and thus it is not natural that there should be men indifferent to the loss of their existence, and to the perils of everlasting suffering. They are quite different with regard to all other things."[12]

What is this dark enchantment that keeps the human race from facing the inevitable? Maturity means living without denial. But you are grasping at every possible means to avoid the inevitable. You give your hopes to all sorts of kingdom counterfeits and substitutes; you give your heart over to mere morsels. You mistake the promise of the kingdom for the reality and give your being over to its shadow.

But when you finally accept the truth that you will lose everything one way or another, utterly, irrevocably, in this life—then the Restoration is hope beyond your wildest dreams.

I don't mean to be unkind, but you do need to be honest about your losses—both those you have suffered, and those that are coming. What exactly in your life can you control? Be perfectly frank about that.

DECEMBER

THAT WILD HOPE

"Your kingdom come, your will be done,
on earth as it is in heaven."
MATTHEW 6:10

You have been looking for the kingdom all your life. When you were a child, you searched for it in ponds and cornfields, attics and bedroom forts you'd make with blankets. You "found" it in fairy tales and your favorite stories. You hear a certain song or piece of music, and it brings you to tears because it is haunting you with the kingdom. All your special places or those you dream of going—the longing you have for them is not because the kingdom is there, but rather because it is calling to you through that place, the aromas, the way you feel when you are there.

God knew he had to woo your heart forward into the Restoration, so he wove the promise of it into the earth. Now you understand why that promise fits perfectly with a wild hope deep within your heart, a hope you hardly dare to name. As you live forward from here, you can now interpret the promise rightly; you can embrace it for you know what it is. These glimpses can help fill the treasury of your imagination.

Browse through some magazines or any of those photo websites. Certain pictures and places will stir your heart. Now you know— they are telling you about the restored earth and the restored you in that new earth.

RECOVERING DESIRE

"What do you want me to do for you?" Jesus asked him.
MARK 10:51

Recovering your true heart's desire may involve facing some deep disappointment. Undoubtedly, it will require painful self-examination. But you do not need to fear what you will find.

Many committed Christians are wary about getting in touch with their desires, not because they want to settle for less, but because they fear that they'll discover some dark hunger lurking in their hearts. The father of lies takes many people out of the battle and ends their journey by keeping them in the shallows of their desire, tossing them a bone of pleasure, thus convincing them that they are satisfied. However, once you begin to move from that place, his strategy changes. He threatens you about going into the deep waters by telling you that your core desires are evil.

Yes, you still struggle with a tendency to kill desire or give your heart over to false desires. But that is not who and what you truly are. If you really believe the new covenant, you'll be able to embrace your desire. Jesus asks you a simple question: *What do you want?* Don't minimize it; don't try to make sure it sounds spiritual; don't worry about whether you can obtain it. Just stay there until you begin to get an answer. This is the way you keep current with your heart.

This would be a good thing to journal about: *What do you want these days?* Don't minimize it; don't try to make it sound spiritual; don't worry about whether you can obtain it. Just stay there until you begin to get an answer.

WORTHY!

Worthy is the Lamb who was slaughtered—
to receive power and riches and wisdom and
strength and honor and glory and blessing.

R E V E L A T I O N   5 : 1 2   N L T

Pilate dares to ask Jesus, "What is truth?" Jesus doesn't even bother answering. You know how the Story goes—though Jesus could call down more than sixty thousand angels to prevent it, he lets the people kill him, and pardons them beforehand for doing it. Because of his extraordinary humility, no one seems to fully grasp just who this is. But nature knows, and cannot bear it—the earth convulses; the sun hides his face. It is only after the resurrection that the full reality begins to dawn on mankind. If it has even dawned on us yet.

And then there comes the touching humility of keeping the scars of those wounds—forever. You'll see them, soon, get to touch them for yourself. Jesus wears them proudly now.

I think three years of this kind of humble generosity and patience is pretty dang impressive. But Jesus has kept right on at it—for two thousand years. Teaching you, including you in the mission, sharing in the glory, being playful, being honest, helping you along. No wonder when he steps into the heavens to accept the throne the cry goes up, "Worthy! Worthy! Worthy! Make him king!"

We have hardly touched on worship in this devotional. But worship is so important for the soul. Find some songs you love, and just tell Jesus he is worthy!

MADE PERFECT

Just as we are now like the earthly man, we
will someday be like the heavenly man.
1 CORINTHIANS 15:49 NLT

You'll be made perfect. Finally, the totality of your being will be saturated only with goodness. Think of all that you're not going to have to wrestle with anymore. The fear that has been your lifelong battle, the anger, the compulsions. No more internal civil wars; no doubt, no lust, no regret; no shame. What has plagued you these last many years? What has plagued you all your life? Your Healer will personally lift it from your shoulders.

What tender intimacy is foretold when you're promised that your loving Father will wipe every tear from your eyes *personally*— not only tears of sorrow, but all the tears of shame, guilt, and remorse. That moment alone will make the whole journey worth it.

Yet there's more. You will be free, alive, whole, young, valiant. You'll have the character, the internal holiness, of Jesus himself.

You'll finally be everything you've ever longed to be. Not only that—it can never be taken from you again. "Eternal" life means life unending, life that never dims nor fades away. You'll be in your glory to live as you were meant to live and take on the kingdom assignments God has for you.

Again, it is so good for our hearts and souls just to linger a moment with these beautiful promises. Think of all that you're not going to have to wrestle with anymore. Let the relief of it lift your heart today.

EARTH'S HEALING

Then the angel showed me a river with the water of life,
clear as crystal, flowing from the throne of God and of
the Lamb. It flowed down the center of the main street.
On each side of the river grew a tree of life, bearing
twelve crops of fruit, with a fresh crop each month.
The leaves were used for medicine to heal the nations.

REVELATION 22:1–2 NLT

I believe your healing brings about something of the healing of the earth, and I'm certain the healed earth helps to usher in your healing.

Your enemy is the great divider. His most poisonous work takes place at the level of fragmentation, dividing families, churches, and fomenting racial hatred. He uses pain and suffering to create deep divisions within your being. He traumatizes human beings, then separates them from the earth that could bring about their healing. Your life has become cut off from the Garden you were meant to flourish in. Nature heals. God has ordained that in the new earth it is *river* water that brings you life and *leaves* that are used for healing.

You will hear nature in full chorus. It will mingle with the laughter, music, and aromas of the feast itself, and you'll drink it all in, practically swimming in the healing powers of creation, feeling Life permeate every last corner of your being.

What parts of nature do you love? Is it the beach? Your garden? Songbirds? Horses? Let your imagination think about what they will be for you in the next chapter of our Story!

EVIL DEFEATED

"All mankind will know that I, the LORD,
am your Savior, your Redeemer."
ISAIAH 49:26

Once upon a time the earth was whole and beautiful, shimmering like an emerald, filled with glory, bursting with *anticipation*. Such wonders waiting to be unveiled, such adventures waiting to be yours. Creation was like a fairy tale, a great legend—only true.

Once upon a time we were whole and beautiful too, glorious, striding through the Garden like the sons and daughters of God. We were holy and powerful; we ruled the earth and animal kingdom with loving-kindness.

But Eden was vulnerable; something dark slithered in the shadows. Something most foul and sinister. Banished from heaven, Satan and his fallen warriors came seeking revenge.

If the coming Restoration is to be fulfilled on the earth and in your life, Satan and his armies must be destroyed. He must never be allowed in again.

You are letting the great stories awaken your imagination to the coming kingdom, fill your heart with brilliant images and hopeful expectation. Seize the moment crucial to the climax of every story and the redemption you long to see: that glorious moment when evil is defeated.

Back to the movies you love—you should go watch the scene again when the enemy is defeated, and let it remind you of the day your true enemy is cast down. Forever.

YOU LONG FOR THE DAY

*Hallelujah! Salvation and glory and power belong
to our God, for true and just are his judgments.*

REVELATION 19:1–2

Evil judged and utterly destroyed. Forever and ever. Not just in the fairy tale, but in *your* story. Satan, his armies, and *every* form of evil are destroyed with a punishment that never ends.

What will it be like to no longer be assaulted? To look in the mirror and hear no accusing thoughts or voices? To be completely free of all temptation and the sabotage of your character—not because you are successfully resisting it in a moment of great resolve, but because it no longer exists? Imagine having the dark clouds lifted between you and your beloved Jesus, that veil that clouds your relationship with him. Imagine when all the physical affliction, emotional torment, abuse—all the evil in this world has vanished.

Oh, the joy you'll experience when you get to watch with your own eyes the enemy brought down for good, cast into his eternal torment! What hope rises at the thought of a world where the enemy no longer gets to do what he does? To see your loved ones released from their lifelong battles? To be released from your own lifelong battles? The kingdom of death and darkness is forever destroyed.

You long for this day, and you long for it in very particular ways. Someday, it will come.

Think of it—what evils will you no longer have to live with personally? What will this moment mean for you?

ENFORCE LOVE

*Because of his great love for us, God, who is
rich in mercy, made us alive with Christ.*
EPHESIANS 2:4–5

It's important to grasp what's taking place in the world, so you know how to live and how to respond. Hatred has become the new "spirit of the age"; the mounting tensions in this country are symptoms of a much deeper reality. The more you understand the essence of human nature and human conflict, the more you understand what Jesus was pointing to.

When sins rages, when cruelty, selfishness, and hatred rule the day, love is hard to cultivate—even in the best of us. Never before has love been more important to cling to, to pray, to invoke. You are going to need to be vigilant—no little grievances, no offense, no revenge. Jesus will keep bringing you back to love, to pray love, to enforce love. Forgiveness, mercy, overlooking offenses, breaking any agreement with violation, hatred, or violence.

God is love, and as you call down love you call down the heart of God himself, and you call down the power of his kingdom.

Jesus, I love you. I turn my heart toward you and receive your love. I choose love and align myself with love and command the love of God to flow through my life.

YOUR TRUE GLORY

*Anyone who belongs to Christ has become a new
person. The old life is gone; a new life has begun!*
2 CORINTHIANS 5:17 NLT

We haven't yet seen anyone in their true glory. Including you. Yes, Mozart wrote symphonies as a child, and Picasso could draw before he could talk. But most human beings are profoundly thwarted in their "calling" because of circumstances that would never let them fly. This is not what God intended. How many Mozarts are there right now, hidden across the globe?

Imagine, all your creativity and gifting will be restored and then some when you are restored. All of that latent potency inside of you—never given the opportunity to grow and develop and express itself—completely restored, including your personality. From there you are able to act in the new world in ways far greater than Adam and Eve were able to. You will have absolute intimacy with Jesus Christ, and his life will flow through your gifts unhindered. Imagine what you will be capable of, how vast your powers in the new earth! You know you can walk on water, for Peter did on this earth at Jesus' bidding. How far do your creative and artistic capacities reach?

What will you do in the life to come? Everything you were born to do. Everything you've always wanted to do. Everything the kingdom *needs* you to do.

∽

What dreams have gone unfulfilled in your life? What part of your calling has not had a chance to soar? Name it. It's important to name it. And then tell yourself, *But it will! Very soon!*

TAKE REFUGE

*Let the morning bring me word of your unfailing
love, for I have put my trust in you. Show me the way
I should go, for to you I entrust my life. Rescue me
from my enemies, LORD, for I hide myself in you.*

PSALM 143:8–9

David wrote this—the man who could often be found hiding in the desert, in the forest, on the mountain. He was no coward. He was no fool. Nor was Jesus, who practically begs you to hide yourself in him. Six times in the opening lines of John 15 he urges us to "remain in me," then caps it off a seventh time with "Remain in my love" (v. 9).

As men and women warriors we must not always live at war. Your enemy will first try to prevent you from embracing the warrior within. If he fails at that, he will then try to bait you into battles that you should not take on or bury you in battle after battle. There is a time to take refuge.

It's a choice, a posture of heart, a prayer, and a practice. We pray to receive him as our refuge. We bring reality into being. God is ever present to be our refuge, but he never forces it upon anyone. As soon as our hearts turn his direction for refuge, he is there to become so to us.

I give myself to you, Father. I consecrate my life to you again, body, soul, and spirit. I take refuge in you. I take refuge in your love.

YOU WILL BE VINDICATED

*The fire will test the quality of each person's
work. If what has been built survives,
the builder will receive a reward.*

1 CORINTHIANS 3:13–14

You know your every sin is forgiven. So if you can remove all fear of exposure from your heart, and set it safely within the context of your Father's love, it helps you toward a great moment in the kingdom when your story will be told rightly.

How wonderful it will be to see Jesus Christ vindicated. He has endured such slander, mistrust, and grotesque distortion by the religious counterfeits paraded in his name. All the world will see Jesus *as he is.* Every tongue will be silenced, and his vindication will bring tremendous joy to those who love him!

Friend—that vindication is also yours.

You probably have many stories you'd love to have told rightly—to have your actions explained and defended by Jesus. I think you'll be surprised by what Jesus noticed. The thousands of unseen choices to overlook a failure, to be kind to that friend who failed you, again. The things you wish you had done better, but at the time no one knew what you were laboring under—the warfare, the depression, the chronic fatigue. The millions of ways you've been missed, and misunderstood. Your Defender will make it all perfectly clear; you will be vindicated.

What do you most look forward to seeing vindicated? If you are wrestling with this thought, take your concerns to God, and ask him to replace them with joy.

PROMISE OF JUSTICE

*Commit yourself in love, in justice! Wait for
your God, and don't give up on him—ever!*
HOSEA 12:6 THE MESSAGE

Without naming evil for what it is, and without a day of reckoning, there can be no justice. (This is where other religions that deny or ignore the actual and personal existence of evil fall short.)

Imagine, friend, a world without evil. Every demon swept away. A world without evil people, where everyone loves God and overflows with his holy love. Imagine being surrounded only by people you can trust completely. Holiness will permeate all things. No wonder joy is the constant mood of the kingdom!

Our age cries out for justice. I believe in those justice movements. But I fear a great heartbreak is coming unless we understand the timing of things. Until the evil one is bound and cast into the lake of fire, our efforts here will be only partially successful. A dear man who runs an orphanage for abused and trafficked girls wrote me of his ache due to turning away girls every week. There's simply no room to take them all in. This is a terrible reality: our best efforts must be carried on, but they will not achieve justice on the earth until our Lord's return.

How do we carry on? *Only* with the anchor of your soul; only with the sure and firm hope that this Day *is* coming. Justice is coming. You must place this hope in front of you daily.

*O Jesus—breathe this deep into my mind and heart. Justice is coming.
Let me believe it, Lord, with the help of your Spirit in me.*

LIFE ETERNAL

This is exactly what Christ promised:
eternal life, real life!
1 JOHN 2:25 THE MESSAGE

Jesus' offer of eternal life has gotten "interpreted" by well-meaning people to say, "Oh, well. Yes, of course . . . God intends life for you. But that is *eternal* life, meaning, because of the death of Jesus Christ you can go to heaven when you die." And that's true . . . in a way. And in the meantime? Isn't there a whole lot more to the relationship *in the meantime*? (It's in the meantime that we're living out our days, by the way.) What did Jesus mean when he promised us life?

Jesus talks about a life available to you, a glorious, unending life *that begins in this age.* So does Paul: "Godliness has value for all things, holding promise for both the present life and the life to come" (1 Timothy 4:8). Your *present* life, and the next. When we hear the words *eternal life,* most of us have tended to think, *A life that waits for me in eternity.* But eternal means *unending,* not *later.* The Scriptures use the term to mean you can never lose it. It's a life that can't be taken from you. The offer is life and that life starts *now.* The Renewal begins *now.*

O Jesus—I pray for every bit of renewal and restoration that can come to me now, while I rest in the promise I will have all I want very soon.

ANIMALS IN HEAVEN?

Then I saw Heaven open wide—and
oh! a white horse and its Rider.
REVELATION 19:11 THE MESSAGE

The child-heart wants to know, "Will there be animals in heaven?" The calloused heart dismisses this as theologically unworthy. Friend, the whole debate ends when you realize that heaven comes to *earth*. How could your creative God renew his precious earth and not fill it with a renewed animal kingdom? That would be like a village without people.

You know there are horses, for Jesus and his company return on horseback. I wonder what Jesus named his horse. Does he come to his whistle? Does he need a saddle? Oh yes—there are horses in the kingdom.

Now, unless you want to dismiss this as completely allegorical, we have wolves, lambs, leopards, lions, and bears in the kingdom as well. The kingdom of God operates in its fullness on earth. And animals are clearly a part of it, praise our loving Father.

The animal kingdom will be your joyful partner. They will not be afraid of you, nor you of them. They will long to love and serve.

Dream, my friend. What animals would you love to have come to your call, to have a deep and holy friendship with? Will your childhood dog run to meet you? (God makes all things new.) Will you fly on a golden eagle? Ride the waves with a whale? What does it look like to you, to partner with nature as God intended?

YOUR PERSONAL DESTINY

*Dear friends, now we are children of God, and
what we will be has not yet been made known.
But we know that when Christ appears, we shall
be like him, for we shall see him as he is.*

1 JOHN 3:2

There's an expression that is used to describe someone who's out of sorts, who's not acting like the person she's known to be: "She's just not herself today." It's a marvelous, gracious phrase, for in a very real way, no one is quite himself today. There's more to you than you have seen. I know my wife is more beautiful than she imagines. I've seen it slip out, seen moments of her glory. Suddenly, her beauty shines through, as though a veil has been lifted.

You have moments like this, glimpses of your true creation. They come unexpectedly and then fade again. Life for the most part keeps your glory hidden, cloaked by sin, or sorrow, or merely weariness. How truly wonderful it will be to see the entirety of this restored to you.

When the disciples saw Jesus on the Mount of Transfiguration, they got a peek at his glory. He was radiant, beautiful, magnificent. He was Jesus, the Jesus they knew and loved—only *more so*. And you shall be glorious as well. Jesus called himself the Son of Man to state clearly that he is what mankind was meant to be. What you see in Jesus is your personal destiny.

Have you dreamed about who you will be when your full restoration is complete? It might do you good to let your heart go there.

YOUR HEART CAN BE PURE

"God blesses those whose hearts are
pure, for they will see God."

MATTHEW 5:8 NLT

According to the Scriptures, the heart can be troubled, wounded, pierced, grieved, even broken. How well you know that. Thankfully, it can also be cheerful, glad, joyful, rejoicing. The heart can be whole or divided—as in "Well, part of me wants to, but the other part of me doesn't." It can be wise or foolish. It can be steadfast, true, valiant. (All of these descriptions can be found by perusing the word *heart* in any concordance.) It can also be frightened, cowardly, wandering, dull, proud, hardened. Wicked and perverse. I think you know that as well.

But friend, according to Jesus, your heart can also be pure. The Bible sees the heart as the source of all creativity, courage, and conviction. It is the source of your faith, your hope, and of course, your love. It is the "wellspring of life" within you (Proverbs 4:23), the center of your being, the fount of your life.

There is no escaping the centrality of the heart. God knows that; it's why he made it the central theme of the Bible, just as he placed the physical heart in the center of the human body. The heart is central; to find your life, you must make it central again.

Jesus—I keep losing track of my heart every week. Thank you that you keep calling me back. Where am I needing to "come back" today, Lord?

THOSE YOU LOVE

They will enter Zion with singing; everlasting joy will crown their heads. Gladness and joy will overtake them, and sorrow and sighing will flee away.

ISAIAH 35:10

What will it be like to be crowned with everlasting joy? To be "overtaken" with gladness and joy? There is certainly the joy of *relief*. People who survive accidents often break out in giddy laughter afterward, relief overtaking the fear of the event. But there is also the joy of *anticipation*, the joy that comes when you know the road has opened before you and life will now happen the way you've always wished it would. Both shall be yours, the relief, followed by the thrill of anticipation—probably in that order.

It may be a difficult thing to imagine your soul's complete restoration. But perhaps you can get there by thinking of the restoration of the ones you love. Think of the joy it will be to see them young and well, alive and free, everything you knew they were! You always knew there was a shining greatness in there, though they never could quite take hold of it for themselves. And you *see* it. How many times over will we hear at the feast, "Look at you! You're glorious!"?

Oh, to see again the ones we have lost and know they can never be taken from us again. Imagine the tears of joy and the very long embraces!

Whom are you looking forward to seeing again?

WHAT IF?

I saw Heaven and earth new-created.
REVELATION 21:1 THE MESSAGE

What if? A large golden eagle in this world can carry a sheep. What load can a renewed eagle bear? I would love to ride a golden eagle, with their permission of course. And friend—what about the angels? Heaven comes to earth, and the angels shall walk in fellowship with man. What do the angels have to teach us? What sort of games do they play? The entire earth will be our playground.

This is why you don't need a bucket list. It's *all* yours, and you can never lose it. To wander the beautiful places, without the end of vacation always looming. You've longed to see the fjords of Norway? Done. You've secretly hoped to wander the jungles of Africa? Yours too. What next? It shall all be yours.

Good thing you have all the time in the world that has no time to explore and tell the tales. To take up new adventures with those who want to sail the seven seas or climb the peaks of the Andes or range the universe itself.

You think I am being fanciful. I am being utterly serious. I am being as serious as Jesus when he warned that only the child-heart can receive the kingdom. It was your creative Father who gave you your imagination; and his creative majesty will certainly do yours one better in the world to come.

Do you have some secret dreams you are hoping will come true for your life? Now you know—those will be fulfilled! You don't need a bucket list because your life is unending!

GOD'S CREATIVE ORDER

"Look ahead with joy. Anticipate what I'm creating."
ISAIAH 65:18 THE MESSAGE

Certainly storytelling is one of the great pleasures in the kingdom. Would you like to write? Illustrate? Act? Produce? These are not obliterated when you step into the life to come; God renews all things. Dallas Willard assures:

> We will not sit around looking at one another or at God for eternity but will join in the endlessly ongoing creative work of God. It is for this that we were each individually intended, as both kings and priests (Exodus 19:6; Revelation 5:10). . . . A place in God's creative order has been reserved for each one of us from before the beginnings of cosmic existence. His plan is for us to develop, as apprentices to Jesus, to the point where we can take our place in the ongoing creativity of the universe.[13]

Just as Adam and Eve were commissioned to, only this time around on a higher level, with greater powers, creatively engaged in very real and tangible things. You eat in the city; surely the joy of eating doesn't end with the feast. Who grows the food? Who brings it to market? What chefs prepare it? It's unlike God to just "zap" these things into existence while you sit around doing nothing. No, friend, he creates you to create—in your full glory.

If God allows our gifts to be fully used in his coming kingdom, what gifts would you love to bring to the Story? What would you love to do?

YOUR REWARD

"Look, I am coming soon, bringing my reward with me."
REVELATION 22:12 NLT

Reward—it fills the pages of both Testaments. C. S. Lewis writes: "If you consider the unblushing promises of reward and the staggering nature of the rewards promised in the Gospels, it would seem that Your Lord finds your desires not too strong, but too weak."[14]

Unblushing means boldfaced, unashamed. Did you know the promises of reward offered to you in Scripture are bold, unashamed, brazen? Reward is a central theme in the teachings of Jesus, in the Bible as a whole.

God seems to be of the opinion that no one should sustain the rigors of the Christian life without very *robust* and *concrete* hopes of brazen reward.

Consider that pastor who serves a small and petty congregation for forty years. What about the believer who struggled under mental illness, largely alone? What do they have to look forward to? No doubt every noble deed of their hidden faithfulness, every misunderstood action of love will be *individually* and *specifically* rewarded.

Oh yes, rewards will be given out in the kingdom with great honor and ceremony. And I believe one of our greatest joys will be to witness it happen.

I know very few contemporary Christians who have a hope of coming reward. The old saints did, but not our age. Is reward something you allow yourself to hope for? If not . . . why not?

FILLING YOUR TREASURY

*Then I looked, and, oh!—a door open into Heaven. The
trumpet-voice, the first voice in my vision, called out,
"Ascend and enter. I'll show you what happens next."*

REVELATION 4:1 THE MESSAGE

The dreams I have about the kingdom only started this year.
Then one day it struck me: *Maybe I don't get pictures from
God because I don't ask for them.* So I began asking.

And God began answering. Not only in dreams, but in all sorts
of ways (he is eager to fill your heart with hope!). The sunrise out
my window has become a regular reminder for me; I've come to
look for his *promise* there every morning. I cut pictures out of magazines for a scrapbook of images of the new earth, images that have
a special magic for me of the Great Renewal.

Dear friend, you will be greatly helped by filling the treasury
of your imagination with images of the coming Renewal; without
them, it will be nigh impossible to make this the anchor of your
soul. If you would take hold of this hope with both hands and
never let go, you need to know what it is you are taking hold of. If
you can't imagine it, you can't hope for it. The foggy and vague do
not inspire, ever.

Ask God to show you his promises, and then hold tightly
to them.

☙

Take some time to look at photos that speak the promise of the
Restoration to you. Create a journal with these and revisit the
hope it offers regularly. It will feed your heart with goodness and
the joy it needs.

MORE THAN HUMAN

And there was the baby, lying in the manger.
LUKE 2:16 NLT

Much of the famous artwork depicting Jesus is beautiful, but the artists also make it difficult to remember that Jesus was *human*. The incarnation is one of the greatest treasures of your faith. The world keeps pushing God away, feeling more comfortable with him up in the heavens somewhere. But in the coming of Jesus he draws near. *Incredibly near.* How could he possibly get closer? He nurses at Mary's breast.

One of my favorite meditations comes from this passage by G. K. Chesterton: "The strange kings fade into a far country and the mountains resound no more with the feet of the shepherds; and only the night and the cavern lie in fold upon fold over something more human than humanity."[15]

Savor that—the manger Mary used as a cradle held something *more* human than humanity. Do you think of Jesus as the most human human-being who ever lived? It's true.

The ravages of sin, neglect, and abuse have left you but a shadow of what you were meant to be. Jesus' favorite title for himself was the Son of *Man*. Too much "heavens" stuff pushes Jesus away. His humanity brings him close again.

O Jesus—thank you for embracing humanity in order to rescue my humanity. I give my humanity to you again this day, to be restored in your image.

FROM HEAVEN'S POINT OF VIEW

*Her child was snatched away from the
dragon. . . . Then there was war in heaven.*
REVELATION 12:5, 7 NLT

I would pay good money to have a nativity scene with Revelation 12 included. Not only would it capture the imagination, but it would also better prepare us to celebrate the holidays and to go on to live the Story Christmas invites us into.

Your vision of the nativity was shaped by classic Christmas cards and lovely crèche displays. And while I still love those tableaus very much, I'm convinced they're an almost total rewrite of the story. I understand this traditional imagery is probably dear to you, but friend, it's also profoundly deceiving by creating all sorts of warm expectations—many quite subconscious—of what the nature of the Christian life is going to be like.

But war in heaven the instant Jesus was born—this is an essential part of the Story. Yes—Christmas is the glow of candlelight, and a baby sleeping in a manger. It is starlight, shepherds in a field. But Christmas is also an invasion. The kingdom of God striking at the heart of the kingdom of darkness with violent repercussions. And victory.

Christmas is meant to remind us each year of the Great Story we live in. Not something cute and quaint from time gone by, but the most epic Story unfolding right now, all around us. What will help you remember that this year?

IT WORKED!

The angel was joined by a vast host of others—
the armies of heaven—praising God and saying,
"Glory to God in highest heaven, and peace on
earth to those with whom God is pleased."

LUKE 2:13–14 NLT

As I reflect upon the mystery of the incarnation, and the great invasion of the kingdom that began under cover of darkness in a remote village in the Middle East, so many wonders flood my heart. The wild plan of God to come the way he did, where he did, when he did, as he did. The great battle in the heavens. The immense cost. The staggering series of events that began to unfold. It really is breathtaking, more than any other story ever told.

But above all, what I wanted to offer you this Christmas is this one simple thought: It worked.

God came for you, and all that he planned and all he intended in Jesus Christ has come true. The rule of evil has been broken. You are ransomed. Your life is now filled with the life of God. The kingdom of God has broken through. Redemption is unfolding all over the earth, and will come to a glorious climax with the return of Jesus. Sin no longer reigns over you. Restoration is yours, now. And *so* many other glories.

It worked. Hold on to that truth this Christmas, dear friend.

This glorious victory needs to be celebrated! How can you celebrate this wonderful truth today?

HIS UNIQUE GIFT

*They will call him Immanuel, which
means "God is with us."*
MATTHEW 1:23 NLT

I was listening to a few refrains from "O Holy Night": "A thrill of hope, the weary world rejoices" and something deep in my spirit said, *O yes, dear Jesus, we need hope. Come for this weary world.* Actually, this world is more than weary, it's coming apart at the seams. Something deep is unraveling. I wonder if you've felt it too. The barrenness of spirit, a desolation creeping across the earth.

You can see this through the great ache of social concern—the rallying to offer a helping hand, which is easier than offering Jesus. Now, we are to care for the poor and the oppressed. Yes. But let me ask: *What is the unique contribution of Christianity to this weary world?* It's not social concern. It is Jesus and his kingdom. God didn't offer the shepherds a grant for their micro economics, or the little outcast family an apartment. He offered them a Savior. He offered them himself. There's simply no other way to save this weary, unraveling world.

Think again about the gift in the manger. God saw what the world most desperately needed, and what he chose to give us was . . . himself. To care for the world is to offer Jesus Christ. This is the message of Christmas. "Let every heart prepare him room." Then heaven and nature will sing. Then will break the new and glorious morn. *Jesus, may your hope and glory come.*

*Father—I receive the gift of Christmas. I receive the gift of Jesus
Christ and all it means for my life. Thank you, with all my heart.*

THE INCARNATION CONTINUES

[My] labor pains for you . . . will continue until
Christ is fully developed in your lives.
GALATIANS 4:19 NLT

And so you've celebrated Christmas, the coming of Jesus to this world. And what a thing to celebrate! The entire pageant comes down to this: Jesus took on a genuine humanity.

And of course, this late in the Story, I hope it's nearly impossible for you to celebrate Christmas without your heart turning toward his return. One day soon, Jesus will return to this earth, with his army, to make a final end of evil and to usher in the coming of a Golden Age. This is referred to as the "Second Coming."

But what struck me this Christmas was this: the Second Coming is actually . . . the Third Coming. Christ came to Bethlehem. And then he comes to dwell in you. The Second Coming is actually *in you*—right now.

Christ was first formed in Mary's womb; now he's being formed in you. It's a truth unique to Christianity and no other religion. "Christ in you, the hope of glory" (Colossians 1:27 NASB). Jesus made his first invasion into Bethlehem. His second great act of indwelling happens when you open your heart to him.

Think of it—Jesus Christ is inside of you this very moment. The incarnation didn't finish but continues . . . in you.

I receive it, Lord! I receive Jesus Christ into every part of my life and my being! Yes, Lord—come and be formed in me today!

LISTEN FOR THE TRUMPET

*What is our hope, our joy, or the crown in which we
will glory in the presence of our Lord Jesus when
he comes? Indeed, you are our glory and joy.*

1 THESSALONIANS 2:19–20

Where is this supposed coming? The current expression of that is often: "But *every* age has thought Jesus was about to show up. It might take another thousand years." It sounds so reasonable. Yes, every age has thought that Christ would return any moment, and they were right to do so because "any moment" could have been their moment. They were right to have expected his return because they were commanded to by Christ himself. They were wise to do so because it's the *antidote* to so many harmful things; when it's embraced that the master is still far off, the heart turns toward indulgences of this world, trying to slake kingdom thirst with everything within reach.

Friend, turn your soul toward meditating on Christ's return. As we draw closer to the Day itself, the church begins to turn its focus from "heaven" to the coming kingdom, the restoration of all things. (The church at the end of Revelation is crying out for his return!) I guarantee you one thing—we are closer now than ever before. There is every reason to expect to hear that trumpet blast any day. If what this world is going through does not count as birth pangs, I honestly don't know what will.

Are you looking for signs of Christ's return? We are supposed to be; in fact, we are commanded to! Begin to turn your heart toward the return of Jesus right now—what if it happened today?!

YOUR HEART'S LONGING

"Come!" say the Spirit and the Bride. Whoever hears,
echo, "Come!" Is anyone thirsty? Come! All who will,
come and drink, drink freely of the Water of Life!
REVELATION 22:17 THE MESSAGE

Two ideas are absolutely basic to a Christian understanding of this world: first, you are created for happiness and second, that you'll not truly be happy until Jesus brings into fullness the kingdom of God. So what's with the awkwardness of Christians talking about his return, and, more fascinating (and troubling), how come no one really prays for it?

I want to venture an observation: if you're not personally longing for and praying for the return of Jesus, you're still committed to making life work here and now. Your prayers reveal what you are after. If you're not praying for the return of Jesus, you're not banking on it or looking forward to it much. But . . . you're created for happiness, and you're not going to truly find it until the kingdom is yours.

In the book of Revelation we see the church longing for and praying for the return of Jesus: "Please come! Come now! We want you to come!" This isn't a fear of dying. This is *hopeful*, eager *expectation* of every dream you ever had coming true. This is the expectation of life coming to you in all its fullness. Not to mention your Jesus coming to you. And never ever losing it again.

Dear friend, pray for it daily! It will do you good to begin to pray for Jesus to return!

YOUR PARTICIPATION

"After a long absence, the master of those three
servants came back and settled up with them. . . .
His master commended him: 'Good work! You did
your job well. From now on be my partner.'"

MATTHEW 25:19–21 THE MESSAGE

You are created to accomplish a work worthy of God; it is one of your deepest yearnings. And you will, in the kingdom; not just once, but many, many times over. Are you employed in the actual restoration itself? I don't know for certain. "They will rebuild the ancient ruins and restore the places long devastated" (Isaiah 61:4) certainly hints at it. And you know your God is a God of *process*—look at how long your sanctification is taking.

You might think I am merely daydreaming about what we actually do in the kingdom. But remember—God creates you to be a creator like he is. You are promised you will reign; you will be given estates; you will have a vital role in the kingdom.

He says to you, "Be my partner"—that's the perfect way to put it. The idea behind the parable of the three servants in Matthew is promotion. And notice that the servants are promoted in the very things they are good at! God puts his renewed sons and daughters—creators like he is—in a re-created world and tells them to do exactly what he told Adam and Eve to do in the beginning.

As the old year fades, and the new year approaches, what are you hoping to do with your life? You should let yourself dream . . . and then let those dreams carry right on into your wonderful, unending life!

HOPE ABOVE ALL HOPES

*Out of that terrible travail of soul, he'll see
that it's worth it and be glad he did it. Through
what he experienced, my righteous one, my
servant, will make many "righteous ones," as
he himself carries the burden of their sins.*

ISAIAH 53:11–12 THE MESSAGE

If you woke each morning and your heart leapt with hope, knowing that the renewal of all things was just around the corner—might even come today—you would be one happy person. If you knew in every fiber of your being that nothing is lost, that everything will be restored to you and then some, you would be armored against discouragement and despair. If your heart's imagination were filled with rich expectations of all the goodness coming to you, your confidence would be contagious; you would be unstoppable, revolutionary.

Dear friend—don't you let anyone or anything cheat you of this hope. You have barely begun to take hold of it. Do not let anything diminish the beauty, power, and significance of this hope above all hopes. Jesus lived the way he did in this world, for this world, because his hope was set beyond this world; that is the secret of his life.

You need to take this hope so seriously you sell everything to buy this field. You must make this utterly real and tangible, so that your soul becomes truly anchored by it.

It's true—you must make this utterly real and tangible. Begin to journal about your plans to enjoy your unending life.

JOY WILL BE YOURS

*He who testifies to all these things says it again: "I'm
on my way! I'll be there soon!" Yes! Come, Master Jesus!*
REVELATION 22:20 THE MESSAGE

There's nothing like stepping out your door into the beckoning world. This is why people vacation in beautiful places. It's also the secret to the stories you love—that magical moment when the hero or heroine steps into a "brave new world."

Dear friend, you're preparing your heart to receive the hope that alone can be the anchor of your soul. One day soon you will step into a renewed earth, sparkling like an orchard of cherry trees after a rain shower. Joy will be yours. How do you open your heart to this after so much pain and disappointment? You have lost many things as you've passed through the battlefields of this war-torn world; your humanity has been stripped of such essential goodness. One of your greatest losses is the gift of wonder, the doorway into the kingdom heart. But you have special places and favorite stories that will awaken it.

Sometimes even a single phrase like "they strode away into the night" can awaken a sense of longing that almost pierces. There are parts of you, no matter how deeply buried, that still remember you were made for this. You have been looking for the kingdom all your life. It is the most beautiful, hopeful, glorious promise ever made. And it is *real*. And it is *yours*.

Just stay with that for more than a second: It is *real*. And it is *yours*. Repeat that to yourself. *The restoration of all things is real. And it is mine.*

OUR DAILY PRAYER

My dear Lord Jesus, I come to you now to be restored in you, renewed in you, to receive your life and your love and all the grace and mercy I so desperately need this day. I honor you as my Lord, and I surrender every aspect and dimension of my life to you. I give you my spirit, soul, and body, my heart, mind, and will. I cover myself with your blood—my spirit, soul, and body, my heart, mind, and will. I ask your Holy Spirit to restore me in you, renew me in you, and lead this time of prayer. In all that I now pray, I stand in total agreement with your Spirit and with all those praying for me by the Spirit of God and by the Spirit of God alone.

Dearest God, holy and victorious Trinity, you alone are worthy of all my worship, my heart's devotion, all my praise, all my trust, and all the glory of my life. I love you, I worship you, I give myself over to you in my heart's search for life. You alone are Life, and you have become my life. I renounce all other gods, every idol, and I give to you, God, the place in my heart and in my life that you truly deserve. This is all about you, and not about me. You are the Hero of this story, and I belong to you. I ask your forgiveness for my every sin. Search me, know me, and reveal to me where you are working in my life, and grant to me the grace of your healing and deliverance and a deep and true repentance.

Heavenly Father, thank you for loving me and choosing me before you made the world. You are my true Father—my Creator, Redeemer, Sustainer, and the true end of all things, including my life. I love you, I trust you, I worship you. I give myself over to you, Father, to be one with you as Jesus is one with you. Thank you for proving your love for me by sending Jesus. I receive him and all his life and all his work, which you ordained for me. Thank you for including me in Christ, forgiving me my sins, granting me his righteousness, making me complete in him. Thank you for making me alive with Christ, raising me with him, seating me with him at your right hand, establishing me in his authority, and anointing me with your love and your Spirit and your favor. I receive it all with thanks and give it total claim to my life—my spirit, soul, and body, my heart, mind, and will.

Jesus, thank you for coming to ransom me with your own life. I love you, worship you, trust you. I give myself over to you to be one with you in all things. I receive all the work and triumph of your cross, death, blood, and sacrifice for me, through which my every sin is atoned for, I am ransomed, delivered from the kingdom of darkness, and transferred to your kingdom; my sin nature is removed, my heart circumcised unto God, and every claim being made against me is cancelled and disarmed. I take my place now in your cross and death, dying with you to sin, to my flesh, to this world, to the evil one and his kingdom. I take up the cross and crucify my flesh with all its pride, arrogance, unbelief, and idolatry [and anything else you are currently struggling with]. I put off the old man. Apply to me all the work and triumph in your cross, death, blood, and sacrifice; I receive it with thanks and give it total claim to my spirit, soul, and body, my heart, mind, and will.

Jesus, I also receive you as my Life, and I receive all the work and triumph in your resurrection, through which you have conquered sin, death, judgment, and the evil one. Death has no power over you, nor does any foul thing. And I have been raised with you to a new life, to live your life—dead to sin and alive to God. I take my place now in your resurrection and in your life, and I give my life to you to live your life. I am saved by your life. I reign in life through your life. I receive your hope, love, faith, joy, your goodness, trueness, wisdom, power, and strength. Apply to me all the work and triumph in your resurrection; I receive it with thanks, and I give it total claim to my spirit, soul, and body, my heart, mind, and will.

Jesus, I also sincerely receive you as my authority, rule, and dominion, my everlasting victory against Satan and his kingdom, and my ability to bring your kingdom at all times and in every way. I receive all the work and triumph in your ascension, through which Satan has been judged and cast down. All authority in the heavens and on this earth has been given to you, Jesus, and you are worthy to receive all glory and honor, power and dominion, now and forever. I take my place now in your authority and in your throne, through which I have been raised with you to the right hand of the Father and established in your authority. I give myself to you, to reign with you always. Apply to me all the work and triumph in your authority and your throne; I receive it with thanks and I give it total claim to my spirit, soul, and body, my heart, mind, and will.

I now bring the authority, rule, and dominion of the Lord Jesus Christ and the full work of Christ over my life today: over my home, my household, my work, over all my kingdom and domain. I bring the authority of the Lord Jesus Christ and the full work of Christ against every evil power coming against me—against every foul spirit, every foul power and device. [You might need to name them—what has been attacking you?] I cut them off in the name of the Lord; I bind and banish them from me and from my kingdom now, in the mighty name of Jesus Christ. I also bring the full work of Christ between me and every person, and I allow only the love of God and only the Spirit of God between us.

Holy Spirit, thank you for coming. I love you, I worship you, I trust you. I receive all the work and triumph in Pentecost, through which you have come. You have clothed me with power from on high, sealed me in Christ, become my union with the Father and the Son, the Spirit of truth in me, the life of God in me, my Counselor, Comforter, Strength, and Guide. I honor you as Lord, and I fully give to you every aspect and dimension of my spirit, soul, and body, my heart, mind, and will—to be filled with you, to walk in step with you in all things. Fill me afresh, Holy Spirit. Restore my union with the Father and the Son. Lead me into all truth, anoint me for all of my life and walk and calling, and lead me deeper into Jesus today. I receive you with thanks, and I give you total claim to my life.

Heavenly Father, thank you for granting to me every spiritual blessing in Christ Jesus. I claim the riches in Christ Jesus over my life today. I bring the blood of Christ once more over my spirit, soul, and body, over my heart, mind, and will. I put on the full armor of God: the belt of truth, breastplate of righteousness, shoes of the gospel, helmet of salvation; I take up the shield of faith and sword of the Spirit, and I choose to be strong in the Lord and in the strength of your might, to pray at all times in the Spirit.

Jesus, thank you for your angels. I summon them in the name of Jesus Christ and instruct them to destroy all that is raised against me, to establish your kingdom over me, to guard me day and night. I ask you to send forth your Spirit to raise up prayer and intercession for me. I now call forth the kingdom of God throughout my home, my household, my kingdom, and domain in the authority of the Lord Jesus Christ, giving all glory and honor and thanks to him. In Jesus' name, amen.

BIBLIOGRAPHY

ARTICLES BY JOHN ELDREDGE

"Agreements"   "Five Agreements That Are Killing Millennials." *And Sons Magazine.* January 2018. http://andsonsmagazine.com/31/five-agreements-are-killing-millennials.

"Beauty"   "Beauty Heals." *And Sons Magazine.* October 2015. http://andsonsmagazine.com/18/beauty-heals.

"Mission"   "Finding Your Mission." *And Sons Magazine.* August 2014. http://andsonsmagazine.com/05/finding-your-mission.

"Navigation"   "Navigation 101." *And Sons Magazine.* April 2014. http://andsonsmagazine.com/01/navigation-101.

"Normandy"   "Normandy: Pilgrim at War." *And Sons Magazine.* July 2017. http://andsonsmagazine.com/29/normandy-pilgrim-war.

"Remembering"   "Remembering." *And Sons Magazine.* April 2016. http://andsonsmagazine.com/24/remembering.

"What"   "What Do You Do When You Find Yourself Hating Your Life?" *And Sons Magazine.* January 2017. http://andsonsmagazine.com/27/what-do-when-you-find-yourself-hating-your-life.

BLOG POSTS BY JOHN ELDREDGE

"Bethlehem"   "I Am Bethlehem." Ransomed Heart Ministries. December 20, 2011. https://www.ransomedheart.com/blogs/john/utterly-unique-gift-christmas.

"Christmas"   "One Christmas Thought: It Worked!" Ransomed Heart Ministries. December 24, 2013. https://www.ransomedheart.com/blogs/john/one-christmas-thought-it-worked.

"Come"   "Will You Come with Me?" Ransomed Heart Ministries. January 13, 2015. https://www.ransomedheart.com/blogs/john/will-you-come-me.

"Deliverer"   "God as Deliverer." Ransomed Heart Ministries. June 3, 2010. https://www.ransomedheart.com/blogs/john/god-deliverer.

"Dragon"   "Remember the Dragon." Ransomed Heart Ministries. December 5, 2014. https://ransomedheart.com/blogs/john/remember-dragon.

"Easter" "Easter." Ransomed Heart Ministries. April 18, 2017. https://ransomedheart.com/blogs/john/easter.

"Encounter" "A Fresh Encounter with the Love of God." Ransomed Heart Ministries. April 5, 2013. https://www.ransomedheart.com/blogs/john/fresh-encounter-love-god.

"Envy" "Envy." Ransomed Heart Ministries. May 22, 2017. http://ransomedheart.com/blogs/john/envy.

"Experiencing" "Experiencing the Fullness of God—Really." Ransomed Heart Ministries. April 6, 2014. http://ransomedheart.com/blogs/john/experiencing-fullness-god-really.

"Long" "But Don't You Long for It?" Ransomed Heart Ministries. January 20, 2014. http://ransomedheart.com/blogs/john/dont-you-long-it.

"Loving" "Loving Jesus in the Pain." Ransomed Heart Ministries. November 29, 2011. https://www.ransomedheart.com/blogs/john/loving-jesus-pain.

"Prophecy" "The Prophecy All Around You." Ransomed Heart Ministries. July 12, 2016. https://ransomedheart.com/blogs/john/prophesy-all-around-you.

"Reality" "How Are You Interpreting Reality?" Ransomed Heart Ministries. February 21, 2013. https://ransomedheart.com/blogs/john/how-are-you-interpreting-reality.

"Recovering" "Recovering the Romance." Ransomed Heart Ministries. July 31, 2017. https://ransomedheart.com/blogs/john/recovering-romance.

"Refuge" "Taking Refuge." Ransomed Heart Ministries. March 16, 2015. https://www.ransomedheart.com/blogs/john/taking-refuge.

"Soul" "Soul Care." Ransomed Heart Ministries. September 26, 2016. http://ransomedheart.com/blogs/john/soul-care.

"Spirit" "Spirit of the Age." Ransomed Heart Ministries. July 25, 2016. https://ransomedheart.com/blogs/john/spirit-age.

"Start" "A Fresh Start." Ransomed Heart Ministries. January 11, 2012. http://ransomedheart.com/blogs/john/fresh-start.

"Table" "Table for Two." Ransomed Heart Ministries. October 31, 2012. https://www.ransomedheart.com/blogs/john/table-two.

"Unique" "The Utterly Unique Gift of Christmas." Ransomed Heart Ministries. December 20, 2009. https://www.ransomedheart.com/blogs/john/utterly-unique-gift-christmas.

"Urged"   "Why We Are Urged to Remember." Ransomed Heart
                 Ministries. September 11, 2013. https://www.ransomedheart
                 .com/blogs/john/why-we-are-urged-remember.
"We"   "We Must Be." Ransomed Heart Ministries. March 23,
                 2015. https://ransomedheart.com/blogs/john/we-must-be.

BOOKS

Beautiful   Eldredge, John. *Beautiful Outlaw: Experiencing the Playful,*
                 Disruptive, Extravagant Personality of Jesus. Nashville:
                 FaithWords, 2011.
Captivating   Eldredge, John and Stasi. *Captivating: Unveiling the*
                 Mystery of a Woman's Soul. Rev. ed. Nashville: Thomas
                 Nelson, 2005, 2010.
Epic   Eldredge, John. *Epic: The Story God Is Telling.* Nashville:
                 Thomas Nelson, 2004.
Fathered   Eldredge, John. *Fathered by God: Learning What Your Dad*
                 Could Never Teach You. Nashville: Thomas Nelson, 2009.
Free   Eldredge, John. *Free to Live: The Utter Relief of Holiness.*
                 Nashville: FaithWords, 2013.
Journey   Eldredge, John. *The Journey of Desire: Searching for the*
                 Life You've Always Dreamed Of. Rev. ed. Nashville: Nelson
                 Books, 2000, 2007, 2016.
Lions   Eldredge, John and Sam Eldredge. *Killing Lions: A Guide*
                 Through the Trials Young Men Face. Nashville: Nelson
                 Books, 2014.
Moving   Eldredge, John. *Moving Mountains: Praying with Passion,*
                 Confidence, and Authority. Nashville: Nelson Books, 2016.
New   Eldredge, John. *All Things New: Heaven, Earth, and the*
                 Restoration of Everything You Love. Nashville: Nelson
                 Books, 2017.
Sacred   Curtis, Brent and John Eldredge. *The Sacred Romance:*
                 Drawing Closer to the Heart of God. Nashville: Thomas
                 Nelson, 1997.
Waking   Eldredge, John. *Waking the Dead: The Secret to a Heart*
                 Fully Alive. Rev. ed. Nashville: Nelson Books, 2003, 2016.
Walking   Eldredge, John. *Walking with God: How to Hear His Voice.*
                 Rev. ed. Nashville: Nelson Books, 2008, 2016.
Wild   Eldredge, John. *Wild at Heart: Discovering the Secret of a*
                 Man's Soul. Rev. ed. Nashville: Nelson Books, 2001, 2010.

SOURCES BY DATE

JANUARY

1. "Start."
2. *New*, 16–17.
3. *New*, 17.
4. *Beautiful*, 60–62.
5. *New*, 142–143.
6. *New*, 46–47.
7. *New*, 44–45.
8. *New*, 44–46.
9. *New*, 45–46.
10. *Beautiful*, 56–57.
11. *Captivating*, 122–123.
12. *Beautiful*, 202–203.
13. *Beautiful*, 202–203.
14. *Free*, 165–167.
15. *Journey*, 212–213.
16. *Walking*, 45–46.
17. *Free*, 73–74.
18. *Waking*, 169–170.
19. *Walking*, 82.
20. *Sacred*, 42–43, 46.
21. *Walking*, 85–86.
22. *Free*, 80–83.
23. *Free*, 84–86.
24. *Journey*, 74–76.
25. *Sacred*, 168–170.
26. *Free*, 14–17.
27. *Sacred*, 170.
28. *Journey*, 223–224.
29. *Lions*, 84–86.
30. *Free*, 169–171.
31. *Free*, 53–55.

FEBRUARY

1. *Free*, 169–171.
2. *New*, 3–4.
3. *Journey*, 86–89.
4. *New*, 117–118.
5. *New*, 6–7.
6. *Journey*, 12.
7. *Journey*, 172–173.
8. *Walking*, 182.
9. *Wild*, 134.
10. "Urged."
11. *Walking*, 17–18.
12. *Journey*, 204–205.
13. *Beautiful*, 69–71.
14. *Free*, 49–51.
15. "Loving."
16. *New*, 8–10.
17. *Journey*, 40–41.
18. *Wild*, 113–115.
19. *Wild*, 123–124.
20. *Sacred*, 137.
21. *Wild*, 139–140.
22. *Beautiful*, 159–160.
23. *Waking*, 78–79.
24. *Wild*, 178–179.
25. *Sacred*, 126–127.
26. *Moving*, 176–178.
27. *Journey*, 65–66, 69.
28. "Come."
29. *Lions*, 73–74.

MARCH

1. *Waking*, 119.
2. *Captivating*, 119.
3. "Deliverer."
4. "Deliverer."
5. *Moving*, 141–143.
6. *Free*, 77–80.
7. *Beautiful*, 31–34.
8. *Beautiful*, 38–40.
9. *Sacred*, 79–80.
10. *Journey*, 114–115.
11. *New*, 44–45.
12. *Walking*, 41–42.
13. *Moving*, 34–35.
14. *Free*, 179.
15. *Beautiful*, 146–147.
16. *Fathered*, 92–93.
17. *Captivating*, 100–101.
18. *Moving*, 7–8.
19. *Captivating*, 216.
20. *Beautiful*, 154–155.
21. *Beautiful*, 140–141.
22. *Epic*, 10–11.
23. *New*, 173–175.

24. *Walking*, 142–143.
25. *Beautiful*, 64–65.
26. *Walking*, 204–205.
27. "Experiencing."
28. *New*, 175–177.
29. *Beautiful*, 76–77.
30. *Beautiful*, 101–102.
31. *Moving*, 15.

APRIL

1. *Beautiful*, 21–23.
2. *Fathered*, 11–12.
3. *Beautiful*, 102–103.
4. *Free*, 45–47.
5. *Free*, 96–97.
6. *Beautiful*, 113–114.
7. *New*, 202–203.
8. *Epic*, 39–40.
9. *Epic*, 55–56.
10. *Sacred*, 116–117.
11. *Free*, 162–163.
12. "Envy."
13. "Envy."
14. *Epic*, 78–80.
15. *Fathered*, 57–58.
16. *Beautiful*, 103–104.
17. *Sacred*, 107–108.
18. *Sacred*, 53–54.
19. *Moving*, 182–184.
20. *Waking*, 161–162.
21. *Captivating*, 101–102.
22. "Reality."
23. *New*, 183–185.
24. *Beautiful*, 213–214.
25. "Table."
26. *Walking*, 192–193.
27. *Epic*, 22–24.
28. *Walking*, 90–91.
29. *Waking*, 219–220.
30. *Sacred*, 39–41.

MAY

1. *Epic*, 52–54.
2. *Epic*, 49–50.
3. *Lions*, 74–75.
4. *Journey*, 143.
5. *Waking*, 80–81.
6. *Walking*, 9–10.
7. *Beautiful*, 217–218.
8. *Lions*, 8–9.
9. *Fathered*, 209–210.
10. *Beautiful*, 127–128.
11. *Journey*, 159–160.
12. *Journey*, 122–124.
13. *Lions*, 17–18.
14. *Moving*, 164–165.
15. *Walking*, 37–39.
16. *Waking*, 209–210.
17. *Beautiful*, 189.
18. *Waking*, 101–102.
19. *Sacred*, 97–98.
20. *Free*, 5–7.
21. *Lions*, 105.
22. *Sacred*, 50–53.
23. *New*, 154–156.
24. *Epic*, 84–87.
25. *Epic*, 103–104.
26. *Lions*, 91–92.
27. *Journey*, 2–3.
28. *Sacred*, 10–11.
29. *Moving*, 142–143.
30. *Moving*, 144–147.
31. *Waking*, 126–128.

JUNE

1. "Prophecy."
2. *New*, 207–208.
3. "Encounter."
4. *Lions*, 33–34.
5. *Beautiful*, 206.
6. *Beautiful*, 145–146.
7. *Beautiful*, 208–209.
8. *Moving*, 129–130.
9. *Beautiful*, 67–68.
10. *Journey*, 37–39.
11. *Free*, 111–112.
12. *Beautiful*, 156–157.
13. *Waking*, 162–164.
14. *Free*, 172–174.
15. *Journey*, 83–84.
16. *Beautiful*, 205.
17. *Fathered*, 147–148.

18. *Fathered*, 101–102.
19. *Waking*, 130–131.
20. *Beautiful*, 177–178.
21. *Beautiful*, 209–210.
22. *Waking*, 50–51.

23. *Beautiful*, 139–140.
24. *Moving*, 4–6.
25. *Moving*, 26–30.
26. *Journey*, 186–188.
27. *Moving*, 57–59.

28. *Moving*, 71–72.
29. *Moving*, 77–79.
30. *Free*, 112–113.

JULY

1. *Moving*, 81–82.
2. *Waking*, 103–104.
3. *Moving*, 97–98, 108.
4. *Moving*, 108–110.
5. *Moving*, 201–203.
6. *Moving*, 111–115.
7. *Moving*, 55–56.
8. *Moving*, 122–123.
9. *Moving*, 132–135.
10. *Moving*, 138–139.

11. *Moving*, 139–141.
12. *Moving*, 151–154.
13. *Moving*, 185–186.
14. *Moving*, 217.
15. *Lions*, 53–54, 62.
16. *Sacred*, 88.
17. *Beautiful*, 88.
18. "Agreements."
19. *Journey*, 43, 45.
20. *Beautiful*, 160–161.
21. "Navigation."

22. *Sacred*, 35–36.
23. *Walking*, 25–26.
24. *Beautiful*, 130.
25. "Mission."
26. *Lions*, 164.
27. "What."
28. *Free*, 172–173.
29. *New*, 110–112.
30. *Beautiful*, 129–130.
31. *Moving*, 224–225.

AUGUST

1. *Journey*, 195–197.
2. *Journey*, 217–219.
3. *Waking*, 224–226.
4. *Sacred*, 95–96.
5. *Journey*, 136–139.
6. *Journey*, 25–26.
7. *Fathered*, 113–114.
8. *Waking*, 85–86.
9. *Waking*, 81–83.
10. *Wild*, 135–136.
11. *Sacred*, 71–72.

12. *Beautiful*, 121–122.
13. *New*, 158–160.
14. "We."
15. *Wild*, 136–138.
16. *Wild*, 138.
17. *Journey*, 216.
18. *Beautiful*, 41.
19. *Fathered*, 27–29, 31.
20. *Fathered*, 60, 62.
21. *Fathered*, 32–34.

22. *Lions*, 160–162.
23. *New*, 64–66.
24. *Free*, 32.
25. *Beautiful*, 148–149.
26. *Waking*, 111–112.
27. *Beautiful*, 143–145.
28. *Moving*, 48–49, 52.
29. *Moving*, 39–40.
30. *Walking*, 5–6.
31. *Beautiful*, ix–x.

SEPTEMBER

1. *Beautiful*, 11–12.
2. *Beautiful*, 13–16.
3. *Beautiful*, 20.
4. *Free*, 33–34.

5. *Beautiful*, 44–46.
6. *Free*, 49–51.
7. *Captivating*, 34–35.
8. *Moving*, 92–95.

9. *Beautiful*, 54–55.
10. *Captivating*, 29–31.
11. *Beautiful*, 104–106.
12. *Beautiful*, 108–109.

13. *Beautiful*, 113, 116.
14. *Beautiful*, 117–119.
15. *Beautiful*, 132.
16. *Beautiful*, 137–138.
17. *Beautiful*, 147–148.
18. *Beautiful*, 198–199.
19. *Beautiful*, 36–37.
20. *Beautiful*, 36–37.
21. *Moving*, 64.
22. *Wild*, 129–130, 132–133,
23. *Fathered*, 177–178.
24. *Beautiful*, 90.
25. "What."
26. *Journey*, 13–14.
27. "Easter."
28. *Beautiful*, 81–83.
29. *Beautiful*, 8–10.
30. *Moving*, 218.

OCTOBER

1. *Free*, 8–9.
2. *Moving*, 190–191.
3. *Free*, 133–134.
4. *Free*, 145–148.
5. *Free*, 149–150.
6. *Free*, 151–152.
7. *Beautiful*, 215.
8. *Moving*, 32–34.
9. *Captivating*, 40–41.
10. *Moving*, 219–221.
11. *Beautiful*, 207–208.
12. *Sacred*, 190–191.
13. *Fathered*, 132–133.
14. *Free*, 132–134.
15. *Journey*, 48.
16. *Waking*, 5.
17. *Waking*, 136–137, 139.
18. *New*, 92–94.
19. *Moving*, 198–199.
20. *Moving*, 200.
21. *Wild*, 130–131.
22. *Walking*, 61–62.
23. *Beautiful*, 164–165.
24. *Fathered*, 23–24.
25. *Moving*, 187–189.
26. *Waking*, 141–143.
27. *Free*, 138–141.
28. *New*, 91–92.
29. *Lions*, 130–131.
30. *Wild*, 18–19.
31. *Beautiful*, 190–191.

NOVEMBER

1. *Epic*, 13–15.
2. *Moving*, 42.
3. "Normandy."
4. *Moving*, 225–226, 228–229.
5. *Lions*, 57–58, 63–64.
6. *Beautiful*, 185–186.
7. *Free*, 63–66.
8. *Captivating*, 95–96.
9. *Walking*, 36–37.
10. *Epic*, 50–51.
11. *New*, 198–200.
12. "Soul."
13. "Recovering."
14. *Waking*, 100–101.
15. *New*, 57–59.
16. *New*, 147–148.
17. *New*, 204–205.
18. *Waking*, 10–11.
19. *New*, 205.
20. "Remembering."
21. *Epic*, 87–88.
22. *Epic*, 66–67.
23. *Journey*, 202–203.
24. "Beauty."
25. *Walking*, 178–179.
26. *Epic*, 82–83.
27. *New*, 24–27.
28. *New*, 33–35.
29. *New*, 35–36.
30. *New*, 52, 55–57.

DECEMBER

1. *New*, 208–209.
2. *Journey*, 174–176.
3. *Beautiful*, 119–120.
4. *New*, 95–96.
5. *New*, 100–102.
6. *New*, 129–131.

7. *New*, 134–136.
8. "Spirit."
9. *New*, 170–171.
10. "Refuge."
11. *New*, 118–119.
12. *New*, 145–146.
13. *Waking*, 11–12.
14. *New*, 70–72.
15. *Journey*, 120–121.

16. *Waking*, 42–43.
17. *New*, 97–98.
18. *New*, 76–79.
19. *New*, 161–163.
20. *New*, 114–116.
21. *New*, 206–208.
22. *Beautiful*, 47–48.
23. "Dragon."
24. "Christmas."

25. "Unique."
26. "Bethlehem."
27. *New*, 181–183.
28. "Long."
29. *New*, 169–170.
30. *New*, 200–201.
31. *New*, 62–63, 208, 210.

NOTES

1. Lilas Trotter, quoted in *Many Beautiful Things*, directed by Laura Waters Hinson (Oxvision Films LLC, 2015).

2. "Outlandish Proverbs," ed. George Herbert, in *The Complete Works in Verse and Prose of George Herbert* (1640; repr., London: Robson and Sons, 1874), 3:324.

3. Dallas Willard, *The Divine Conspiracy Participant's Guide* (Grand Rapids, MI: Zondervan 2010), 29.

4. "Envy," *The Hipster Conservative*, published August 3, 2013, http://hipsterconservative.com/2013/08/03/dorothy-l-sayers-on-envy.

5. A. W. Tozer, *I Talk Back to the Devil: The Fighting Fervor of the Victorious Christian* (Camp Hill, PA: WingSpread Publishers, 2008).

6. Frederick Buechner, *Wishful Thinking: A Seeker's ABC* (San Francisco, CA: HarperCollins, 1993), 95.

7. Edward M. Bounds, *The Complete Works of E. M. Bounds on Prayer: Experience the Wonders of God Through Prayer* (Grand Rapids: Baker, 2004), 70.

8. G. K. Chesterton, *St. Francis of Assisi* (New York: Random House, 2001), 7–8.

9. Oswald Chambers, *My Utmost for His Highest* (New York: Dodd, Mead, 1963), 219.

10. J. B. Phillips, *Your God Is Too Small* (New York: Simon & Schuster, 2004).

11. C. S. Lewis, *Mere Christianity* (New York: HarperOne, 1980), 135.

12. Blaise Pascal, *Pensées* (Indianapolis: Hacket, 2004), 219.

13. Dallas Willard, *The Divine Conspiracy* (San Francisco: HarperCollins, 1998), 399.

14. C. S. Lewis, *The Weight of Glory* (New York: Touchstone, 1975), 26.

15. G. K. Chesterton, *The Everlasting Man* (Radford, VA: Wilder, 2008), 116.